Advance praise for Anna Arutunyan's book

"Why do so many Russians go on giving uncritical support to Putin? Arguing that Russians hold a quasi-religious respect for the state and its leader, this illuminating book delves into the intertwining of the sacred and the political in history and today. Fresh vignettes of Putin in action illustrate both the supreme leader's attitude to his subjects and their needs, desires, and fears that make him the kind of leader he has become."

Caroline Humphrey, *University of Cambridge*

Praise for foreign language editions

"Anna Arutunyan's book is an excellent description of Putinland, where corruption and the abuse of power makes Russia fall even further down the international corruption list, to Latin American levels."

Gävle Dagblad, *Sweden*

"Arutunyan gives the reader a fascinating history of Russian identity, with extensive use of the long strands of literature and history… Arutunyan's collection of stories is a dramatic eye opener on the Russian soul, with poignant stories about her own experiences…"

Politiken, *Denmark*

"*The Putin Mystique* makes us wiser about a significant phenomenon in Russia's past and present."

Berlingske Tidende, *Denmark*

"A great experience… lively and interestingly written."

Leif Davidsen, *Danish writer and journalist*

ANNA ARUTUNYAN

THE PUTIN MYSTIQUE

Inside Russia's power cult

OLIVE
BRANCH
PRESS

An imprint of Interlink Publishing Group, Inc.
www.interlinkbooks.com

First American edition published in 2015 by
OLIVE BRANCH PRESS
An imprint of Interlink Publishing Group, Inc.
46 Crosby Street
Northampton, Massachusetts 01060
www.interlinkbooks.com

Originally published in the United Kingdom by
Skyscraper Publications

Library of Congress Cataloging-in-Publication Data
Arutunyan, Anna.
The Putin mystique : inside Russia's power cult / by Anna
Arutunyan.
pages cm
Includes bibliographical references and index.
ISBN 978-1-56656-913-2
1. Putin, Vladimir Vladimirovich, 1952---Influence. 2.
Putin, Vladimir Vladimirovich, 1952---Public opinion. 3.
Putin, Vladimir Vladimirovich, 1952---Cult. 4. Political
culture--Russia (Federation) 5. Power (Social sciences)--
Russia (Federation) 6. Russia (Federation)--Politics and
government--1991- I. Title.
DK510.766.P87A78 2014
947.086'2092--dc23
2014022831
Cover and design by Chandler Book Design

Printed and bound in the United States of America

To request our complete 48-page, full-color catalog,
please call us toll free at 1-800-238-LINK,
visit our website at www.interlinkbooks.com, or send us an
e-mail: info@interlinkbooks.com

CONTENTS

Introduction   1
Prologue: To Give unto Caesar   9

PART I THE SUBJECTS

1. To See Putin and Die   29
2. The Petition   43
3. Playing God   55
4. The Pikalevo Effect   67

PART II THE OPRICHNIKI

5. Men of the Sovereign   87
6. The Audience   105
7. Agent Loyal and his Little Racket   121
8. The Police Major   139

PART III THE BOYARS

9. Doing Business with Putin   155
10. The Inner Circle   169
11. In Favor   181
12. The Regent   203

PART IV THE SOVEREIGN AS GOD

13. The Cult   213
14. The Sect   227
15. The Heretics   235
16. The Church, the Tsar, and the Holy Fool   251
17. The Living Law   269

Epilogue: Russia without Putin   293
Acknowledgements   309
Notes   311
Index   325

Introduction

I WANT THE President of the Russian Federation to decree what I should think, what religion to profess, where to work, the number of children to bear,[1] how to live, and when to die.

Depending on whether his most supreme instructions bring me profit or ruin, I will swear fealty to him as a guarantor of stability, or decry him as a ruthless despot, a gangster, a corrupt oprichnik.[2] For whether I am his vassal, his serf, his victim, or his foe, there is always the option of blaming him for the quotidian scurrying of life in this impossible country.

For ten years I have been recording the first draft of his rule, for readers who cared only about his nukes and his spies, and who asked endlessly, "Who is Mr. Putin?"—missing the point entirely, for there is no mystery in the "inimitable" stare of his "pale blue eyes,"[3] nor in the intent and the will that they may or may not conceal.

I have been in the presence of the sovereign on ten occasions. I have suffered his dreary aluminium stare for a total of about thirty seconds. My mind concealed no treacherous thoughts, no unpaid taxes, no unfulfilled obligations, and most of all—no unspoken ridicule— and thus did not shrivel in terror. I found no soul there, nothing "interesting"[4] at all. In fact, the closest approximation to what I saw when he stared at me for a few moments—as he would at a wallpaper decoration, after his bored, impatient glance flitted all over the room— was a reflection of whatever I wanted to see.

"Those who wanted to understand who Putin is have already

understood him," his press secretary, Dmitry Peskov, told me cryptically, smiling under his mustache and staring that same aluminium stare. "Those who do not want to, well, they never will."

No, the mystery lies with whoever that stare is directed at—be he a quavering official, a defiant journalist, a loyal or betrayed soldier, a friendly or corrupt businessman, or a harried petitioner, kneading his cap in his hands as he waits for his ruler to sort out his problems.

Russia's involvement in the Ukraine crisis and its annexation of Crimea has shaken the international community, confounding it about what kind of country Russia really is and what its ruler is truly after. After over 20 years of transitioning towards democracy, with Putin, even before his incursion into neighboring Ukraine, being labeled the most powerful man in the world, there is little doubt that democracy hasn't really happened in Russia. It is also becoming evident that democracy won't simply "happen" when Vladimir Putin departs. In the literature that seeks to understand why, one concept is being cited with increasing frequency: the country is described as being a dual state. Some, like Russia scholar Richard Sakwa, describe a country in the throes of a battle between a legal-rational and a neo-patrimonial state.[5] The sociologist Vladimir Shlapentokh has described Russia as a segmented society containing both liberal and feudal elements.[6] The lawyer and political analyst Vladimir Pastukhov has compellingly described a competition between an external and an internal state—if the external is a failed state of laws and political institutions, then it is the internal, with its religious, personified identification of state power (as opposed to the law) that has repeatedly interceded to rule the country, like a co-pilot stepping in for his partner who is drunk or sleeping.[7]

In a legal-rational state, power rests with laws, institutions and the bureaucracy. Officials will often abuse their positions for personal gain, a phenomenon which is referred to as corruption and which exists, to various extents, in any country. When officials abuse their positions to the extent that the institutions stop functioning, the country can become a failed state, a condition which usually presumes a collapse of governance. In a patrimonial state, power rests individually with the person of the leader; when the feudal element is introduced, it means that power also rests with an oligarch or a local or regional official who, to a large extent, can control a certain territory as a personal domain.

On the outside, Russia is governed by a legal-rational state. It has a system of laws, institutions, and a bureaucracy that, at first glance, struggles to govern the country but is abused to such an extent that Russia is in constant danger of becoming a failed state. On second glance, however, it becomes evident that those laws and institutions often simply clash with the reality on the ground. Whatever Russia has, it's not a failed state because it's not really collapsing—largely because the more fluid, informal, and often irrational system of patrimonialism kicks in to govern the country.

This book aims to take the reader on an inside journey through that modern patrimonial-irrational state that steps in to rule Russia: the inner government, unwritten and quasi-divine, whose unspoken rules and psychology are either concealed from, or misunderstood by, the Western world. To understand why that is the case, I examine how the citizens—or subjects—experience state power, and delve into the basic, primordial relationships between the people and their ruler that end up violating the legal-rational state.

What often emerges from those relationships is a startling propensity to deify supreme government authority and to inadvertently participate in a cult of power. Within the patrimonial state, where social roles are reduced to the relative strength or weakness of an individual, the central government, ever distant and perennially autocratic in its constant efforts to ensure order over such a vast land, is ascribed near supernatural powers, even in cases when it is actually weak and inefficient. This is not deification in the common understanding, it is far from the transcendent, religious worship of something benevolent and omnipotent. Rather, it is the acceptance of a force beyond influence, beyond logic. "State power, not law, holds a sacred status in Russia," Pastukhov writes. Russians experience state power as a "mystical entity," a "life-giving substance," a "deity" that, in hardship, they will expect answers from. Whoever happens to occupy that sacred post can be simultaneously feared, admired, hated, or even ignored and ridiculed for inevitably failing to live up to that with which he has been endowed.

Vladimir Putin's tenure has presented me with a unique opportunity to study these relationships and experiences. Obviously, as a journalist working in Russia during his rule, I have had a chance to report on his administration rather than someone else's.

But the uniqueness stems from the fact that Putin, initially a small, soft-spoken, unimposing former intelligence officer, was never naturally endowed with the charisma, ambition, or popularity that are typical of a successful patrimonial leader. He never led a coup to seize power, nor did he run the gamut of a political career, which would have allowed him to expand his base with successive elections. Instead, he found himself at the apex of Russian state power largely by accident in 1999, having been chosen by the moneyed elite surrounding President Boris Yeltsin, who named him as his successor and then hastily abdicated. Putin's popularity, then, was swiftly engineered by political scientists loyal to Yeltsin's administration in order to ensure a smooth transition of power. In the 2000 election, the Russian people largely (53 percent) accepted what they were told to—much as they would a new Tsar, even if he was handpicked by an exceedingly unpopular predecessor.

Putin appeared to have flaunted somewhat of an autocratic streak when he reined in independent television stations and chased out or jailed disloyal oligarchs. But compare him to the spectrum of Russian rulers, and he emerges as less of an autocrat than we have habitually assumed. In a historical context, Putin has demonstrated a lack of any easily identifiable ideology or even agenda, other than remaining in power, accumulating wealth for the loyal segment of the elite, and, where possible, restoring the semblance of order and imperial grandeur (semblance, here, is the key word). While he has definitely demonstrated a willingness to "resolve issues" by extrajudicial means and instigate repressions where necessary, he hasn't inherently shown himself to be a strong leader—his notorious performances berating errant oligarchs notwithstanding, he has demonstrated, as we shall see, a laxity in firing and punishing corrupt officials even while promoting a campaign to fight corruption. Instead, by virtue of character and profession (and very much through an extension of his often noted personal character trait of reflecting the tone, gestures, and mood of whoever he is listening to), he has acted as a mirror of society, a product of his times, reflecting what was desired of him on a subconscious level. If he set out, as he claims he did, to impose a "dictatorship of the law"—essentially the Weberian legal rational state—then he has failed. Instead, he has succeeded in bringing out the complexes that

Russians had forgotten they had. Seeing the need for a good Tsar and a patrimonial lord, he played the part expertly; seeing the need for a despot to be feared, he played that too. And where necessary, of course, he was the businessman, one who could easily strike a deal or offer protection in a lawless country.

By acting as a mirror, Putin exposed and entrenched ancient habits that had never gone away, offering us an opportunity to see them in action. He served, essentially, as an easily recognizable caricature of Russian state power itself—quasi-divine, corrupt, at times brutal, and in charge of the country's vast economic resources. Struggling to rule at the apex of a legal-rational state (as witnessed by his efforts to impose a "dictatorship of the law"), he has, to a large extent, allowed himself to be subjugated by the inner, patrimonial state. With Putin at the helm, the patrimonial state has in turn subjugated the legal-rational state, particularly its layered, tangled bureaucratic apparatus. Finally, acting within the unwritten paradigm of the patrimonial state, Putin has allowed society to mold him into a sort of sacred king, a role that many Russian leaders inadvertently assume.

As I traverse the inner, patrimonial state, I try to reveal how that has happened in this book.

For approximately four years, beginning in late 2008, I gathered interviews and case studies, trying to shed light on the patterns and expectations that molded the Russian leader. Closely watching his interactions with his people, I studied how he responded to these expectations and how he reinforced and took advantage of existing psychological and economic patterns. My work on this book was aided by the fact that these four years marked a peculiar period of what has been termed by Russia watchers as "tandemocracy": the apotheosis of the legal-rational world clashing with the neo-patrimonial. Russia, *de jure*, was governed by elected President Dmitry Medvedev, but, *de facto*, ruled by Prime Minister Vladimir Putin. Seeing Putin up close during that period presented me with a chance for an unprecedented experiment: how do we, his subjects, the journalists, the businessmen, the officials, know, at gut level, that he, Prime Minister Putin, and not President Medvedev, is our real leader?

The Putin Mystique is structured to reflect how various groups of people along the social hierarchy experience supreme power in Russia. The titles of its four parts use sixteenth century caste terminology to suggest the patrimonial parallels and historical origins, but should not be taken literally.

I begin with an examination of how people—including myself—behave in the ruler's immediate presence, in a chapter that opens the first part of this book. Featuring examples from several regions outside Moscow, the first part deals with the economic aspects of how Russians relate to local, regional, federal, and, ultimately, supreme authority. When institutional authority fails, people will resort to supreme authority, with appeals that are sometimes as irrational as those to a deity.

The second part of this book deals with the government's security and repressive apparatus—and the feudal "understandings" that govern that apparatus in the weakness of the rule of law. Ostensibly, it is a section about corruption—but as several of the cases I describe show, corruption may not be the right word for a far more endemic phenomenon of tax farming and protection rackets, mechanisms that, in the absence of functional institutions to protect property rights, get the job done.

The third part details how businessmen interact with state power and what role is played by their personal connections to Vladimir Putin. Given the murky rules in a world that struggles to play by the arcane, contradictory network of formal laws, business in Russia can be a deadly gamble that depends on patronage, luck, and, ultimately, your favor at court.

The fourth and final part examines the mythical, psychological, and ideological packaging of supreme state power in Russia—quasi-divine, sacred, and thus prone to personality cults that have taken on a curiously sexual dimension in the twenty-first century. In a patrimonial setting, displays of affection can take place spontaneously from below—and some of the most fascinating material I was able to gather was the testimony of members of pro-Kremlin youth groups seduced by the state through glamor, money, and the exploitation of a primordial relationship to authority. The recent popular street demonstrations against Putin's return to the Kremlin in 2012 provided valuable evidence of the experience of patrimonial power from the perspective of dissent. The case of Pussy Riot—three female members of a punk band jailed for singing an anti-Putin song from the sacred altar steps of Moscow's Christ the Savior Cathedral—hit at the heart of the mystical foundations of the patrimonial-irrational state, and is an important case study in this book. The penultimate chapter traces the Kremlin's closeness to the church—or, rather, the church as an appendage to the Kremlin—in the context of power cults through history.

At first glance, economic micromanagement, corruption, personality cults, and divine mandate appear to be largely unconnected themes. Indeed, I initially conceived this book as a far less ambitious investigation into the outward displays of Putin's personality cult. It became clear, however, that those displays could not be understood without delving into the deep patrimonial state that predated Putin.

I realized that economic dependency and endemic corruption were crucial factors without which it would be impossible to answer my central question: what makes the deification of the state, and of the state personified, possible in a modern society?

What has emerged in this book is a problem that has permeated Russia's history but has far wider implications, that, as the Ukraine crisis has shown, go beyond its borders but may not necessarily be unique to Russia: a superb confusion about the role of Caesar and God. It is a confusion that affects those who hold power, but it rests with those who give up their powers in exchange for order, abundance, and justice. It is also a confusion that has hampered even recent efforts by Russia's fledgling opposition movement to build the foundations of a functioning civil society. This creates a persistent paradox in any attempt to forge a functioning legal-rational state in Russia: change cannot happen as long as such gargantuan expectations are placed squarely on a government seen as so absolutely omnipotent that it is expected to transcend itself and curb its own powers. Without a clear delineation between secular and temporal power, there is little room for the rule of law, regardless of who assumes the role of Caesar.

Finally, I should address some questions and misunderstandings that have come up since the first edition was published in Danish. Part of the complexity of this book (aside from its eclectic scope) stems from the fact that I examine a current phenomenon through a historical prism, becoming a journalist treading on academic ground.

I am writing about Putin and his subjects as though they have long passed away; as though the author is separated from her subject matter not just by time, but by space. In reality, of course, as a Russian living under Putin's rule, I am very much in the picture. This book does not seek to be an academic study of modern patrimonialism and its causes. Instead, it seeks to reflect the real experiences—both objective and subjective—of living in a patrimonial state.

For that reason, I also feel I need to answer one question up front: what is my own opinion of Vladimir Putin? Is this book a critique, an apology, or an indictment?

Even from this introduction, it may sound as though I am shifting the blame for Russia's current problems from Putin to the people themselves. When I describe Putin as being molded into a sacred king, it may give the mistaken impression that he is blameless and powerless in this process. This, of course, is not so—Putin has cunningly taken advantage of social phenomena that predate him to further the livelihood of his friends and to ensure his hold on power. However, his agency in this process should not be overestimated: when examining leaders, we tend to focus on the *the will to power*, forgetting that to make the domination of one man possible, it also takes the will of millions to follow.

Putin's rise to power is not the subject of this book, since I seek to go beneath politics and policy to look at how human beings experience state power within the patrimonial state. The aim is not to shift the blame from the person in power to the people, or to deny that Putin is responsible for what he has become, but to look at a previously unexamined process—what role the people have played in molding a patrimonial leader. Despite the controversial material described, this book is not meant to indict either the Russian leader or, more importantly, Russians themselves.

Readers have asked me whether the first lines of this book are to be taken literally. I wrote them more as an expression of the collective unconscious than as a statement of a rationalized desire, for I believe that such yearnings, when unmitigated, are incompatible with human integrity and dignity.

And yet they exist, and exist in all of us.

Prologue:

To give unto Caesar

Let every soul be subject unto the higher powers.
For there is no power but of God: the powers that be
are ordained of God.
—**Romans 13:1**

Render therefore unto Caesar the things which are
Caesar's; and unto God the things that are God's.
—**Matthew 22:21**

Shit, shit, holy shit. Shit, shit, holy shit.
Virgin Mary, Mother of God, banish Putin, banish Putin,
banish Putin.
—**Pussy Riot's Punk Prayer**, February 2012

1.

IT WAS A few months after Russia annexed Crimea, after thousands of its armed men, whether mercenaries or volunteers or both, flooded into east Ukraine in the spring of 2014, christened by nationalists the "Russian Spring," to fight alongside the separatists there, when a woman said it, spoke the thing that had, for the last sixty years, been inappropriate to say out-loud: "America has attacked us. Putin is our sovereign. We are for him, with all our soul. And *body*."

The way she said it—the way she used the Russian expression—the immortal soul was given first, the profane body after, almost as an afterthought. The woman, Tatyana Gruzdeva, appeared to be in her late thirties; she may have been an accountant or a schoolteacher or a housewife, it didn't seem to matter by then. She was standing in the rain holding up a sign at a rally asking Putin to give aid to the people of Ukraine's breakaway region of Donetsk and protect them from Kiev's "punitive operation." It didn't logically follow that America had "attacked us" from the events in Ukraine, or from the "scepter of fascism" that she spoke of, or how that connected to Putin being our sovereign. She wasn't going to rationalize any of that: suzerainty over Ukraine was a metaphysical necessity of one empire, one true manifest destiny, just as it made necessary to hand over one's soul, and the body after, to the one true emperor, the vice regent of God on earth, for God only knew what purposes.

The body part was actually pretty easy to understand, given how modern spin had, on occasion, propped up the national leader as a sex symbol and succeeded quite well amid the contingency that Tatyana Gruzdeva represented. What was darker, and what in effect propelled me to start writing this book five years ago was that the soul was dragged into it. Ukraine, the annexation of Crimea, the cold Holy War that was brewing on state television, all that was just the logical outcome of Gruzdeva's statement. Putin's rule over one eighth of the world's oil reserve, over the world's largest gas reserves, over the world's second largest nuclear arsenal, over Sochi, and the Winter Olympics he had secured there, were worth nothing unless Tatyana Gruzdeva said those words and meant them. But what, exactly, had made her say them? Many, many things, from the salary she drew to the icons she saw on television each night. As for the peculiarly Russian trinity of body, soul, and government, we would need to go back hundreds of years to understand their ties; fortunately, however, Russian history presented an illustration of that phenomenon as recently as 2012.

★ ★ ★

Father Boris flashed his eyes and turned away momentarily. "That's interesting. The church and state. But why not? What's wrong with that? It has been like that, the [harmony] of the powers, the spiritual and the material."

He was referring to *Symphonia,* the harmony and interdependency of spiritual and temporal authority that had been a hallmark of Orthodox Christianity since the Byzantine Empire. But there was a contradiction: the Russian Constitution explicitly separated church and state, but implicitly, that separateness just didn't make any sense. Not to church authorities, who had implied that summer that the separation of church and state was bad for Russia and hence did not exist, and not for the priest.

We were sitting on the only bench in the priest's rural church. He had looked, for a second, as though he had thought a lot about my question, and yet seemed startled, as if I had come at him from a different ethical plane. I had asked him about the relationship between the Kremlin and the Russian Orthodox Church in the wake of possibly the most bizarre court verdict in Russia's recent history—that in the Pussy Riot case.

"The Bible says that Man was created as one whole, [body and soul]. I am not against that harmony," the priest said, his eyes crinkling and shining as he looked directly at me. "Power comes from God; the people get the ruler that they deserve."

It was August 2012. His rural church was in the throes of reconstruction, as a bearded, Orthodox-looking worker drilled outside, with a view towards a river and a rolling, grassy meadow. We were on the edge of the Moscow Region, about 100 kilometers (62 miles) from the capital, about a half-hour's bike ride on a dusty road to the nearest settlement. With its forests on the horizon, the lifestyle there seemed to have changed little in the past couple of decades, perhaps centuries.

Built in the 1830s, the church had stood in ruins for as long as I could remember. During the 1930s, on orders from the new Bolshevik authorities, it was—not demolished, no, but its bricks were taken to build a pig farm nearby. Around 2007, I had noticed that it was being reconstructed. Then a wooden cottage and a garden went up nearby, with a few milk goats, and Father Boris was sent to serve in the church. His parish consisted mostly of Muscovites who had bought *dachas,* or summer homes, in the vicinity; natives were becoming increasingly scarce.

In his fifties, with a bushy brown beard and laughing eyes,

he was originally a Muscovite himself, who became an Orthodox Christian well into adulthood, after years of atheism. He married and was ordained, then found himself here, living in a wooden house with no plumbing, between a forest, a field, and the church. In his faith, he tended to lean towards the conservatism of those who had found God later in life.

"Like the army," he said of the orders to serve in the rural church, and smiled. It wasn't clear if he was joking, or if the humor was dark or merely gray.

For half an hour, I had been trying to get him to talk about Pussy Riot, five female punk artists who had donned colored balaclavas and tights, and tried to lip sync in Moscow's biggest church, Christ the Savior Cathedral. In their song, they had appealed to the Virgin Mary to deliver them from Vladimir Putin. Two weeks after their performance, Vladimir Putin was elected President of Russia for a third term, after a four-year hiatus as prime minister under the nominal presidency of Dmitry Medvedev. Just days after the March 4 election, three members of the band were arrested and charged with hooliganism. Hardly anyone had heard of them or their radical art group; if average Russians were preoccupied with anything in that remote realm of power and politics, it was with the unprecedented opposition protests that had spilled out into the street ahead of Putin's presidential campaign. While Pussy Riot's church stunt outraged religious Russians, no one paid much attention, not until the church started publicly condemning them, not until Vladimir Putin condemned them himself.

Five months later, on August 17, a court found the three women guilty of hooliganism motivated by religious hatred, sentencing them to two years in a penal colony.

Father Boris didn't want to discuss the case or the verdict. Initially, on the phone, he demurred and suggested I talk to someone higher up in the church hierarchy, explaining that they would be more knowledgeable.

"I'm telling you, it's being blown out of proportion," he kept saying with a smile. He was convinced, for instance, that, according to Russian state television there had been a copycat performance in Europe and the participants had been sentenced to jail. In reality, they had been fined for causing a disturbance, not imprisoned for a federal crime.

The truth was that, like many average Russians who reluctantly shared their views with me about the Pussy Riot case, he didn't seem to have an opinion about the verdict. The group and what they had done disgusted him; as he saw it, their careless, self-serving affront to their own people, a people they did not even try to understand, was not worth the words that we were wasting on them.

But there was a clear sense that the only reason we were talking about them was because the government decided to put them on trial. And that just didn't seem to be any of his business.

"What can we do, if something political happens?" he said at length. "Do everything with love."

2.

"So can you just translate the word itself into Russian, or not?" Vladimir Putin asked the journalist provocatively, "or does it make you uncomfortable?"

It was the second time he'd tried to get Kevin Owen, his British interviewer for RT, the state-owned, English-language Russia Today channel, to say "Pussy Riot" in Russian—with no success. The band had an English name that everyone understood to be far cruder in Russian; the group was referred to using the English words. Owen tried to laugh it off; Putin smiled and tried again. "Maybe you can't, for ethical reasons," he said finally, smiling no longer.

Owen tried changing the subject. "Actually, I'd thought it was referring to a 'cat', but maybe I'm missing a point… Anyway, do you think that… the case was handled wrongly in any way?"

But Putin cut him off, raising his voice slightly. "You understand everything perfectly. Don't pretend you don't understand."

Owen, who was not a native Russian speaker, could be forgiven for misunderstanding. While crude, the English "pussy" is still a euphemism, not nearly as obscene as "cunt." But Pussy Riot—as the group had named itself—was clearly aiming for the only Russian equivalent—*pizda*.

And Putin would try to make another journalist, this time a Russian, also translate the English name of the band into their native language, pushing him towards saying an obscenity on national television.

"I want to ask you about the punk group Pussy Riot," Vadim Takmenev, a presenter at the federal NTV channel, asked in a two-hour long documentary that purported to portray the "real" Putin—with his dog, at breakfast, at the gym, and at the pool, where he spent most mornings. Takmenev, a seasoned prime time host and, unlike Owen, a Russian, asked the more "uncomfortable" questions with a self-conscious nervousness.

But Putin seemed to have his own agenda. "How is the name translated?" he asked back.

"Yes, I know," the presenter tried to smile, trying to nod away the obscenity.

"Can you say it?"

"I can't say it."

"Can you say it to your audience?" Putin insisted. "For people who don't study foreign languages?"

Instead of saying the obscenity, the presenter said something unintentionally revealing.

"I can't say it in front of you," he gave in.

Putin laughed out loud. "If you can't say it in front of me, then it's an obscene word. You see? Those were talented girls. They forced all of you to say it. What, is that good?"[8]

It was early October 2012, nearly two months after the verdict that sent Nadezhda Tolokonnikova and Maria Alyokhina to a penal colony (the third and oldest participant, Yekaterina Samutsevich, would be freed on probation at an appeals hearing just days after the interview aired). Putin no longer had to worry about his statements pressuring the court. He was using crudeness to make a point about how the women had undermined society's moral norms.

He also seemed, unbeknownst to him, to be following in the footsteps of Nicholas I, who had the poet Alexander Polezhayev brought into his presence in the middle of a winter's night in 1836, to force him to read a far less crude poem.

Before the audience, someone had made sure that all of Polezhayev's buttons were in place, for Nicholas was notoriously pedantic. After sizing up the student with his serpentine gaze, Nicholas handed him a notebook with his poem. "Read it out loud," he ordered, but Polezhayev, feeling the Tsar's eyes on him, was too petrified.

"I can't," he said. This was not just terror of the Tsar, who had clearly already read the poem: Polezhayev's work contained words that, in those times, were considered indecent; and he could hardly bring himself to utter something dirty in that sacred presence.

"Read!" the Tsar ordered. Polezhayev read. The Tsar lectured him for a moment, then suggested that the young poet join the army as a soldier, recommending that he use the opportunity of military service to cleanse his soul. As they parted, the Tsar kissed him.[9] Polezhayev would spend the rest of his life as a soldier; at the age of thirty-four he died in a military hospital from tuberculosis.

Like Nicholas facing an upper class revolt, Putin seemed to have found himself suddenly becoming a guarantor not just of the Constitution, but of the moral norms that often contradicted it. He was privatizing God, he was proclaiming his rights to the souls of his subjects, and he hadn't the strength to conceal it any longer.

It was as though a façade had cracked: with the jailing of three women for dancing in a church, something that had lain dormant underneath, that we had thought we'd outgrown, was spilling out onto the surface, to ours, and to Vladimir Putin's dismay, amid haphazard efforts to patch up the hole with repressive measures that only made it grow. It was as though the unmitigated relationship between a human being and his government was laid bare, along with the underlying mandate of Russian governance: a mystical mandate that preceded democratic institutions by thousands of years, a mandate that came down to something as simple as strength versus weakness, food or death, master or God. That an unlikely, poker-faced former KGB officer found himself at the apex of this primordial chaos and had initially tried to suppress it only accentuated its resilience.

It had started with the Dmitry Medvedev conundrum. For four years, Vladimir Putin had ruled from the seat of the prime minister, to where he had withdrawn in 2008 to preserve the letter of the Constitution, which forbade more than two consecutive presidential terms. For president, he handpicked a lawyer he had worked with for decades. And while Russians implicitly understood who the real boss was, there was an eagerness to play the political game, to bet on the soft-spoken liberal, to speculate whether he would run for a second term. Indeed, until the very end, the question of whether Dmitry Medvedev was merely a placeholder or a true successor remained shrouded in intrigue. Most importantly, even Putin—known to make decisions at the last minute—seemed eager to give him a chance, to test whether institutional—rather than personal—authority was strong enough to survive.

For months running up to the 2012 decision, rumors of a rift between the two men festered, fueled deliberately by the Kremlin itself. The suspense seemed necessary to uphold a façade of politics, as if getting politicians to take part in the rehearsal would eventually usher in the real thing. Then, sometime during the summer of 2011, the decision was quietly made between Putin, Medvedev, and a few key insiders: the president was not going to run for a second term, and Putin would return to the Kremlin.

When Putin and Medvedev finally announced their decision in September 2011, admitting that they had reached it privately "years ago," it came as a demoralizing blow to a whole swath of society that had got used to the motions of democratic process, even if they understood that those motions were flawed. No one was surprised that Putin was returning to the Kremlin—they were shocked that he had admitted, so nonchalantly, that it wasn't any of their business and never had been. It was as if, standing before 11,000 delegates of his majority United Russia party, he had admitted that it was all just a game used to bewilder his subjects, but that it had become too confusing, arcane, and risky to carry on with.

It took about two months for the frustrations in that swath of society to boil over. The December 4 parliamentary elections became the tipping point. It did not matter that Putin's United Russia party, though still winning, garnered far fewer votes than in the previous elections, nor that the alleged vote rigging was about the same—if not less—than last time. The damage had already been done, the gauze curtain had been punctured, and thousands of people began spilling into the streets in protest.

For the Putin generation, who had come of age under the high oil prices of his pseudo-autocracy, it was like a form of psychotherapy as they began articulating their attitudes in an attempt to desanctify state power. "You are not a Tsar, not a God," a group of veteran paratroopers sang at rallies, joining an urban, professional class. After the president ridiculed their white ribbons and compared them to condoms, the protesters turned up with all sorts of creative descriptions for the president as a used condom. Sex—which, under Putin, emerged for the first time as an explicit feature of a personality cult around a Russian leader—proved an easy target. At one rally, a girl boldly proclaimed "I do not want you," in a country where a fifth of the female population did.[10] She may have not meant it, but she seemed to be suggesting that sexual willingness was a key condition of political loyalty. "A president who is not doing it with his wife is doing it to his country," a protest leader proclaimed from the stage at the same rally. A day after Putin won the presidential vote in the first round, another leader proclaimed from the stage that the rigged elections had been tantamount to rape.

The Kremlin's initial response to the protests was to act as though this was a normal part of the democratic process. When rallies broke out in early December, as people feared bloody clashes, city authorities took a consistent line on allowing mass demonstrations. A top government official praised the upper class demonstrators as "the best part of our society" and Putin proclaimed that he was "pleased" to see them protesting—it meant that the civil society he was so eager to foster was taking root.

To demonstrate just how serious he was about democracy, he invited them for dialogue—and even designated liberals in his government as potential mediators.

But within two months of the first protests, in early February 2012, it was already clear that the dialogue just didn't seem to be happening—as one of the mediators told me then.

It may have been that Putin never wanted genuine dialogue, or maybe he didn't immediately recognize that by being open to dialogue he must be open to giving up the reins of power. Maybe he earnestly believed that the kind of democratic façade he had instituted was indeed the real thing, just like those gadgets they had in Europe that he was so keen to import. Maybe dialogue, to him, meant something on his own terms, a recognition of token concessions from him in order to bring the dissenters back into the fold.

But the opposition, too, had little experience in political activity—in a country where, as they said themselves, politics did not yet exist. The most charismatic voice to emerge from the movement, lawyer and anti-corruption blogger Alexei Navalny, initially refused to run for office in a campaign that he did not recognize as real.

When he finally ran for Moscow mayor in the summer of 2013, as we shall see later in this book, it was a forced decision. With Navalny facing a conviction that would bar him from public office, the liberal Moscow mayor Sergei Sobyanin eagerly backed him as a contender to ensure a competitive election, knowing full well Navalny could never pose a real threat.

In early 2012, without a clear political platform, and with demands that were clearly fixated on Putin's personal removal from power, the protest rallies bore all the marks of a carnival—at once hopeful, enlightening, and cathartic—but harboring something darker underneath. If the rallies were a carnival, a true carnival carries the threat of death.[11]

Inadvertently, an underlying current in the protest movement seemed intent on provoking Putin to reveal himself as a true autocrat, a feudal sovereign who would respond to revolt with physical repression, jailings, and torture—either subduing his people, or giving them a pretext to depose him.

For lack of an alternative, the confrontation between the "best part of society" and its ruler began to turn into a mirroring process, a game of chicken between two thugs of clearly unequal strength, staring at each other, waiting to see who would budge. It wasn't about politics, it was about something that predated politics: sheer, brute force, and who had more self-confidence.

When dialogue didn't happen, the Kremlin stopped pretending. Out went the Kremlin official who praised the "best part of society," and in came Soviet-style propaganda. To rival the carnival-like protests, the administration began rallying masses from all over the country—with a gentle mix of financial enticement and coercion. Teachers, accountants, nurses, clerks on the state budget, when given tickets to attend pro-Putin rallies in Moscow, didn't really see it as much of a choice: When your boss tells you it's voluntary, then it's mandatory.

If the inadvertent temptation of the protesting opposition had been to bring out the feudal sovereign in a bureaucrat struggling to play the game of democracy, then they succeeded. With the elections a week away, he wasn't asking for their votes, he was asking them to lease their bodies and souls as the price of economic stability.

Implicit in the role of feudal sovereign were the repressions—

and they had already begun. Activists had been detained for a few weeks at the first unauthorized rallies, in early December 2011. But by 2013, nearly thirty people were in custody for taking part in a rally that had turned violent, some of them simply for standing next to a skirmish between police and protesters; opposition leaders were facing up to ten years in jail, and an activist had been snatched in front of a UN office in the Ukraine[12] and taken to Russia, where he claimed to have been kept in a basement without food until he confessed to planning a mass revolt.[13] (The authorities would deny the activist's claim, saying he turned himself in voluntarily.)

Just as repression was implicit in the role of a feudal sovereign, a sacrificial victim was implicit at a carnival.

★ ★ ★

Vadim Takmenev's documentary aired on national television on Putin's sixtieth birthday on October 7, 2012, and for the first time, fear emerged as a normal part of an interview—something that no longer needed to be concealed, an ironic allusion in a conversation set to tinkling, comic music.

"When someone's sitting in front of you like this, can you sense… if he's afraid of you… if he's embarrassed?" Takmenev asked Putin.

"Of course. It's visible."

"With me?" the journalist laughed nervously.

"With you it's less," Putin said dispassionately, after considering him for a moment. "But you're used to it."

3.

Yekaterina Samutsevich didn't really feel anything when, on February 21, 2012, she climbed to the altar steps of Christ the Savior Cathedral, the holiest section of Russia's biggest church, forbidden, by church canon, to anyone but priests.

"I had to act quickly, clearly, it's very easy for something to go wrong and for everything to fall apart," she described shortly after her release from prison in October 2012. "So it was a desire to do everything right, everything that I had thought through beforehand."

Clad in colored tights, with a balaclava hiding her face, she prepared to dance out the trademark moves of her little-known feminist punk group, Pussy Riot, with four other girls, genuflecting in a mock proskynesis, the gesture of full prostration that, in ancient Russian custom, had been used before both secular and clerical figures. As she tried to remove her guitar from her case to lip sync the words to the song they intended to perform, a church guard seized her and removed her from the cathedral. She did not resist.

The words she intended to lip sync were, "Shit, shit, holy shit, Holy Mother, banish Putin, banish Putin, banish Putin."

As Pussy Riot would later underline in their defence, they saw themselves as holy fools—those half-crazy, half-blessed social outcasts of Orthodox tradition.

"There's this situation of utter despair, when there's no other way out, and in that case, in the Orthodox tradition you appeal to the Holy Mother. We quoted this cultural phenomenon."

If she intended to protest at an emerging *status quo* in which her government's power was implicitly based on God, then on another level she wound up reinforcing it. By holding a punk prayer, whether they felt anything at all as they uttered those words, Pussy Riot's inadvertent message was, "only God can replace the man who rules over us."

If their desecration angered Orthodox Christians—by sullying the sacred space of the church with something as corrupt as politics—then it was the duplicity of their message that enraged the church and the Kremlin, a Kremlin bent on legitimizing itself through elections and rule of law.

As a punk group, Pussy Riot had already held several similar performances during that political season, and their anti-Putin song had debuted in other venues. An offshoot of the radical art group *Voina* (War), Pussy Riot could only dream of generating any nationwide publicity outside a fringe audience of protesting performance artists.

In that milieu, their antics were designed to shock. Nadezhda Tolokonnikova, whose pouting, pensive gaze through the bars of her court cage was immortalized during the trial, had taken part in a videotaped group orgy in 2008. Nine months pregnant, she was shown in Moscow's Polytechnic Museum, having sex with her husband, Pyotr Verzilov, in a performance titled "Fuck for the

Successor, Little Bear"—a reference to Putin's protégé, Dmitry Medvedev. Another member of Pussy Riot—who did not take part in the Punk Prayer—was videotaped in a supermarket trying to stuff a raw chicken into her vagina.

Samutsevich herself didn't expect their performance in Christ the Savior Cathedral to generate anything more than a brief media storm.

And yet something in that dubious message, sounded from the altar of Russia's top church, struck an unexpected chord, as if beaming straight into a collective unconscious that had already begun to stir.

The supreme displeasure made itself evident immediately. On the following day, Archpriest Vsevolod Chaplin—a *de facto* mouthpiece for the church—condemned their act. "This is a sin that violates the law of God. The most important law. For the wages of sin is death," he told news media, quoting from Romans 6:23.

Within days, the law of God was neatly discovered in the Criminal Code of the Russian Federation—hooliganism motivated by religious hatred, a sin that merited up to seven years in a penal colony. On February 26, the the girls who had taken part in the performance were named as wanted by the police.

On March 6, two days after Vladimir Putin won the presidential election, his displeasure at Pussy Riot's performance became known for the first time. His reaction to Pussy Riot's performance was "negative," said his spokesman, Dmitry Peskov, calling their stunt "disgusting."

The beauty of a Byzantine power structure is that "rule by signal" can neither be proven nor disproven. There is no record, no personal decree by Putin, that citizens A, B, and C should stand trial for any particular crime. According to several unconfirmed reports around that time, Patriarch Kirill, on close terms with Putin, had asked him directly to take "revenge" on Pussy Riot, while certain investigators on the case allegedly claimed to be reporting about it directly to Putin himself.

Whatever spoken or unspoken instructions passed down from the very top, a signal was sent that was powerful enough to set in motion a whole criminal investigation—and whether it came from the church or from the Kremlin was immaterial, for the result was the same.

That criminal investigation—as though itself a continuation of Pussy Riot's art performance—reflected what, exactly, had displeased the authorities. In the indictment presented by investigator Lieutenant Colonel Artem Ranchenkov, Pussy Riot's stunt served to "diminish the spiritual foundation of the government." Experts recruited by prosecutors stated that the women had violated decrees by the Church Council of Trullo held in Constantinople under Byzantine Emperor Justinian II in 692.

"Imagine if something like this happened under Tsar Ivan the Terrible," a literary expert who would go on to testify in court, wrote in a patriotic publication. "The headless corpses of the heretics would have been thrown to the dogs. Terrible! But what was done in Christ the Savior Cathedral was, in terms of the seriousness of the crime, far worse than the execution I mentioned."[14]

Each side seemed to be forcing the other to assume an ancient role. The "criminals" exposed a divine mandate that the supreme power found itself relying on, in the absence of other forms of legitimization. The criminal investigators responded in kind, identifying the "spiritual foundation of the government" as a legal concept, and initiating what, in effect, could be called an Inquisition. And the defence, opting out of the confused and ineffective paradigm of the law, focused instead on exposing and indicting that spiritual foundation. The effect was the same: both sides were proving that it existed.

"In Russia it is customary, if you are under investigation, to lick the shoe of the judge," the fiery defence lawyer Mark Feygin, an ambitious activist and a former regional politician, proclaimed from the crowded defence bench. Behind him, the three girls of Pussy Riot sniggered from their glass cage, the same one built nearly a decade before to "protect" Mikhail Khodorkovsky, the oil tycoon jailed in 2003 after falling out of favor at court. (The justice system was, of course, about protection—"we are protecting them from you," a stony-faced court bailiff had told me as they led the members of Pussy Riot past us.)

Feygin was on a roll. "You must weep, debase yourself, you must squash your identity. You must allow the government to tear you to pieces. You must turn into a complete nothing."

It was an irony that as Feygin spoke, he was not hauled off

by the guard, as he would in a real Inquisition. It was ironic also that the judge, Marina Syrova, watched this condemnation of her work, her shoes, and her implicit sadistic tendencies with a detached bemusement, as if not really comprehending the meaning of his words, but acknowledging that they must be part of the due process she was charged with overseeing.

What made this scene startling as I watched it was that in an American courtroom, a lawyer making such an unwholesome reference to a judge's shoe could well be held in contempt of court, given the relative independence of an American judge. But Judge Marina Syrova remained silent.

For Yekaterina Samutsevich, the art performance stopped in early October, when she switched lawyers. Accused of that very bootlicking by more radical detractors (and later by her former lawyer, Mark Feygin), she opted for a less politicized lawyer who focused not on the statement she had been trying to make, but the fact that she never had the opportunity to make it—having been removed from the stage before she could start her performance.

That had been enough, to everyone's surprise, to set her free. And with Samutsevich out of jail, her performance stopped. The provocation she had set in motion was, for her, concluded.

"Political art which holds events in public places is of course provocative. It's a test. You make an event, you watch how a system responds," she said.

But if she believed that Russia was a secular state, then why test it, why stage the provocation? If there was a mix of the two, then why deliberately bring out that dormant, primordial matrix, especially if it posed a mortal threat?

And then she said something else: "Harmony of church and state—of course we were trying to disrupt this harmony, and I hope we succeeded."

If there was harmony to disrupt, and a patrimonial deep state that ruled through personalized power instead of the constitutional state that ruled by law, then Pussy Riot should have known they would go to jail for their antics.

There was something else she didn't fully explain, possibly because she didn't fully understand it herself: she seemed to have internalized the role of the sacrificial victim.

"It's as though there's a mechanism for the opposition, created by the government, that the only way to be in the opposition is to be in jail," she said.

"As soon as you get out of jail, you lose that aura of the sacrificial victim. You're not interesting. This image of someone who is behind bars—who is being silenced by force—it's somehow been made more appealing for the opposition. It's an illusion."

What she didn't know—at least, she could not recall it when she spoke to me—was that it was Putin who, about a week after the Pussy Riot performance, made the first reference to sacrifice.

He was talking about planned provocations at protest rallies, and was describing the potential methods. "I know about this. They're even looking for a so-called 'sacrificial victim,' someone famous. They'll 'whack' them, if you'll pardon me, and then blame the government."

There was something about Yekaterina Samutsevich that didn't compute—a double origin, a combination of two matters that did not mix easily.

On one level, Katya, as she had become known, looked and spoke like the kind of person I'd encounter in an American university town, or in Europe. Born too late to attend Soviet schools, she was a teenager in the 1990s, joining the workforce soon after Vladimir Putin became president. For a few years after college, she worked from nine to five in an office as a computer programmer writing code for a nuclear submarine, and then suddenly decided to drop out, downshift, as she put it.

But on another level—in the stunt that became the ultimate product of her yearning for creativity—she had tapped into the ancient identity of the holy fool. Thanks to her stunt and her subsequent punishment, she had helped expose a social paradigm where the holy fool is both a necessary and an inevitable role, a paradigm where all players, as if on cue, assume their positions: the victim and the executioner, who could not exist without each other.

Free from prison, she would never be free from this. "Sometimes I feel like we are being used," she said. She said this, as everything else she told me during our interview, with the air of a person who has very little idea of what is happening to her.

4.

Father Boris was too far removed from all this for the simple reason that he was restoring his church. If the government had once destroyed these churches and sent priests like him to their death, now it was helping restore what its predecessors had destroyed.

No, they were not getting in the way anymore. "Local [authorities] even helped out… there's even a managing role," he said, speaking of both public and private funds that trickled down to restore the rural church. "That unifying, directing role—in many ways it comes from the authorities."

But wasn't he afraid of becoming dependent on them?

"What kind of dependence can there be? To announce from the pulpit who to vote for in the local administration?"

I told him then that Patriarch Kirill had met with Putin in February to proclaim publicly that his presidency had been a miracle of God—precisely the meeting that Pussy Riot sought to ridicule in their church performance—that the Patriarch was endorsing Russia's *de facto* ruler for the *de jure* role of president, and that the would-be president was drawing his legitimacy from the church.

To this the priest replied: "Power comes from God, yes. Any people have the ruler that they deserve."

I saw a glimmer of what this meant in the way that Yelena, a music teacher from the Moscow suburbs who sang in this church on weekends, described her feelings about the Pussy Riot verdict.

"It was disgusting what they did and they needed to be punished," she said reluctantly. "Perhaps not harshly." What certainly annoyed her was how, with the help of the government, the case had become overblown.

And why was that happening? "I am not privy to it," she said. "It will be as they decide, it's not for us simple people to judge what goes on between the church and the state. Only God knows what goes on up there."

I told Father Boris about the kind of book I was trying to write, looking out of the church window onto the fields, and impatient for a swim in that winding river nearby.

"You have to understand the life of the people you are writing about," he said, certain that the life of his people had been misunderstood and distorted. "There are things that are nearly impossible to understand."

I nodded.

He looked at me inquiringly. "You don't have it easy, do you?"

PART I
THE SUBJECTS

Chapter 1

To See Putin and Die

I closed the window and everything ceased being
Only the sun swam and glimmered, shivering and ringing
No one before me, no one around me, no one before me
Only the sun is against me, and around me and before me
I stare into the fire, it's burning and shining and glowing
I fall and lie there afraid they will notice me cowering.
—**Dmitry Ozersky,** poet and songwriter, "Fell"

I wanted to call my next book To See Putin and Die,
but then everyone said that would be a bit too much.
—**Andrei Kolesnikov**, pool reporter, author of
I saw Putin and *Putin saw me,* in an interview with
the author

1.

THERE WAS NO door in our newsroom on that day. Taken off
the hinges for the occasion, it revealed the worn-out woodwork of
economy-class panelling ("Regulations," a manager said reverently
when asked why this was necessary). After about four hours of
queasy anticipation, a woman, wearing a slightly glamorous, low-cut
black suit and white frilly blouse (the same one, it seemed, donned
at countless protocol events at the White House), leaned in through
this opening and told a milling retinue of scrawny security guards,

journalists, and staff that "they are on their way."

The hype had actually started four days ago on Friday, when an ominous memo advised middle managers at the sprawling, government-owned enterprise that "due to a special regime on Tuesday, Feb. 24" guests would not be allowed on the premises of the building. The "movement" of employees outside their offices was to be "minimized" or "limited." The "movement" of employees on the second floor (where our offices were located) was to be "maximally limited." It was even suggested that some people not show up for work altogether. And yet the reason for the special measures was never named. Employees passed news of a "visit" to each other in hushed voices, joking about what they would say to the "guest" if they got the chance.

Everyone was told to clean their desks. All photographs and posters were ordered to be removed—including a little postcard one translator had in her cubicle, with a 1950s-style drawing of Putin and the inscription: "I'm watching you, you are not working!"

A janitor, when asked why the door was taken off its hinges, was incredulous.

"Don't you know who's going to be here tomorrow?" she said. People in the building had been talking like that since Friday—a visit by Prime Minister Vladimir Putin was euphemized down to "a VIP guest" or "a special regime," or, in the case of this janitor, simply "they."

"They are expected at 11 AM, if they deign to drop by. They will walk along this corridor, into the archive, and through there, to the press hall."

The janitor, who only gave her name as Tatyana, knew the itinerary because she had vacuumed these areas three times over the long weekend, when no one was even here. And now she was doing it again—washing every surface of every room the prime minister might or might not cast his eyes on.

"It's always been like that," she said. "We've had to do the same thing, even under Yeltsin. Then they will kick us out, so that, God forbid, we are not seen by them."

Worst of all, it could still be all in vain. "And what if he doesn't even show up?"

But on the afternoon of February 24, after about three hours of waiting, it was finally clear that yes, they would drop in, and Tatyana's three days of scrubbing would not go to waste.

After the press representative announced them, leaning in through the opening, a slow procession lumped in through the doorway. Instinctively, I stood up. A cameraman behind hissed for me to sit down.

Milling around, stepping into their midst and slowly sizing up the immediate surroundings, the prime minister walked with a noticeable swagger, like a CEO checking out his business. Gray and bland, benevolent and sinister, he was boring, glorious, and terrifying all at once.

He nodded and returned the smile of the first pretty girl in the office, then, slightly aloof, allowed himself to be led towards us.

"They have surpassed [their competitor] in terms of online hits," the director of the organization he was touring told him gravely. She was showing him the offices of an English-language newspaper, a brand that had recently come under the control of the state-funded news agency, and that, on the prime minister's orders, had been re-launched anew. He nodded and smiled. He liked what he saw.

"How many people work here?" he asked her in a barely audible voice that was heard all over the room.

"Thirty," she said. In reality, there were a lot fewer; to fill the empty seats, employees from another department had been told, to their great annoyance, to spend half their workday next to us.

When he reached the middle of the room and stood about six feet away from me, I deemed it appropriate to look him in the eyes, smile, and say "hello." He answered soundlessly with a nod, looked directly at me for a quarter of a second, blinked once, like a camera, and, having acknowledged my existence, click, he looked at someone else.

After eye-contact was made with all of the staff, he turned to the director, asked her, "That's it?", turned around and left.

Two foreigners on the staff, who had sat less than a meter away from where Putin stood, pronounced the whole affair anti-climatic and compared it noisily to an episode of M.A.S.H.. Their disappointment was understandable: as they had waited for the prime minister to appear, they were held for two hours in the office of the top manager, who drilled them on how to pronounce "Vladimir

Vladimirovich," how to ask for permission to be photographed together, and how to shake his hand most eloquently.

But paralyzed by his proximity less than a meter away, they did none of those things.

Still, these foreigners and the Russian top manager would never quite understand each other; for the foreigners, Putin's visit was an inconvenient disruption to their working day. For the general director, it was obviously something more: when I asked him, hours in advance, if Putin was actually going to pass through our office, he nodded wordlessly with a look of childlike rapture that I was startled to see on the face of an otherwise intelligent, grown man.

Aside from the memo, no one had instructed me on how to behave in the presence of the prime minister and former president of Russia. Neither to stand when he entered our office, nor to worry about the fact that I was busy writing an article about the trial of his foe, Mikhail Khodorkovsky, widely seen as politically motivated.

Indeed, no one told the director general to have his employees approach Putin to shake his hand. If anything, we were specifically told to "relax" by the head of the organization during her final inspection of the premises prior to the arrival.

And while we were told to clean our desks before his visit, no one even hinted that I remove a pile of books with titles like *Putin's Russia: the Ruins of the Opposition*. Growing up in America, I had once prided myself on refusing to stand for the pledge of allegiance in high school, thinking it servile and totalitarian. But here in Moscow, half an hour away from meeting the *de facto* ruler of Russia, I removed the books from my desk myself. Why?

2.

Dmitry Ryabov,[15] a rookie reporter with an independent weekly, aligned himself with a row of cameramen near the grand stairwell of the State Duma building on Okhotny Ryad, just across the street from the Kremlin, and stood waiting on his tiptoes for about an hour in a setting clearly heralding the appearance of a celebrity. "It was like Cannes," he recalled later, casting his eyes down in a timid disgust. But it was also nothing like it: for to applaud a movie star was not regrettable, but to applaud inadvertently the appearance of Vladimir Putin was.

It was the first time that Ryabov, who identified himself with a democratic intelligentsia that was deeply opposed to a government it had no means to change, had ever seen Putin. And when— either from the pressure of waiting, or at the surprise of suddenly seeing him so close—he applauded, the act of clapping his hands so irritated him that he felt he had to mention it on Facebook the next day. "I hate myself," he wrote, as if by the acknowledgement he made himself clean.

Ryabov's inadvertent applause reflected all the contradictions inherent in a Byzantine regime that kind of wanted to be democratic but could not be for lack of real democratic institutions—and it cut right through the elaborate façade of democracy that was being enacted that April 20, 2011. Constitutionally, Putin was a subordinate to President Dmitry Medvedev—a close colleague he had personally handpicked as his successor in 2008—and yet, regardless of their political preferences, most government officials intuitively sensed who wielded real power. Constitutionally, it was Putin who was reporting to his Parliament—but aside from the perfunctory criticism coming from three emasculated opposition parties, a whole army of deputies from the United Russia party gave him standing ovations and called him, without even the slightest hint of irony, "our leader." Constitutionally, Putin was to provide a progress report in this annual address—but in reality, everyone knew that the coming speech was a chance for the supreme leader to give a blueprint, a set of instructions for life in this enormous, impossible country. It was five months before Putin would unequivocally announce that he would be returning to the presidency in 2012— describing the decision as having been made "years ago"—but by April 2011 most people already sensed that Medvedev was merely a placeholder and that Russia's sovereign ruler was the prime minister, who staunchly insisted on paying lip service to all the formalities of democracy.

The reality of what was happening on the grand stairwell and the makeshift panel partition that separated us from them reflected all those kaleidoscopic contradictions. The very act of waiting, normally for hours—standing on aching feet, with your camera equipment or your laptop, sometimes allowing a colleague you've never seen before to perch her notebook on your shoulder— established the stardom of the moment, enhancing metaphysics of power that not even the American president could match.

The murmur around me intensified, then quieted. Ministers began to appear one by one; Igor Sechin, the dreaded energy chief in Putin's cabinet who was believed to have helped orchestrate the imprisonment and induced bankruptcy of oil tycoon Mikhail Khodorkovsky, walked darkly past; followed by Alexei Kudrin, the liberal finance minister who would leave his post in September and start making overtures to the opposition. Then, flanked by United Russia leader Boris Gryzlov (the bureaucrat who referred to the prime minister as "our leader"), Vladimir Putin, looking more confident than usual, emerged and rushed down the stairs, cast a glance and smiled warmly to greet the press, and disappeared through the doorway.

The appearance couldn't have lasted more than a few seconds, but it drew a strange reaction from the crowd of lesser officials and onlookers who had congregated along the grand stairwell. Where a rockstar or a popular president would be greeted with cheers— possibly of adulation—the sound that came from the stairwell behind us recalled more of a quiet wail, a sigh of relief and desperation, mingled with weak, inadvertent applause that wasn't even supposed to happen. The sound did not seem to express so much the popularity of the star as it did the fear and deference that surrounded him.

That suppressed wail encapsulated an internal confusion about how we were supposed to relate to the national leader. Do we applaud his appearance on the parapet, or do we fall to our knees? What about those, like Ryabov, who do not like him? As it was, everyone was making an effort to pretend that this small, bland, agile man in his late fifties was merely a popular prime minister who had arrived to address his parliament. But if that was really the case, there would be no need to applaud his seconds-long passage along a balcony. In reality, what many felt and what most could not articulate was the presence of a power far more primordial than the highest elected office: for in the absence of rule of law, this was no president or prime minister, but a sovereign who had the power of life and death over you.

Something strange had happened to Ryabov, and he didn't notice the applause or the wail behind him. He wasn't even looking around to make mental notes of his surroundings, but stood instead aloof, concentrating on whoever was supposed to emerge on the stairwell. And when Putin finally appeared and deigned to look in his direction, Ryabov, a journalist who had always opposed this regime, who disliked most of Putin's policies, to his own horror found himself applauding. And he was so irritated by his unconscious behavior that he eagerly deconstructed it, as if by his awareness he could somehow escape it.

"What brings me the most sorrow is the slavish awareness of our people (and myself included)," he wrote to me days later. "Despite all the democratic rhetoric, [we] know exactly who rules the country and are ever ready to demonstrate our loyalty to that ruler. And my actions (my applause) came into direct conflict with my political convictions."

The nineteenth century Count, Vladimir Sollogub, recalled a telling appearance of Tsar Nicholas I during the 1830s. Count Sollogub was walking down St. Petersburg's Nevsky Prospect with the poet Alexander Pushkin and Sergei Sobolevsky, who had recently returned from an extended stay in Europe and was sporting a goatee—at a time when the aristocracy was still forbidden to wear beards in Russia, based on a decree by Peter the Great.

"Suddenly a plume of feathers emerged on a carriage up on Politseisky Bridge. It was the Tsar. Pushkin and I turned to the edge of the sidewalk and stopped; taking off our hats we waited for him to pass. But Sobolevsky disappeared. Seeing the Tsar approaching, he slipped into some store." When Sobolevsky finally caught up with them, wearing the latest Parisian fashions and looking sheepish, Pushkin chided him, "So, what is it, brother? You have a little French beard, and a little Russian soul?"[16]

Pushkin was poking fun at his subservience. Sobolevsky, a modern, well-read, well-traveled member of the elite, who espoused moderately liberal views, was afraid that the Tsar would see his goatee.

Like many Russian poets even in this day, Pushkin had a deeply ambivalent personal relationship with the Tsar—and he already recognized the neurotic tensions inherent in a society pretending to be more modern and democratic than it actually was.

"Power and freedom must be combined to mutual benefit," he wrote in 1832. "To presume humiliation in the rituals dictated by etiquette is sheer foolishness. An English lord, presenting himself to his king, kneels and kisses his hand. This does not keep him from belonging to the opposition, if he so desires."[17]

By ritualizing primordial attributes of power in etiquette, he argued, a society is able to abandon them in substance. An English lord thinks nothing of kneeling in front of the king because the sovereignty of the law stands between them—and only an independent court can deprive the lord of life and liberty. But for an educated Russian who has taken on all the trappings of modernity and Western etiquette, even bowing slightly before his Tsar is demeaning because the reality of life has him falling on his face.

3.

Various people present themselves before Vladimir Putin in different ways based on their caste, upbringing, income, education, and dependence on the state. Not all display awe, adulation, or servility—far from it. Many, in fact, show utter indifference. But no group is racked more with indecision, doubt, and angst about how to behave in his presence—and whether to appear at all, if it can be avoided—than the intelligentsia.

For Alisa Ganiyeva, a writer and a journalist in her late twenties, agreeing to a meeting with Putin was accompanied by a deep ambivalence, as if she was somehow repulsed by the very idea of appearing in the presence of state power. She had expected to see a Tsar; she said she was disappointed to behold a man who didn't evoke any emotions at all.

A young writer from the Muslim republic of Dagestan in the North Caucasus, Ganiyeva initially refused an invitation to a writers' meeting when she learned that it was going to turn into an official audience with the prime minister over tea.

Her ethnicity, in this case, was not very relevant to her unease. While she recognized that she would be used as a multi-ethnic "decoration" in the meeting, the real reason she initially refused was part of a more widespread attitude common among a number of writers who consistently avoided any audience with Russian leaders, as if the leader's mere presence could contaminate them.

"Initially, I decided not to go because I believe that there is very little point in these meetings," Ganiyeva explained a few days after the meeting. "And they cast a shadow on your reputation. For me it's an unconscious feeling. Every time there's a meeting between writers and the government, there is an inexplicable feeling of resistance and some revulsion."

Her editor at the *Nezavisimaya Gazeta* (Independent Newspaper) talked her into going, explaining that it would be "cowardly" not to and suggesting she ask about Mikhail Khodorkovsky—the staple oppositionist question used to demonstrate defiance. Ganiyeva, however, recognized the banality of asking about Khodorkovsky for the hundredth time and listening to Putin's answers about the rule of law. Instead, she decided to bring up the controversial law on extremism, whose broad wording was widely used to jail oppositionists and expand the powers of the FSB (the Federal Security Service of the Russian Federation).

"I decided to go and see this person who was shrouded in so many myths," she said. The day before, she was telephoned and told that she would be sitting right next to Putin during a tea that would follow the meeting. Ganiyeva recalled with irritation how she was even told to wear something nice, "as if I had the intention of showing up in a torn sweater."

If Putin was initially shrouded in myth, Ganiyeva couldn't help feeling disappointed when she saw a small, pale, ordinary man, an official trying to ingratiate himself with a group of writers—that enviable class known in early Soviet times as "the engineers of the soul." Putin seemed to be as curious about the writers as they were about him, eyeing them intently as if they were a bunch of strange animals. He smiled and laughed with the group in what clearly represented a "mask" he wore with the intelligentsia, as if he was trying too hard to make himself liked. Ganiyeva, who was seated just right of Putin during the tea, couldn't help but notice that he filled a whole notebook page with platitudes about writers and power, jotting down every obvious word in his large script.

But the behavior of the group revealed far more than Putin's awkward camaraderie. As they waited for the meeting to begin, some took to drinking the strong alcohol on supply, talking, and joking. Others, like the writer Zakhar Prilepin, struck a pose of defiance, while many others appeared to be obviously enthralled.

"There was a change in mood when he entered the room. Everyone stood. I remained seated [along with another writer], and there were looks of disapproval," Ganiyeva said. She went on to describe a scene involving a popular writer who "nearly melted" when Putin sat down next to her, turning radiant and engaging the prime minister in a whispered conversation. No one, of course, paid much attention to the actual union meeting—all eyes were on the whispering. Ganiyeva described how, following the tea, the popular writer immediately approached Putin with entreaties to visit, and as she grabbed his hand Putin became so flummoxed that he dropped a pile of books he had been forced to take. Flustered, he bent down to pick them up as she continued talking.

For Ganiyeva, however, the chief disappointment wasn't Putin's awkward ordinariness, or the sycophancy of some of the writers (she had anticipated that). It was that she never got the chance to ask a question. She went on at length justifying it, as if suggesting to herself that it was all for the better, and then going back to her regret as if it was all she had left from the meeting. That Prilepin, a member of the outlawed National Bolshevik party, managed to ask Putin about his billionaire friends and embezzlement at state-owned companies without a blink of an eye probably compounded Ganiyeva's regret.

"I didn't like the questions being asked," she said, explaining that Prilepin's was one of the few honest questions. "And I didn't want to be too insistent. Everyone was raising his hand, Putin had to refuse them. And I didn't want to be told to wait my turn. I consoled myself that maybe it was for the better that I didn't ask. I might have just scored some liberal points. I just wanted to sit there incognito and watch, after all."

But by not asking, she appeared somehow to feel that she had failed to justify her compromised presence. "It felt uncomfortable that I was there and didn't ask a question," she admitted.

And without a question, without speaking truth to power, the meeting left her more vulnerable to a perceived "closeness" to power that she was instinctively revolted by. What, apart from the popular writer's ingratiation, did the revulsion pertain to, exactly? That she was in the same room, witnessing the fawning and by proxy taking part in it?

4.

On April 29, 2011, one of Vladimir Putin's routine visits across the country found him in Penza, a provincial capital about 600 kilometers (370 miles) southeast of Moscow. Before chairing a meeting on cultural development in a recently restored local theater where he pledged to help subsidize a six billion ruble ($176 million) theater district, Putin, as has been his custom, convened with his people right in the street.[18]

An unofficial video circulating on the internet shows the prime minister approaching the pavement. As he does, a multitude of cheers are heard from the crowd. The sound, once again predominantly female, is a more intense, louder variant of the curious wails I heard ten days before, in Moscow. And just as in Moscow, these sound less like jubilant cheers and more like desperate cries—either for help, or from relief of finally seeing him (the residents, of course, had been waiting for hours in the rain). Indeed, someone called out, "Vladimir Vladimirovich, please help us!"

In a clear shot of Putin in the midst of the crowd, with his hand extended, a middle-aged woman, with short-cropped hair dyed dark red, is kissing his hand, amid repeated exclamations of "thank you." As she tugs at him, he reluctantly offers his cheek. She kisses him on the cheek, then grabs his neck and kisses him repeatedly on the ear. With an expression of amusement bordering on disgust, he carefully and expertly frees himself from the embrace. Several women shout, "We love you!" He responds, "I love you too."

This grotesque display of adulation was circulated over the internet and met with ridicule—but it was ignored by national television, which apparently recognized the discomfort that this somewhat unconscious behavior elicited not just in those who somehow succumb to it, but in Putin himself. Two hundred, one hundred, or even seventy years ago, it would have been an accepted norm—with Joseph Stalin stoically suffering through better choreographed communions with his people.

Somehow, despite the revulsion of the elites and a muted disapproval from the state, this behavior has survived centuries of violent modernization, occurring in the twenty-first century and contaminating far more orderly displays of deference to power. No one approves of it—not even those who unconsciously take part— but it still manages to surface in the most unexpected places.

The "Putin phenomenon"—the stability of his rule and the entrenchment of key features like bureaucratic loyalty and corruption—has been attributed to his popularity and, by sceptics, to high oil prices that have managed to keep the population complacent. But popularity and oil prices are too temporary to explain the perennial structural relationship Russians build with their state—and this explanation suggests wrongly that the majority of people who voted for Putin actually "like" or "prefer" him in the same way that an American voter would "like" or "prefer" Barack Obama.

Attitudes towards Putin have been examined largely in the context of his popularity on the one hand, and his contrast to his predecessor, Boris Yeltsin, on the other.[19] But Putin's high approval ratings—averaging at over 70 percent before 2011—do not indicate a genuine admiration among respondents who, pollsters have told me, are often simply answering what they feel is required of them. Moreover, based on interviews I conducted in 2010–2011, the same person can show feelings of exceeding gratitude ("we would fall at his feet"[20]) one moment, and attitudes of scepticism, disappointment and ridicule the next ("It's all for show, his behavior. Nothing changes."[21])

Behaviors like the one exhibited by the Penza woman have been attributed to a latent personality cult, but that would not explain the ways these behaviors present themselves on a spontaneous level. The Putin cult doesn't even have to be fostered by the government—much of it springs up from below, from sheer inertia, camp and irony-infused, with the potential of social networking at its disposal.[22] And compared to Stalin, Putin is "no führer and no demagogue," according to Lev Gudkov, the head of the Levada Center, who insists there is no evidence of mass adulation in the surveys. "The basis of the trust in him is quite conservative, and, unlike totalitarian leaders, he is not connected to ideas for a new world order."[23]

On February 24, 2009, the postcard of Putin was removed from the desk of the translator at our organization in anticipation of a visit from Putin himself. But ten years before that visit, when that same building was the home of a Kremlin think tank, the staff—internet-savvy liberals—sported t-shirts bearing the anaemic, expressionless profile of the young presidential candidate, Yeltsin's heir apparent, and the inscription: "Putin is our everything."[24] The words were a pun on "Pushkin is our everything"—a phrase that defined another century-old personality cult, around the poet Alexander Pushkin.

What accounts for that kind of behavior, if neither popularity nor a powerful cult can fully explain it?

Sitting at my desk in February 2009, I felt the contagious excitement of some of our middle managers as they waited for Putin to appear. But it wasn't the excitement of meeting someone famous. There was another even more important reason. Like many organizations, ours was funded by the state. Putin's visit fell at the start of the year, when budgets were confirmed. In the unending, often unconscious scramble to secure funding, one cannot fail to see the advantages of being noticed in a positive light and the risks of being disgraced. And so it is easy to understand both the excitement of someone like a popular writer meeting Putin, and a local in Penza, who will be reaping the material benefits of a Putin visit (repaired roads, a new theater, cleaner streets) for years to come.

When Putin came to power in 2000, contemporaries described it as a spontaneous surrender. Not a single weapon was brandished, not a shot was fired—there was no skirmish, no struggle.

Looking back with horror at the mess that resulted when society was left to its own devices in the wake of a revolution, the sheer despair that one is overtaken with when faced with the futility of organizing infrastructure between communities separated by thousands of kilometers, some people surrendered, others gave up, still others criticized, resignedly, just for the record.

Oligarchs and regional leaders were "stumb[ling] over each other in trying to show their support for Putin,"[25] according to scholar Nikolai Petrov. Alexander Oslon, a pollster for the Kremlin, described people eager to stop swimming against the tide, to let the river have its way, and to revert to habits of subservience that had, over centuries, developed as a coping mechanism for subjects otherwise faced with the vast, flourishing chaos that was one sixth of the world's landmass. [26]

And so, what emerged with the beginning of the millennium in Russia was part Tsar, part General Secretary, part CEO, part patrimonial lord. A guarantor of stability when he could satisfy yearnings for order and profit—and an impotent, corrupt oprichnik when he could not. To understand why that is the case, one needs to move away from Putin, and and look at the people he rules—and the environment which makes up their fabric of life.

Chapter 2
The Petition

It is important to use all means to help a single specific individual resolve his issues, his problems, perhaps even his tragedies.
—**Vladimir Putin**

Jah will give us everything. We have no more problems.
—**Boris Grebenshikov**, leader of the rock band Aquarium

1.

A GROUP OF three women—one middle-aged and two quite visibly old—were seated on a plush, blue, faux leather couch, where, having met in the central reception office for Vladimir Putin, the prime minister, former president, and current chairman of the United Russia party, they shared their woes with each other, as they would at a water cooler.

The older one was trying to keep back tears. It was not a life-and-death issue; but she was visibly upset: having survived German captivity during the War—a victory that was still celebrated with the pious intensity of the nation's only truly religious holiday—she couldn't convince local authorities to provide her with anything better than fourteen meters (150 square feet) of living space.

But Sergei Kvitko sat separately; sat and waited patiently, clutching a small suitcase. He did not appear destitute, he was not a pensioner.

He was not a middle-aged woman. Looking slightly older than forty-one, he had the self-sufficient posture of a man who supported a family of four on less than $500 a month.

A mine worker, he would wake up each morning, and, shivering in the cold, load the furnace with firewood to start heating his home. "You know how hard that is with two children?" he complained. "And we don't have electricity all the time."[27]

Kvitko lived in a mining settlement just outside of Novomoskovsk, a small town in the Tula region. Like many rural homes his had no central heating, but it had a television set. And the evening news showed a repeated image that filled him with hope: his cold-eyed sovereign talking incessantly about the one thing he owns a lot of, when Kvitko has none: gas.

On closer inspection, Kvitko's somewhat sunburnt face (it was a frigid February) looked rustic and tired. There was a scar on his right cheek.

The moment he saw a fellow human being waiting to listen to him, recorder poised, all the grievances started pouring out.

"I had to pay for my own way to help out in the rescue efforts at Lubyanka." It turns out that Sergei Kvitko was contracted in March 2010 to aid rescuers in the tunnels of the Moscow subway, where two suicide bombers detonated themselves just half an hour apart on Lubyanka and Park Kultury stations, killing forty. He had to pay for the trip himself, and now he feels jilted: he helped his government look for dead bodies in subway tunnels, and now his government won't even bring the gas that it promised his settlement in 2007.

"Vladimir Vladimirovich always says that money is being spent on gasification. I think he will help. And if he doesn't, then no one else will bring gas [to our homes]."

2.

Alexei Anisimov, the director of the Central Reception Office for United Russia party chairman Vladimir Putin, made himself comfortable behind his huge, enamelled desk, with a single portrait behind him (and in those days of diarchy, two portraits—not one—was the norm).

"I just hope you're mindful of what you print," he said with a disarming grin, "because when it's about a person of such…" he didn't finish, and motioned vaguely with his hand towards the portrait. "Well, you either say good things or…" He meant to say "or nothing at all," in accordance with the Russian maxim about talking of the dead, but just waved it off cheerily.

That warning made sense later in our conversation, because Anisimov directed a very peculiar socio-political institution. On the one hand, here was a perfectly normal—democratic, even—venue for citizens to share their everyday problems with elected officials, the United Russia deputies, either municipal, regional, or federal, who headed these reception offices.

But unlike functioning Western democracies, these deputies did not seem to be catering directly to their petitioners—and Anisimov's post did not depend on whether he was re-elected by the voters he would receive with their requests. Instead, he had another client—Vladimir Putin. And his motive for doing his job well—solving the problems of these half-destitute citizens—was to seek not votes but the approval of his boss. That approval would come in the form of several subsequent promotions. About a year after we met, Anisimov would go on to serve as deputy campaign manager during Putin's re-election in 2012. Shortly after that, he would be appointed to head a department in Putin's Presidential Administration.

Like many party initiatives, linking these reception offices to its chairman came directly from Putin, who touted them as an effective means to communicate with his citizens. But Anisimov seemed to be struggling as he described Putin's exact role in these reception offices.

"We know how great… er, not great, but how big…", here he stumbled again, self-consciously trying to avoid sounding too Soviet in describing Russia's National Leader, "how big the potential, the rating of the chairman of the party is among the population. And how great his authority is on all official levels."

In other words, having potential voters complaining that their social rights were being violated wasn't enough of a stimulus for local deputies to make sure that regulations were being followed and that people were getting their allotted apartments, gas, electricity, and social benefits. Instead, the deputies needed the direct oversight of the national leader to motivate them.

"All party resources were involved, and not just party resources, since the status of the chairman of the party facilitates this [mobilization]."

Even if the reception offices had turned into a populist gimmick for a former president intent on maintaining control of all spheres of public life after stepping down to the rank of prime minister, they seemed to have a perfectly institutional base.

Indeed, the very idea of a reception office for the party came out of sincere attempts at democracy building. In Russia, every political institution has had reception offices since Soviet times. By 2005, after five years in existence, the United Russia party established its own network, with offices directed by either regional or municipal deputies from United Russia—party functionaries who usually headed committees in their local parliaments that were responsible for the social sphere.

Even local deputies from the opposition Communist and Liberal Democratic parties had a budget of anywhere between $10,000 and $38,000 to spend on social issues in their electoral district, depending on the scale of the community they represented, whether regional, local, or municipal. The funds were set aside for help, such as with buying new homes for the poor, or paying medical bills, but ultimately it was up to the speaker of the regional parliament to approve each request.[28]

But by 2008, several factors converged to mark these sleepy institutions for a convenient overhaul. The President of the Russian Federation, who every year held televised phone-in shows where citizens could ask him directly to sort out their pension problems and their broken pipes, was stepping down from his post, and would hence be known as: Prime Minister, Chairman of the United Russia party, and National Leader.

Politically, the move to establish personalized reception offices fortified Putin's image as a hands-on man of the people, sending a powerful signal that, no matter who was in the Kremlin, Putin was still very much in charge. For United Russia, the reception offices offered a role that the Soviet-era Communist Party used to wield: as an organizer of civil initiative where there was none. Putin's party, as was his wont, was pre-empting and co-opting civil society by reaching out into places where it did not exist.

But examined from a social perspective rather than a political one, the move actually revealed a staggering lack of functioning local institutions that were accountable to the citizens of their district.

In other words, the chances that a request to such an office would have any meaningful rate of success was dim—the papers would be filed away under the glass covering the desk of any official a citizen happened to appeal to.

Linking the reception offices to the national leader ensured direct manual control of how each and every request was being handled. "The very algorithm of the reception office changed," Anisimov said.

"Deputies and their aides were involved in helping ordinary citizens on the orders of the chairman of the party—on the direct orders of Vladimir Vladimirovich Putin."

Deputies and their aides, in other words, are authorized to telephone local officials responsible for red tape, and, by dropping the name of the prime minister, pulling strings on behalf of the citizen. Vladimir Putin, in other words, is brought in to mediate between the residents and their direct, elected municipal officials—the ones in direct proximity to the people making the requests.

3.

Inevitably, the establishment of direct reception offices for the national leader attracted a whole slew of petitioners, some even described by reception officials as mentally deficient. An elderly woman at a Moscow reception office once asked a journalist if Putin would be receiving her in person.

But Sergei Kvitko's case seemed perfectly sound—moreover, it reflected Russia's perennial gap between a self-sufficient, educated elite and a large majority systemically dependant on a paternalistic government. Unfairly written off as destitute, backward, or even crazy, these "average citizens" from the provinces simply could not find a common language with their better-off peers. And the misunderstanding appeared to be mutual.

Had Sergei Kvitko been to "his senator"—his direct, elected representative? He had. But the local deputies in his town proved useless.

"I went to local United Russia deputies. They told me that [my home] was already supposed to have gas," he said. But they would go no further. "'We don't want to fight with the town administration,' they told me. 'We have to live and work with them.'"

The local legislative branch, in other words, was more afraid of the local executive branch than of its voters.

But if that was one reason that Kvitko still didn't have gas in his home, it certainly wasn't the main one. Rather, local parliamentarians answered to local administrative officials because they were powerless to do much in this vast terrain.

And the problem of gasification illustrated this vastness perfectly—and demonstrated the dire limitations of local governance.

Kvitko's case seems to have fallen through the cracks of a local gasification drive that began in 2007. That April, municipal representatives of the Shekino district in the Tula region launched a three-year program to bring gas to all rural settlements in the area.

On April 27, the state-run Vesti (News) channel was "pleased to announce" that the long-awaited "blue fuel" had finally arrived at the Shakhty-22 settlement—the same one where Sergei Kvitko lived. The news report identified the settlement as part of the Shekino district, and noted that 27 homes—and over 70 residents—were already connected to the new gas pipe infrastructure.

But somehow, Kvitko wasn't one of them. By the end of 2010— when the 163 million ruble ($4.7 million) program was supposed to be complete[29]—there was no sign of any gas.

"They kept telling me I was supposed to get gas. But there were only promises," he said. "Vladimir Vladimirovich is always saying that money is being spent on gas. But where does this money go?"

Kvitko earned just 13,000 rubles ($380) a month as a mine worker, and it would take him several years and a number of loans to save up enough money to modernize his home without government help. But the possibility of uniting with his neighbors was an option that Kvitko seemed to discard at once.

"In Tula [the regional capital] deputies were surprised to hear that we don't have gas yet," he said. "But local authorities tell us to do this ourselves, to collect 800,000 rubles ($23,000) from our town, and the gas will be installed. How can we do that when our settlement consists of veteran miners and pensioners? Old women can contribute about 200 rubles ($6) each."

The 800,000 rubles ($23,000) that Kvitko speaks of is far less than the 4.5 million rubles ($130,000) that the Shekino administration, using part federal, part regional and part local funds, set aside to gasify a district that neighbored Shakhty-22. The problem is often one of income disparity. In one case observed by the author, the elected chairman of a dacha cooperative outside the town of Dubna said that residents could pitch in for a new water pipe network. After hours of vocal debates, the issue was stalled—wealthier residents who relied on their own, autonomous, networks did not want to pitch in because they did not intend to use the new system, and pensioners did not want to pay anything unless the wealthier residents paid. In the end, the pipe network remained the same.

A similar conundrum appeared to be plaguing communities like Shakhty-22. Those who could afford to contribute had no incentive to do so because they had the means to modernize their homes on their own. Those who could not were failing to convince their wealthier neighbors to compromise—they simply spoke a different language.

And for someone like Kvitko, surviving on so little, the question of spending hours, days, or weeks first petitioning local authorities, then regional authorities, and then taking a day's journey all the way to Moscow to petition Vladimir Putin made more sense than mobilizing a few dozen people in his community to come up with $23,000 so that all their homes could have gas.

4.

For Vladimir Putin, the status of the gas pipe in Sergei Kvitko's home—as well as a whole lot of other information—was now accessible in real-time through a nationwide database. Putin could simply log on—if he chose to, which he doesn't very often—and see for himself whether Kvitko was still hauling firewood in the mornings. Kvitko had given him that opportunity.

"It's one thing to take very important, necessary decisions in Moscow, in the Kremlin, in the White House," Putin told United Russia leaders in Samara in September 2009. "It's another to solve a number of completely different problems across the whole country…. It is important to use all means to help a single specific individual resolve his issues, his problems, perhaps even his tragedies." [30]

Sergei Kvitko's petition, like requests to Vladimir Putin that fall on the desk of Alexei Anisimov, whether made in writing or in person, is filed in an electronic database that can be accessed by deputies and party officials at any time, from anywhere. Anisimov, asked how receptions report on their progress to their leader, was eager to point out that "even the Chairman of the Party can log on, using his login and password, to check the status of every request."

Anisimov pointed out another telling statistic—in Moscow and St. Petersburg, about 70 percent of the pleas and appeals to Vladimir Putin are filed in writing, while about 30 percent are filed in person. But in the regions, the statistics are reversed—up to 80 percent prefer to file their applications in person.

While Putin was prime minister, institutionally it was still the Kremlin that got the bulk of citizens' pleas—and President Dmitry Medvedev established his own set of reception offices almost simultaneously with Putin. In the first half of 2009 alone, the Kremlin administration received some 172,800 requests from around the country,[31] while the total number of nationwide requests to Putin through the reception network in over two years hit 500,000 in early 2011, according to figures provided by Anisimov.

What this illustrates isn't the relative popularity of Putin and Medvedev (and Putin has consistently led Medvedev in approval ratings throughout the latter's presidential term), but the symbolic power of appealing to the supreme, federal government—and the resilience of this habit on a societal level.

Though Medvedev had struggled to adopt a more legalistic approach, his use of online social networks like Livejournal and Twitter incited a bombardment of similar direct appeals—this time, not from rural residents, but from people who had their own blogs.

Shortly after Medvedev launched a blog on Livejournal in April 2009, another blogger asked him to help rebuild a dilapidated children's hospital in the Ryazan region. Two days after the April 23 post, an official-sounding statement proclaimed that Medvedev had told Ryazan Governor Oleg Kovalev to look into the matter.[32]

In an even more widely-publicized incident in January 2011, the father of Yarslav Kolosov, a one-year-old suffering from cystic fibrosis, posted an open letter to Medvedev on Livejournal on behalf of his wife, who complained that medical personnel at the Moscow hospital where her son was being treated were consistently rude and insensitive to her needs.[33] Medvedev reacted to the letter with a Twitter post—when asked by another well-known blogger if the government could do anything, Medvedev tweeted "It can." He then had children's ombudsman Pavel Astakhov check the hospital for violations. As a result, through an official (rather than informal) request to Health Minister Tatyana Golikova, the child was sent to Germany for treatment.[34]

Medvedev's marathon press conference in May 2011 brought the point home—even Medvedev, a much softer public speaker than Putin and a leader positioned specifically to target the more self-sufficient, modern, and liberal part of Russia's population, was not above issuing decrees on public request, for example promising a journalist that he would order the simplification of procedures for annual car inspections. The micromanaging role of the president was so clear in the press conference that it led one Western journalist to note that "little happens in this country unless the ruler in the Kremlin decrees it, just as it has always been."[35] Medvedev the Modernizer was, reluctantly, responding to deep-seated, unspoken traditions regulating interaction between the Russian sovereign and his people. But Putin, by establishing a venue for him to continue this type of intimate interaction after stepping down as president in 2008, was taking this sovereign function with him to the prime minister's seat.

Asked how Putin's reception offices differed from Medvedev's, Anisimov pointed to Putin's informal influence.

"[Medvedev's] reception offices function within the legal framework, they are limited by the law—article 59, which regulates how long agencies need to take to respond to requests. They have [chains of command], they have officials that work within this framework. But we can go beyond these boundaries using party mechanisms and finance, and, above all, our people. We reach officials from another direction. There is a personal side, other mechanisms are involved."

What Anisimov had essentially described was an extralegal process through which the sovereign could help his subjects solve their problems. Vladimir Putin wasn't acting against the law. He was simply above it.

5.

On December 4, 2008, during Vladimir Putin's first live phone-in as prime minister (he had been holding them yearly as president), the voice of nine-year-old Dasha Varfolomeyeva, a third-grader from Buryatia, was broadcast nationwide.

"Uncle Volodya! New Year is coming soon. We live on Babushka's pension, there is no work in our village. My sister and I dream of getting new dresses. I want to ask you for a dress like Cinderella's."

Putin, whose voice Dasha would later say she was so glad to hear, smiled. "Dashenka, I heard you. I want to invite you and your sister—and your grandmother too—to all come to Moscow for one of our New Year's parties. We'll sort out the business of the presents."[36]

After a frenzy of back and forth phone calls among frantic regional officials struggling to comply with the orders, Dasha came to Moscow with her family and visited Putin at his residence in Novo-Ogaryovo.

The gift was just one of a countless number of gestures Putin made as president and prime minister, having begun in 2001 with the first of these phone-in shows. Once a year, in a live broadcast on all federal television channels, Putin would sit down behind a desk in a Moscow studio before a small audience of selected representatives from around the country, and field apparently random telephone calls from viewers. The requests varied from individual complaints about back wages, late pensions, and poor housing to larger infrastructural issues such as dilapidated hospitals, lack of roads and transport in the remote regions, and allegations of corruption.

Each year, these marathon sessions grew longer and broke new records—and Putin continued the tradition as prime minister, with the show exceeding four hours by 2011. When he returned to the presidency in 2012, the tradition continued as a massive press conference with hundreds of journalists from around the country vying for his attention. While appearing spontaneous, it is widely believed that the shows are actually orchestrated, with many of the callers picked and primed in advance. But with no script and at least a veneer of spontaneity, Putin addressed minute local issues with a competence that no regional official could muster. From memory, he spouted numbers, names and towns, demonstrating a phenomenal knowledge of daily economic details from across his dominion, prompting comparisons with the "all-knowing" Stalin.

The Russian media covered this communion with his people with more than a hint of irony—Putin, for all purposes, was acting as a benevolent parody of Stalin, whom little girls had once thanked for their "happy childhood."

But among the millions of petitions that Russians sent to their Tsars, requests for gas pipes and Christmas presents have intermingled with pleas for mercy.

In a letter dated 1946, kept in the Moscow archives of the Memorial Human Rights Society, the careful, school-age cursive of an eleven-year-old girl asked "Dear Iosif Vissarionovich" to "please find out the truth" and rescue her father from what the child thought to be a miscarriage of justice. "They tortured my father and forced him to sign" a false confession. The girl couldn't have fathomed, of course, that the leader she was writing to personally signed execution orders for thousands of people like her father. And while her fate is unknown, some of her peers to this day refuse to believe that Stalin signed the orders to execute their relatives, even when faced with the documented order itself.

Putin, of course, is no Stalin—at best a parody of him, at worst an empty threat. And while his propaganda machine was certainly exploiting and cultivating these deep-seated, paternalistic sentiments for its political purposes, it would be unfair to say that it had created them in the first place.

A great deal of these requests were genuine and sincere—and whatever these people felt about having to appeal directly to Putin to solve their problems—frustration with local incompetence, the anger that no one is accountable to them—for a large number of low-functioning residents like Sergei Kvitko, it was done with a great degree of relief.

That relief in itself is a beneficial result, perhaps the only one—a year later, the authorities had still not provided Kvitko with gas.

A case worker at the branch where Kvitko applied, speaking on conditions of anonymity, first confused his record with another Sergei Kvitko—a man she described as "mentally unstable" who had applied dozens of times to sort out his criminal record. "We get a lot of people like that," she said.

As for Sergei Kvitko of Shakhty-22, she finally located his application, but said it was difficult to make a decision. "We'd have to investigate what is actually going on," she said. "From the way Kvitko described it, nothing made sense; he seemed to have failed to sort out and identify the problem himself," she said—and so, as it usually is over such vast terrains, no one was actually to blame.[37]

Chapter 3
Playing God

A fire consumed their homes;
I built them new dwellings; then forsooth
They blamed me for the fire!
—**Alexander Pushkin**, *Boris Godunov*[38]

All hope is on him, on his words, on his constant
monitoring.
—A victim of forest fires in Nizhny Novgorod
region following a visit from Vladimir Putin and a
pledge to rebuild her home, August 2010

For a variety of reasons people in this country invested all
their hopes in the kind Tsar, in the state, in Stalin, in their
leaders, and not in themselves.
—**President Dmitry Medvedev**, in an interview
with the *Financial Times*, June 2011

1.

IT WAS STARTLING and more than a little eerie to listen to just
how much hope a resident of the village of Verkhnyaya Vereya, who
had lost her home to a spate of unprecedented forest fires, placed
personally in the prime minister of her country.

"All hope is on him, to be perfectly honest with you. On his words, on his constant monitoring," Julia Volkhova told me. Just days before our conversation, in August 2010, Vladimir Putin had promised the residents of what was once the village of Verkhnyaya Vereya that he would personally ensure that their homes, which were among the thousands destroyed in the forest fires that swept Russia in the summer of 2010, would be rebuilt. Volkhova had been in Vyksa's central square when Putin arrived in that neighboring town, though she admitted that she hadn't seen him up close. "He said that on November 1 we would all move in to our homes. We would have gas and water. If anyone else had said that, the people probably wouldn't have believed it."

The timid Volkhova, who admitted after speaking to me that she was concerned about getting in trouble with local officials for talking with a journalist, may have embellished her gratitude towards Vladimir Vladimirovich due to her fears.

But the way her gratitude gushed out revealed something far deeper than the square meters of living space that she was promised—it revealed that she had little other choice.

"Everything that the people had pent up inside them they expressed to Putin and [local governor Valery] Shantsev," Andrei Gorelov, a factory worker who organized residents to fight fires in the absence of firefighters, explained. "You have a boss, right? And he has a boss. Well, imagine what happens when the very top boss, the boss of all bosses, comes down and says 'I'm going to show you what's what.' What happens then? This is what happened here."

By late July 2010, even the atheists in Moscow felt as if God had forsaken the city. A pungent, pink-gray-brown smog had enveloped the capital in a relentless grip, the product of a record-breaking heatwave that fixed temperatures at 38°C (100°F) and sparked a series of wildfires so brutal that the prime minister's trust rating plummeted to levels not seen since 2006.

But in Vyksa, a town of 56,000 people in the Nizhny Novgorod region, billows of dark-gray clouds had been engulfing the horizon for weeks—and they were not signs of a pending thunderstorm, but a reflection of raging forest fires that were closing in on the town.

By July 29, Verkhnyaya Vereya, a settlement of 321 homes about 20 kilometers (13 miles) southwest of Vyksa, was fighting for its life. Throughout the month, locals, frustrated by fruitless efforts to bring firefighters to their towns and save their homes, had gathered in groups with their cars, shovels, buckets, and whatever else they could find, and fought the forest fires themselves. Vyksa, a relatively prosperous town with a metallurgical plant that produced pipelines for Putin's pet gas project, Nordstream, couldn't muster the basic infrastructure to protect residents on its outskirts from forest fires.

As a result, programmers, factory workers, pensioners, and young women found each other through a local internet forum, Wyksa.ru, which coordinated who would do the driving and who would do the spade work, and set out into the forests, facing the fire.

Local authorities were insisting they had brought in troops, Emergency Ministry officials, and soldiers to help in the efforts, but residents saw little sign of help. As fires were closing in on Verkhnyaya Vereya, the region's governor, Valery Shantsev, boasted that no additional help was needed from the federal center—even though Putin had publicly offered him federal aid.

But residents saw no signs of the local efforts. The soldiers, who often weren't even equipped with radio transmitters, had to be fed by the residents themselves, and fire engines had to be supplied with fuel. When a fire engine did arrive, it was often out of water and thus useless. The firefighters would help residents put out their own fires with buckets of water.

And so, partly owing to the forces of nature, and partly because of a social infrastructure lulled into despair and inaction by the blistering heat, when the fire reached Verkhnyaya Vereya, the town succumbed instantly.

"We only had two fire engines," Julia Volkhova recalled one month later. "And it all came down on us with such force that firefighters wouldn't have helped. It was a hurricane of fire, you can't call it anything else. If only to quiet the souls of residents, they should have sent more than eighteen-year old conscripts to dig ditches."

Having fought ground fires, no one was prepared for the crown fires that swept over the village, levelling it to the ground in one night. Not a single house was left standing. Nineteen people were killed.

The prime minister, arriving on July 30, walked through the ruins, his mood as black as the earth.

But he was hardly prepared for what awaited him on the steps of Vyska's district administration.

Amateur footage of that spontaneous meeting relayed that same wail that seems to greet the prime minister every time he appears in public. But this one was desperate, grief-stricken ,and even hateful. "Down with this government!" a shrill woman shouted as Putin approached the crowd. "We're standing here with nothing [in Russian the word she used was 'undressed']!" a woman cried.[39]

Accosted at once by dozens of people, the prime minister struggled to talk over the cries. The anger, of course, wasn't so much directed at him as at the bald man standing next to him—the governor of the Nizhny Novgorod region, Valery Shantsev.

"We're burning, don't you understand?" a woman said.

"I understand," the prime minister told her.

"And no one will listen to us, you understand?"

"I understand. That's why I'm here."

"No one is extinguishing the fires."

Then, Putin gave in to a momentary frustration. He faltered. "There's nothing left to extinguish," he said angrily. "Everything has burned down."

"What do you mean nothing?! Our homes! Our homes are still there! You're not doing anything! Stop promising!"

A man facing Putin was not weeping or screaming, and the prime minister used the pause to get his message across. "We're going to transfer money to the region. Everyone will get compensated. And all the houses will be built anew. All of them."

Interrupted by another man on one side, Putin flashed his eyes angrily at him: "Give me a second, wait please."

Kommersant (Russian business newspaper) reporter Andrei Kolensnikov, pictured in the crowd with a look of unwonted bewilderment, would write the following day that Putin indeed nearly lost his temper.

"A man shouted something at the prime minister. [The prime minister] turned and was about to go towards him, but then turned away and went towards his car."[40]

As Putin was leaving, another woman yelled at his back, "Our administration is working very badly. It should be tried. And hanged by the balls."

2.

Andrei Gorelov, a local factory worker who had been organizing volunteer brigades to keep the raging ground and crown fires around Vyksa in check for the third week in a row, told a story that local officials didn't seem to want to hear.

After an emergency situation was declared in fourteen regions, news wires and state television channels had been reporting hourly updates on the volume of troops, machinery, and equipment involved in fighting the forest fires in the Nizhny Novgorod region. The powerful Emergencies Ministry chief, Sergei Shoigu, was on the spot, giving regular updates, together with Valery Shantsev, the governor just fresh from being chastised by Vladimir Putin.

But to hear Gorelov speak, it sounded as if he was talking from a different region altogether.

"Me and the guys from Vyksa are still fighting the fires. Yesterday a brigade from Nizhny Novgorod came to join us."

An Emergencies Ministry brigade?

"No. Volunteers," he said with some disappointment.

Just a few moments ago, I had spoken with Yevgeny Muravyov, an official spokesman of Governor Shantsev in Nizhny Novgorod.

"There are no volunteers there," he said. "They aren't being allowed anywhere near the fires. Maybe there's one or two or three. What kind of volunteers are you talking about? It's an emergency situation!"

Shantsev, the official spokesman said, started every morning at the site of the fires near Vyksa. "Our residents are soon going to start setting fire to their own homes once they see the kind of houses that are being built. All the necessary equipment and troops—military and civilian—everything was working even before all this started."

Officially, 1,800 federal and regional troops were deployed to fight fires in the area. But Gorelov and other volunteers only saw them on paper.

"I saw the amount of equipment that we had officially. When

I saw the numbers, I couldn't figure out: then how come we're burning?"

Vladimir, a local programmer who gave only his first name, said the soldiers that were sent weren't equipped with basic necessities like food, fuel, and radio transmitters.

"There was no coordination. To have coordination, you need radio receivers. They didn't even have those."

Vladimir, a Muscovite by birth, may have been overwhelmed by a sense of adventure. He said he had never seen anything like a crown fire—a wall of flame that literally overtook his car as he and other volunteers were trying to escape it. But perhaps because of his urban upbringing, he was more skeptical than others about relying on the government—and that motivated him to take matters into his own hands. If other volunteers like Andrei Gorelov didn't hide their outrage at the negligence and inaction, Vladimir seemed to take it in his stride.

"There are still more volunteers than firefighters. No one is under the illusion that the government will help," he said, days after Putin's visit. "The government will not help. Nothing helped. Not Putin, not Shantsev, not Shoigu."

Considering the natural disaster that the summer of 2010 was turning into, one obvious approach was to collaborate with volunteers to help fill the holes in the dilapidated municipal and regional political infrastructure. Moscow understood this—and President Dmitry Medvedev, shortly after declaring an emergency in fourteen regions, issued a decree allowing firefighting brigades— which came under Shoigu's Emergencies Ministry—to include the kind of volunteer brigades that Andrei Gorelov was organizing.

But that wasn't happening—either Shantsev's office hadn't had time to distribute the orders, or commanders on the spot had no intention of complying with them.

"There's only one [approachable] person in the forces, a certain Alexander Alexandrovich," Gorelov said. "We talk to him. All the others—whether firefighters or emergency officials—refuse to deal with civilians."

Despite Medvedev's decree, volunteer efforts like Gorelov's were not condoned by local officials. For one thing, they represented a grass-roots organizational effort that, whatever the rhetoric from

Moscow, local governments were reluctant to tolerate.

Gorelov said that shortly after the forum began organizing volunteers, it underwent a series of hacking attacks, while local security officers checked employees at the Vyksa Metallurgical Plant for any evidence that they had logged on to the town forum.

Such seemingly useless intimidation measures were common in areas that posed threats of social unrest, and went back to mechanisms used by the KGB. I have encountered them in regional cities across Russia faced with unemployment, natural or technogenic disasters, or any other problem that threatened to spark genuine mass dissent. Rather than dealing with the problem, the measures serve to create a climate of fear amid the workforce which, when supported by the management, discourages local initiative.

In the case of Vyksa, it was also becoming clear why local authorities were unwilling to tolerate a grass-roots volunteer effort. Whether the volunteers ended up collaborating or not, their sheer existence revealed that local government services were so deeply dysfunctional that they could not be relied upon in a natural disaster. By taking the firefighting into their own hands, the volunteers were demonstrating, in spite of themselves, that the money being spent on fire engines, interior troops, and Emergencies Ministry equipment was going to waste. They were unmasking local inefficiency, making it particularly vulnerable to the displeasure of the federal center.

Shantsev's press secretary was not trying to impress the general population. Just like his own boss, he was trying to impress the boss in Moscow—or at least conceal local shortcomings.

3.

In his rambling 1839 work, *Empire of the Czar: A Journey Through Eternal Russia*, the French Marquis de Custine marvels, among other things, that Russian newspapers were forbidden from reporting on the notorious St. Petersburg floods during the 1820s. After all, one could accuse the Autocrat of All of Russia, Nicholas I, of many things—but certainly his conscience should be spared from floods and other natural disasters, so why the censorship?

One mystical explanation for this kind of squeamishness—which continues to plague Russia's government to this day—was offered by the historian and novelist Vladimir Sharov: "Even the intimate tie that Russian power has with God is perilous. It has created that unique responsibility of a Tsar before his people that is only encountered in antiquity. He could not be faulted for any of his own deeds; a Tsar could only be blamed for that which is in the hands of God."[41]

In a nation that thought itself the Third Rome ruled by the steward of God on Earth, famines, droughts, and earthquakes could only mean one thing: God had turned away from his chosen people, for a false Tsar had usurped the throne, and he must be deposed.

Towards the end of the nineteenth century, anthropologist Sir James Frazer collected accounts of the treatment of sacred kings among aborigines. A single pattern emerged, carried over from pre-history: primitive tribes from all over the world worshipped a sacred sorcerer king, prostrating themselves before him when the rain fell, and killing him in times of drought. Frazer's work forms part of the foundations of anthropology, but the chief criticism against him was that, as he tried to separate his own world from that of the "savages," he failed to acknowledge the extent to which such primordial practices were incorporated into modern governance.

In their incessant drive to rein in, level, and civilize an inhospitable and unwilling landmass, Russia's rulers primarily sought to suppress and censor those natural manifestations of chaos that threatened their power the most.

But whether they succeeded or not is another question.

The responsibility of a sacred monarch requires him to transcend simply populist measures and to ensure his superiority over a natural calamity through both economic and spiritual means. In Putin's case, this was doubly important, since the fires had demonstrated a systemic vulnerability that is common to feudal social structures: a near total lack of control over the local fiefdoms of regional governors, and the resulting absence of an infrastructure aimed at responding to cataclysms.

When examining Putin's regime as inherently authoritarian, it is hard to reconcile this fact with the weakness of the central government in the regions. Western scholars—and, at one point, even this author[42]—have stumbled over this paradox, arguing that Putin's regime is less authoritarian than believed, because the chain of command is so weak and inefficient. If autocracy implies centralized control, then Russia's lack of it in the regions defies the autocratic model. But this lack of control over the regions is not evidence of autonomy, but of feudalism—and once we recognize the feudal elements that have coexisted with autocratic ones, things start falling into place,[43] and we begin to understand the underlying factors that dictate relations between the regional leader and the Russian ruler on the one hand, and the Russian people and their sovereign on the other. And the key aspect that reinforces the sacred, transcendent nature of whatever ruler occupies the Kremlin (or White House) is exceedingly simple: he is very, very far away.

Opinion surveys point to a telling dichotomy. Muscovites and residents of remoter regions were asked in October 2010 (with the experience of the summer heatwave fresh in their minds) who their own local situation depended on the most—the federal center, the regional governor, or the local administration.

In Moscow, some 47 percent attributed the most power to the federal center. But in the regions, just 16 percent of local businessmen, when asked who has most power over their towns, pointed to the federal center.

"The principle of the [chain of command], which is indeed feudal in character, does in fact control each subsequent level—but only one," Alexei Levinson of the Levada Center argued, citing several polls.[44]

From the perspective of the feudal lord, the vassal of his vassal is not his vassal. And the broken chain of command that emerged in the course of the wildfires of 2010 illustrated this problem perfectly.

In Vyksa on July 30, accosted by dozens of fire victims who, locals say, were close to tearing Governor Valery Shantsev to pieces on the spot, Putin was protecting Shantsev from his people, and his people from Shantsev.

"Comrade Shantsev should be strung up by a certain [bodily organ]," someone shouted.

"Down with him!" shouted someone else. "Down with him! To jail!"

"Calm down!" Putin told them.[45] Standing within an arm's reach of an angry mob, he was being tested to prove that he could hold them at bay. As locals called for Shantsev's blood, Putin decreed, on the spot, that thousands of dollars in compensation from the federal and local budgets be paid out to victims and their families, so that houses could be rebuilt for those who lost them.

"If Putin hadn't come down here, there would have been a revolution," Gorelov told me weeks later, in August. "If only Shantsev had come out to the people [alone], then I'm one hundred percent certain that even his security wouldn't have been able to protect him. No one would touch a woman—but it's the women who would have attacked him. And no one could have stopped them. Putin saved Shantsev's life."

4.

On August 10, Putin was shown on television in the co-pilot's seat of a Russian-built Be-200 amphibious aircraft. He was pressing a button to dump 34 tons of water on forest fires in the Ryazan region.

That month, with the fires still raging, the first homes starting going up like mushrooms in Verkhnyaya Vereya—with officials working directly under the watchful eye of the prime minister (in the form of a CCTV camera), who had promised his people that all the fire victims would have new houses by November 1.

Made to sparkle before the cameras (and the eyes of the National Leader), these homes looked picture-perfect on television, straight out of Pete Seeger's "Little Boxes" of American suburbia. But residents were not surprised to find them flimsy and inadequate when it actually came down to living in them.

In Vyksa, officials had made spectacular efforts to fulfil the expectations of the prime minister, whose mere presence had inevitably made an example out of the town.

"Local firms were bending over [backwards] for Putin," Tatyana Sergeyeva, one of the local volunteers, said a year later. "They would load families with five refrigerators. Just in case Putin noticed them. It was disgusting."

Residents noticed a marked change in the way they were being treated by local authorities.

"After Vladimir Vladimirovich came here, our town was transformed," said Julia Volkhova, tellingly using a false name and patronymic after I asked her if Putin should have visited the town.

"All the officials became polite and efficient. They started saying 'please' and 'thank you,'" she said, attributing the change to Putin's visit. And this positive attention—rather than the material compensation—seemed to be key. "Aren't we people too? Why don't they trust us? Why do they need orders from the very top?"

A year later, having survived the winter in their new homes, residents complained about flooding in the basements due to poor foundations—the houses were built either too deep or too shallow. Panelling would chip away and doors wouldn't close properly, making the homes cold and drafty in the winter.

Then there was the inevitable problem of corruption. Putin had promised residents that they could have new homes built for them or opt for cash compensations equal to the market value of their homes. Though it was obvious that when building one's own home, the care and special focus on a quality foundation would avoid the expected problems of leaks, cracks and basement flooding, residents in Verkhnyaya Vereya said that they didn't know anyone who opted for the cash compensations.

According to Tatyana Sergeyeva, local officials were probably getting kickbacks from construction companies and had been instructed to avoid the cash compensations at any cost. It was cheaper for them to erect jerry-built block homes within a few months than pay out market values. Residents who had witnessed hell on earth, who had watched their homes consumed by fire and people burned to death, had little strength for additional court battles before the ordeal of building their own homes again.

They were habitually exhausted—and this exhaustion may help explain the peculiar gratitude that people continued to express for Putin, despite the cracks in their walls, the Potemkin villages, and the bribery that the billions of rubles in federal funds fueled in local administrative offices.

Against that backdrop of perennial exhaustion, the Sisyphean prospect of fighting court battles against powerful local officials and then rebuilding one's own home, the fact that such a leader could come down and walk amid the ruins as if it was his own land, who listened to their desperate cries, and who essentially rebuilt their homes for them, could not fail to elicit relief. The statements of people like Julia Volkhova were not an admission of love or admiration, they were a cry for help—attributing far more powers to Putin than he actually wielded.

The reality for most of the population is that less than 30 percent of homes have a basic insurance policy to protect them against any fire, let alone a natural disaster.[46] For those residents, however corrupt, however cynical, however dishonest, the leader in Moscow must have the potential, at least, to transcend the natural disasters they are vulnerable to, and to instil fear in the local officials that they depend upon so much. Right or wrong, these qualities are often a matter of life and death. And woe betide the Russian ruler who fails at least to demonstrate those qualities.

Chapter 4

The Pikalevo Effect

*I had one [woman] come in and tell me, "Sveta, I love
Putin so much." And I told her, "You go on ahead loving
him, dear. I don't love anybody."*
—**Svetlana Antropova**, Pikalevo factory union
leader

*Why did everyone scatter like cockroaches just before
my visit? Why weren't there people here who could
make decisions?*
—**Vladimir Putin**

1.

ON JUNE 4, 2009, Yelena Matuzova, an employee of the Pikalevo
Alumina Plant and a mother of two teenage boys living on a monthly
salary of $427, stood before Vladimir Putin and demanded to know
when the privately-owned factory she worked at would start up
again so that she could get paid.

That month, she was one of four hundred people who nearly
started a revolution over months of wage arrears. The residents of
Pikalevo had managed to waylay Vladimir Putin on a planned trip
to St. Petersburg, forcing him to make an emergency stop in their
town. They wouldn't end their revolt any more empowered than
when they had begun. But for the moment, having spent months

without their salaries, they just wanted to feed their children. So Yelena Matuzova cried out to Putin. She had stood there for hours waiting for him, and was determined to tell him "how we live."

Without knowing the economic intricacies and feudal relationships behind what had just transpired, the incident had all the trappings of a miracle: within minutes of Putin appearing before the people huddled in the rain, text messages informed them that their salaries had been deposited.

Two years later, the management of Pikalevo Alumina Plant would proudly show us the furnaces that were restarted on Putin's orders. And then, a little sheepishly, as if they felt that Putin himself wouldn't approve, they would show us something else: the generic black office chair where Putin sat as he threw his own pen at factory owner Oleg Deripaska. They still kept the printed tag with Putin's name on it taped to the back of the chair. For on June 4, 2009, Putin had displayed a sovereign wrath so genuine, so seemingly humiliating for the oligarch who bowed his head and covered his eyes, that the people forgave the prime minister the fact that they didn't believe much of anything he said, and were, for a time, consoled.

2.

The story of what actually happened in that single-industry town of 22,000 people between 2003 and 2009—the break-up and privatization of three Soviet-era minerals plants that fed the entire town, the mismanagement, the corruption, the mass layoffs and wage arrears during the crisis, the road-blocking protests, and Putin flying in to force owners to restart the plants—was no miracle. It was a study in survival when laws and institutions prove useless, and when the people resort to patrimonial habits, the only ones that work under the circumstances. The story of Pikalevo was the story of a whole feudal fiefdom that was Russia in miniature. On some level, it was also the story of factory workers colluding in their own exploitation.

In that dimension, the searing deprivation that Pikalevo residents experienced in spring 2009—subsisting on garden plot produce with hundreds laid off and hundreds more owed months of salaries—wasn't only about the hunger. It was about a factory that they loved as peasants love the earth they till, a unique plant that produced enough aluminium for Soviet war planes. As in any Soviet single-industry town, the three joint factories didn't just feed Pikalevo, they *were* Pikalevo, connecting the people of this hilly, northern town in the middle of nowhere with their country's grand, spiritual mission.

The collapse of the Soviet Union—as it would for many remote places in Russia—changed little in that respect, with Pikalevo's production of cement, alumina, and potash remaining at profitable levels throughout the 1990s. So when private businesses moved in on the consolidated plants around 2003, privatizing each cherry-picked factory separately in accordance with profit margins—or as Putin said, "picking raisins out of a bun"—it was perceived by many locals as a crime nothing short of treason. In the case of the alumina factory, Deripaska broke no laws in his handling of the Pikalevo crisis. If anything, he was the one who had drawn the short straw in the complex chain, saddled with an expensive production process, and the two other plants refusing to sell raw materials at a loss to themselves.

When the salaries stopped, it was Oleg Deripaska, however, who came to be reviled by many locals with the kind of hatred normally reserved for a feckless father who goes out whoring while his family starves. But with no legal leverage against him, they could only appeal to the one higher force above him.

3.

Nearly a century before the Bolshevik Revolution, the poet Alexander Pushkin captured the dread of the quintessential Russian revolt in *The Captain's Daughter*, a story about the Pugachev Rebellion of 1773, with two words: "pitiless and senseless." The revolt in the town of Pikalevo in May–June 2009—tiny by national standards, with just 400 people taking part to block the St. Petersburg-Vologda highway—was, thankfully, not pitiless. But for many participants, the senselessness would later ring true.

The complex economic chain that should have connected the people to the factory management and the owner on the one hand, and to the city administration and the regional government on the other, proved not only useless, but for all purposes meddlesome. For in the end any meaningful decisions on whether the alumina factory and the power station that supplied heat to the whole town could start up again rested on two people: the minerals magnate Oleg Deripaska, who stood well above the town's soft-spoken mayor, and Vladimir Putin, the only person who could put any pressure on Deripaska and the other owners.

While the media presented the incident as a clear-cut consequence of the economic crisis, the problems at Pikalevo actually began much earlier—they were embedded in the unique production process to make alumina—a snow-white powder that plant managers proudly called the "noblest, purest in the world."

Working as a single enterprise with two other plants—Pikalevo Cement and Pikalevo Soda (the soda and potash unit)—the less profitable Pikalevo Alumina Plant could rely on the two more profitable units for its raw materials.

This meant that structurally the plants and their production process were incompatible with a market economy that allowed the privatization of the three assets by different owners. Built in 1957, it was a quintessentially Soviet resource chain that mobilized each separate factory, and each separate single-industry town involved in the chain towards a single aim: building war planes.

That structure, prior to privatization, sheltered the three Pikalevo plants from the economic turmoil of the 1990s. Union leaders, managers, and even locals admitted that they had been "spoiled" by the relative comforts the plants provided them during that transition period.

"Working as one, production could react to market changes. It was profitable and effective," the plant's general director, Sergei Sofyin told us. But when the three parts were privatized by three different owners, each one of them "went his own way" in the rush for profits. Production burdens fell on the least profitable unit, the Pikalevo Alumina Plant, controlled by Oleg Deripaska's Basic Element (Basel) minerals holding.[47]

If a ton of alumina sold for $160, it effectively cost $500 to produce—a margin of loss made even worse by the time demand for cement, aluminium, and its oxide, alumina, fell in the wake of the economic crisis. This loss of demand wiped out some 70 percent of Deripaska's fortune, saddling him with $20 billion in debt—including 20 billion rubles (about $660 million) from Basic

Element alone.[48]

To raise margins, the company opted to diversify production at its alumina factory in Pikalevo and switch to cement production rather than the more costly alumina. In summer 2008, before the crisis hit, BaselCement Pikalevo—which controlled the Pikalevo Alumina Plant—stopped shipments of nepheline by-products to its sister plant, Pikalevo Cement—forcing the plant to close by October, laying off hundreds of people. The move triggered a domino effect that paralyzed production at all three plants by 2009, with Pikalyovskaya Soda, the soda and potash factory operated by Metakhim, also being forced to close.

BaselCement Pikalevo cut production and put half of its 3000-strong workforce on enforced leave, paying them two thirds of their salary.

By February 2009, with production in Pikalevo at a standstill, the wage arrears began.

The perennial scourge of back wages, well-known to Russians from the 1990s, frequently kicked in at debt-saddled companies as the first signal of impending ruin. When short on cash, an oligarch could always skimp on paying his workers—at least, this was how average Pikalevo residents interpreted the events of spring 2009.

As union leader, it came down to Svetlana Antropova to take action. She began petitioning regional authorities and organizing protests. She wrote repeated letters to Governor Serdyukov—only to be ignored.

"Sooner or later, all requests turn into demands. That's what the union is about," she told us in June 2011 as she recalled those events. Nothing worked—she was kept out of meetings with Serdyukov and stonewalled by company management.

"I've only met once with Deripaska," she said. "When I started telling him about the factory's problems and our questions, he only said, "'I don't like labor unions.' And made it understood that he would not talk to me."

Then she started taking workers out into the streets, prompting security officers to move in. Both private and undercover agents from the FSB made their persistent presence known both to her and to the locals.

But there seemed to be another aim apart from quelling social tension—security was bent on making sure that their top boss, in this case Oleg Deripaska, was not displeased.

"His company warned us, 'you can have protests, rallies, do whatever you want,'" Antropova said. "'As long as you don't have the word "Deripaska" anywhere.' I said I couldn't promise that."

The vague statements coming from the governor and the Kremlin only increased the panic. Governor Serdyukov met with President Medvedev in March, but no decisions came out of the meeting. In the coming months, he continued to complain that he had no leverage over the owners.

"We have no law on nationalization or deprivatization," he was quoted as saying. The government, he said, needed to step in and solve the problem.[49]

On every level, attempts to put pressure on the owners seemed to be failing.

Sergei Veber, the hapless, soft-spoken mayor, would find himself answering very difficult—often violent—questions from the residents.

"From our position, as local authorities, it was difficult to affect the owner," Veber told us in June 2011. "We worked with plant managers, with law enforcement, with prosecutors."

What he didn't say was that the "work" yielded no results. That was only achieved by the district prosecutor, Fyodor Veretinsky, who told a crowd of angry locals that his agency was "considering launching a criminal probe," and that they were looking into ways of putting additional pressure on the owners. By June, he would report that prosecutors had filed 4,000 lawsuits on behalf of workers over back wages. In May a court ruled to disqualify the director general of BaselCement Pikalevo, Anatoly Maslikov, from his job.

But key to each of these endeavors was that they were conducted as if in a vacuum—most of the lawsuits went nowhere, and the rulings were not enforced, making negotiation impossible. Each attempt by outsiders to force owners to do something had absolutely zero effect on the owners themselves—in order for workers to get their jobs and their salaries back, three different owners needed to reach a joint agreement on the cost of the raw materials and by-products that they shipped to one another. But Russia's muddled legislation had no legal framework that could force them to do that. There was no law on nationalization that they could be threatened with, and Russia's largely corrupt courts were only a symbolic mechanism.

With neither side listening to the other, the network of administration—from municipal to local to regional—was left to make feeble signals that some higher force needed to get involved to avert disaster.

That disaster occurred on May 15, 2009, when Pikalevo's only power station, which was controlled by the alumina factory, was shut down by Gazprom over a $4.5 million debt.[50] That last measure left the entire town without hot water, causing the built-up tension to reach a tipping point.

4.

On May 20, about 200 desperate residents stormed Mayor Sergei Veber's administration building. Yelena Matuzova was one of them.

Andrei Petrov, an electrician at the factory power station, described how word of the meeting had spread spontaneously. "There was no information. Some co-workers called me up, said there was something happening that very day, an unsanctioned rally in front of the mayor's office or something like that."

Inside, the mayor was holding a meeting with BaselCement Pikalevo management, as well as the district prosecutor and Federal Security Service officers, on how to get the power station running again.

"I felt this excitement, this fear," Petrov recalled. "It concerned me personally, I couldn't have imagined this in a nightmare. The meeting inside—there was no information about it getting out to the people, they were standing there for an hour. Once in a while someone would come out and say something, but it wasn't very informative. So some of the stronger men started pushing their way in, and they burst through."

Petrov, like other residents, believed this spontaneous collective action to be organized by Svetlana Antropova. But judging by the random way people congregated, there was very little "organization" to this event or to the march of June 2, when about 400 people went to block the highway between Vologda and St. Petersburg.

On May 20, footage[51] showed residents randomly gathering

in front of the administration building, huddled around in groups talking quietly to one another.

Then slowly, almost lazily, the crowd started trickling up to the administration entrance. Mostly women, they filed up slowly and looked on as two men started trying to open the doors. "Break them, break them," a woman said. Another joined her. "They broke our [factory.]" And another middle-aged woman added, shaking her head in dismay, "This isn't life."

When the doors opened, they piled in slowly and crowded through the narrow corridor. By the time they reached the police guard in front of the meeting room, they had worked themselves into a state of frustrated desperation. "You have everything, we have nothing!" the women yelled as they haggled with him to let them in. They didn't see the guard as one of their own at that moment, although to all intents and purposes he was—but they could not tell the difference. Their unformulated demands targeted the people they perceived as more powerful than themselves, and not necessarily the people who could actually help them solve the conflict.

They started chanting "Water!", "Work!", and "Salary!", behind the closed doors as the tension mounted. Finally the crowd, joined by several men hammering loudly on the doors, broke through and spilled into the meeting room, crying "What is this?" and "Our children are cold and hungry. What have you done?" A security guard was knocked over, and he rushed to pick up his papers from the floor.

"There wasn't so much fear as panic," Andrei Petrov, who was in the crowd, said of the officials in the room. "It was an effect of unexpectedness. There, inside, in the crowd there were emotions. They weren't necessary, but they were there. It was a crowd, after all, it was powerful, and they started trying to use it."

Two years on, Veber tried to downplay what happened in that room. "They didn't burst in," he told us in an interview. "They stood outside listening, because they had some questions to ask. The door couldn't hold them. But you can't say they burst in. They came in."

Did he feel the blame was directed at him?

"At that moment, everyone could be blamed," he said. "Especially since from the point of view of the worker, any representative of power, any boss, first and foremost has to decide and help."

Video footage showed that Veber was in no position to answer their questions—nor was the crowd prepared to hear out his "lies."

"You're not letting us [talk]," he told the crowd. "Unless you leave the room you won't let us decide anything. No one is going to turn on the water right now, and no one is going to pay you your salaries right now."

They tried to figure out who was to blame, but to a room full of women in raincoats, any man wearing a suit or a uniform was the enemy.

"You think I am personally to blame for your salaries not being paid?" Anatoly Maslikov, the factory director general, stood up and said.

"Yes!" the women cried in unison.

The prosecutor, Fyodor Veretinsky, tried to reason with the crowd, telling them he was on their side. "We're the ones who can defend your rights. If we deem the wage arrears greater than two months, we will consider... launching a criminal case against company directors."

The people listened quietly, but it was becoming increasingly clear that the prosecutor had no real leverage.

"You understand that the [technical issues] are not within the competency of the municipal authorities."

It was building inexorably towards a solution that was on everyone's mind. Finally, a woman interrupted the prosecutor.

"Why not go straight to Medvedev and Putin?"

"Excuse me, please name yourself," the prosecutor said. But the woman, who could not be seen behind the crowd, remained silent.

On June 2, Petrov, Matuzova, and about 400 others blocked a highway to St. Petersburg—the same road that Vladimir Putin was expected to travel along on his way to Finland, for an official trip.

"It was the people's despair. They didn't understand what was happening to them and why," Petrov recalled two years later. "We couldn't understand—why had everything been working for so long, and why did everything suddenly stop working? For so long the country has needed aluminium—what's changed? Aren't airplanes flying anymore? And I think that's what people wanted to know."

Just as before, Veber, Prosecutor Veretinsky, and representatives of the regional administration came out to talk to the people. But no one was listening to a word of what they said. All was "lies."

"These four hundred people broke up into groups," Petrov said. "In one group was Veber, in another was Maslikov. And people surrounded them. They weren't so much asking questions as making demands. 'Give us our salaries back and our jobs.' And the officials were trying to make promises, but the people … were in such a state of emotional excitement that they didn't hear the answers anymore."

Their one unformulated demand was an appeal to supreme state power—i.e. that Putin should learn about what was happening on the ground and intervene.

"Our actions were aimed at our government, so that they would finally hear us and see how we live," Yelena Matuzova recalled.

When Petrov was approached by a journalist during the march, he blurted out the only course of action that seemed likely to help.

"Pass it on to Putin and Medvedev, what is happening here," he said.

5.

Reports that Putin would change his itinerary to come to Pikalevo began appearing as early as the evening of June 2. The visit itself wasn't officially announced; instead, scared plant officials were told to prepare, leaking cryptic statements to the press about a pending meeting.

At approximately 8 AM on June 4, hundreds began gathering in the rain on the wide, green lawn by the town's swimming pool, expecting the prime minister to arrive there by helicopter. A helicopter did indeed land at around noon, but Putin was not on it. He would arrive later by train.

Hundreds more surrounded the factory, where Putin finally toured the plant and met with management and owners. They stood in the rain and waited for him for about eight hours, insisting on speaking to him personally and hearing his message before it was distorted and misinterpreted by his underlings.

"First they told us he would not come out [to the people]," Yelena Matuzova recalled. "But when we learned that the meeting was over, we started shouting to him, 'Putin! Putin!' And he came out, very quickly, just for five minutes." Matuzova asked only if the plants would start running. And he told her and the small circle of people that had surrounded him that they would.

"We wanted to hear it from him, really, we wanted to learn more," she said when asked why they needed to speak directly to Putin.

Andrei Petrov, who stood in the circle, also wanted to talk to Putin but didn't get the chance. "I wanted to say something about the regional management. About [Governor] Serdyukov."

As the people waited for Putin to emerge from the meeting, they got text messages from their banks informing them that their salaries had been deposited. By the end of that day—and for some people, by the end of the visit—thousands of dollars in back wages had been paid in full.

When they went home that evening to their television sets, they were rewarded further. For if the meeting itself yielded thousands of dollars in back wages (Petrov said he bought a car with that single payment), the experience of watching their errant master, Oleg Deripaska, being publicly berated by the only person in Russia who had that right, was priceless.

6.

It was Putin's most brilliant performance as the angry Tsar, a performance that overshadowed President Dmitry Medvedev's keynote speech at the St. Petersburg Economic forum, where Western investors gathered later in bars to discuss the latest thrashing of an errant oligarch.

The broadcast that night was the circus that came after the bread. Touring the plant, Putin asked plant managers why they had "turned it into such a dump."

At the meeting, he turned up in jeans and a beige jacket that he didn't bother to take off. He slouched in his chair, and he had only one hand on the table. He perfected a look of boredom and annoyance more terrifying than any flash of anger.

"I didn't have to come here. We could all have met in Moscow. But I still decided to come here—not because I wanted to look at the empty factory, but because I wanted the authors of all this to look at this —" he paused and scowled. "Everything. That happened. Here. For them to come and look at it themselves." The dull thud of the fingertips of his right hand on the table next to his microphone punctuated each word.

"You've made thousands of people hostage to your unprofessionalism and your greed. That is absolutely unacceptable."

And there it was—the popular legend of a benevolent, unknowing Tsar, and his vassals, the *boyars*, who lead him astray:

"No one can convince me that regional authorities did all they could to help the people. They didn't want me to come here. They tried to convince me to see another new plant. I'm sure it was a great plant. But why did everyone scatter like cockroaches just before my visit? Why weren't there people here who could make decisions?"

Deripaska was shown close up, bowing his head and covering his eyes with his fists—the lowest any oligarch had fallen since Mikhail Khodorkovsky was shown in a courtroom cage. Then followed the most humiliating moment: Putin produced a contract enabling all three plants to restart production.

"Oleg Vladimirovich, did you sign this? I don't see your signature," Putin said quietly and motioned with his fingers for Deripaska to stand up. "Come here and sign it." Putin placed the contract at the edge of his table, took his pen—the one he had in his right hand throughout the meeting—and threw it on the contract just as Oleg Deripaska came up to the table.

"That contract right there," Putin motioned.

Standing up, clearly a head taller than the seated Putin, Deripaska bent and bowed over the contract as he signed its pages. He looked up questioningly at Putin (there was a reason for that) when he was finished and quietly walked away.

As he turned, Putin delivered a final coup de grâce: "Give me my pen back." He said that phrase so quietly, so deprecatingly, that there is still no absolute certainty about the exact words he used.

Whatever consolation the bread and circuses provided, it was temporary for a very simple reason: most people fully understood not only that Putin's performance was just that, a mere performance, but that very little of what he said at the meeting was true.

To start with, the very contract that Deripaska was forced to sign was widely believed to be fake—sources at BaselCement

Pikalevo repeatedly pointed out that a contract on raw materials could only legally be signed by the general directors of the actual factories—not by the chief of the Basic Element empire.

It did not go unnoticed, too, that Deripaska had just benefited from a $4.5 billion bailout from the government, after lobbying Putin personally for the first of many such bailouts throughout the crisis.

But the very fact that Putin noticed his people's plight and castigated an oligarch for neglecting his ancient duties as baron was met with immense gratitude.

"We would fall at his feet," a woman said two years later in Pikalevo—even as she brushed off Putin's appearance with Deripaska as an orchestrated spectacle. Obviously Putin was on the side of the barons, but at least he made it known that mere subjects deserved care and better treatment.

An opinion poll released in late June 2009 found that an overwhelming 69 percent of respondents felt that Putin did the right thing by resolving the problems at Pikalevo. But when asked who was at fault over the situation itself, just 12 percent blamed the federal government, with 34 percent placing responsibility on plant owners, and 31 percent blaming local government.[52]

But in the daily reality of life in Pikalevo, the actual feelings towards Putin and the government were far more ambivalent—the people still saw Putin as doing far less than he could have.

"Putin could nationalize us if only he wanted to," Svetlana Antropova, the union leader, told us. She had sat in the first row, right next to general director Anatoly Maslikov, and reported to Putin about the wage arrears during the June 4 meeting. "But they're trying to keep everyone happy. Every time I see Putin on TV, there's Deripaska. But he could stamp his foot and say, 'Oleg, you're going to sell today…. I allow you to do this and that, under the following concessions.'"

On the one hand, the knee-jerk gratitude appeared to be genuine. "The people associated Putin with these salaries, that it was all thanks to him," Antropova recalled. "Especially the women. I had one come in and tell me, 'Sveta, I love Putin so much.' And I told her, 'You go on loving him, dear. I don't love anybody.' Because first they had to let it get so out of hand. For things to heat up. For people to block the roads. And only then come down and sort things out."

On the other hand, almost everyone we spoke to admitted that there was something deeply wrong with calling in Putin as a way to solve their problems. At the same time, no one could pinpoint what, exactly, could have been done without Putin's personal intervention in what were, essentially, the workings of three private enterprises.

Andrei Petrov described a mix of hope and regret in the way people interpreted Putin's intervention.

"It was unusual. It was probably… [he paused] what [the people] had been waiting for, though they hadn't said it themselves, and didn't understand. But they were happy that it happened. Though they understood that this was wrong, that it's not the way [to solve problems]. But they were glad.

"At that moment, the people were trying to change things in any way possible. Whether they understood that this was wrong—I think a lot of them didn't—they were [overwhelmed by emotion]. I understood this only subconsciously. Only after so much time has passed did I begin to understand that this was wrong."

And if Putin's intervention gave them their salaries and jump-started the factories, it solved none of Pikalevo's underlying problems.

"They heard us, but not quite. We got our salaries, yes, but they haven't gone up. Not much has changed really," Yelena Matuzova said.

"We had this hope that he would come here and change something. We hoped that they would fire Serdyukov. [Putin] promised long term agreements within a year. But there are no agreements."

By December 2011, Yelena Matuzova had turned against Putin. She had trusted him, but he had betrayed that trust, and nothing had changed at her factory.

Indeed, the lack of interest in any potential legislation that could help empower the workers was striking. In the wake of Putin's visit, the State Duma held the first reading of a law on nationalization that would allow the government to take over control of failed enterprises like those of Pikalevo, but this was clearly a publicity stunt and the law was never passed. Meanwhile, when locals were asked about nationalization, they nodded with lukewarm approval at best. The intricacies of management didn't seem to concern them, for their domain was their work and their salaries—the rest, they seemed to be saying, was none of their business.

Andrei Petrov was just one of several locals who noticed this passivity in conversation with us. He described seeing workers unwilling to talk to one another about the events they were taking part in; at the plant, they hardly communicated their plans—not because they were afraid or because their communication took on a conspiratorial air, but because there was little constructive communication to speak of.

"The people that took part in the events—on the road, at the mayor's office—they are very passive. When they're sitting in their own kitchens, they care about what happens. But when it comes to action, they don't do anything."

Were they afraid to lose the little they had? Were they afraid of a reaction from the authorities? Andrei shook his head.

"No. It's just a passive reaction of the Russian man. Especially in a small town. He's interested in very little. He's not interested in public life. This participation used to be forced, there were demonstrations and *subbotniks* [Saturdays of obligatory volunteer work]. But there's none of that left. On the clock, within the gates of the factory—and then home—that's his world."

The origins of that kind of behavior go back to the archetypical Soviet enterprise, but their autocratic nature was clearly embedded over centuries—a survival mechanism that often favored a dysfunctional *status quo* over a potentially "free" future where there was no work at all, and thus no hope of sustenance from an inhospitable land.

The writer Alexei Ivanov describes a telling incident involving iron ore factories in the Urals during the eighteenth century. When, in 1773, the Pugachev Rebellion promised land to factory workers and peasants—all under the yoke of serfdom—the factory workers refused, and turned violently on the peasants. In this miniature civil war, "All were unfree. But they each wanted their own captivity. The workers didn't want lands, for they had forgotten how to till them.... The workers chose their factories over freedom."[53]

During the Soviet Union, despite ownership being in the hands of the state, the local administration of factories remained deeply patrimonial.

Sociologist Simon Clarke, for instance, described a Soviet

enterprise as headed by an all-powerful director who answered straight to Moscow for implementing the production plan and making sure that the workers were cared for. "The ideal general director would be the subject of stories of legendary achievements and enjoyed the loyalty and even the affection of his employees, symbolizing the enterprise and the achievements of its labor collective."[54]

The very fabric of life proved to be so difficult that having a capable and just leader—one who could provide food, shelter, water, and benefits—under the given conditions was often a matter of life and death. But over centuries, this evolved into a disempowerment process that was often initiated by the workers themselves.

"Workers attributed their relative good or bad fortune to the personality of the chief...," Clarke writes. "There was therefore a high degree of collusion by the workers in their own exploitation...."[55]

In a single industry town like Pikalevo, these archetypes are easily recognizable. The ideal plant director was Koren Badalyants, who managed alumina production with an iron fist from 1960 up through 1980. It was Badalyants who was credited with maintaining the highest salaries in the region, and, working within the Soviet allocation system, winning the choicest vacations for his workers. He built Pikalevo's swimming pool—the pride of the town, which still bears a memorial to his name upon its entrance—and established some of the best kindergartens and schools.[56]

Sergei Sofyin—who, like Badalyants, was a home-grown director and thus an exception to a string of managers sent in from Moscow—elicited a similar awe due to his strong authoritarian and paternalistic streak.

An imposing man in his sixties with piercing eyes, Sofyin demonstrated a sincere connection with his plant that was valued by his workers. "Badalyants would say, the plant is my life," he told us of his career at the plant, with tears welling up in his eyes. "I can't add anything else to that."[57]

But he was also efficient in making sure workers' needs were met, locals said, calling him "strict but fair." Yelena Matuzova, who got a two-room apartment from Sofyin, said that he should be the mayor instead of Veber, but doubted that he would choose to run after being fired from the plant.

Strong, popular local plant managers like Sofyin and Badalyants can serve as a key to understanding local attitudes towards supreme power in Russia. If they were seen as demigods, the awe and affection was also tempered with a fierce independence, and, most of all, an awareness of the leader's "otherness." For in the unwritten system of rules and rights that governed working relationships, the boss could enjoy the privileges provided by his caste as long as he never neglected to care for his workers.

In this sense, an expletive-ridden characterization by Pikalevo factory driver Kirill Karpov[58] spoke volumes about the ambivalence that workers felt both for Putin and for "good" managers like Badalyants and Sofyin.

"They say all the right things. Seems to be a sensible guy. [Putin] can say [something so awful], then you see he's not mad. Badalyants was like that. Could tell everyone to fuck off. He could lie to you and punish you [pertaining to both Badalyants and Putin]. But he was objective."

Karpov claimed that he wasn't afraid of his boss. When Badalyants raised his voice at him, Karpov said he threw his keys on the table and refused to work. "He didn't raise his voice at me again. He was an [excellent] psychologist."

And reverently, he said of Badalyants: "He was a boss." As if there were no other real bosses in his experience.

Those contradictory experiences of management reflected the way locals experienced power on all levels—as a force that had an unwritten, God-given right to exploit them in exchange for bringing order to their lives. That meant that Putin's interference, regardless of whether what he said was actually true or not, was an act of order in itself.

As Sofyin told us, "I think Putin's visit was received as a manifestation of reason."

PART II
THE OPRICHNIKI

Chapter 5

Men of the Sovereign

It's the Tsar on a horse, in a golden brocade,
With a posse of butchers around him,
Armed with axes and ready to hack and to hang,
And to execute at the Tsar's pleasure
And in anger Potok reaches down for his sword,
"Who's this Khan come to Rus, who's this tyrant?"
And he hears the reply, "That's a living god there,
That's our father, deigning to slay us!"
—**Count Alexei Konstantinovich Tolstoy**,
from "Potok Bogatyr," 1873

Everyone turned into a vassal. Because there were no new
rules of the game, and to this day they don't exist.
—**Kirill Kabanov**, former FSB officer, 2010

1.

EVER SINCE HIS teens, when students had to decide on a career path and either leave for trade school or finish two more years and go to college, Kirill Kabanov wanted to be a KGB officer.

For Kabanov, it wasn't the movie allure of spies, as it was for Vladimir Putin, who came from the previous, post-war generation. Born in 1967 and growing up during the stagnation and lower-tier corruption of the Leonid Brezhnev era, Kabanov wasn't interested in espionage or traveling abroad, he just wanted to fight crime, and fighting crime as an officer of the KGB was more interesting than being a cop.

Now in his mid forties, Captain Kabanov carries a gun to work every day. His office has a vintage Mauser hanging on the wall next to his desk, with its green glass lamp, KGB paraphernalia, and a framed letter of gratitude from the Investigative Committee. On the wall above his chair hangs the obligatory picture of Vladimir Putin.

Except that nothing is as it seems. The picture is a print-out of a photograph of Putin counting thousand-ruble bills. For some reason, it is surrounded by cartoon drawings of pigs and a vintage Soviet-era poster warning against taking bribes. And the gun he carries to work is for self-protection, just in case. Clearly, this is not the office of an FSB captain.

It wasn't that Kabanov never realized his aspirations—he did. In 1984, after completing school, he studied at the military academy. After a brief stint working for the Soviet Communist Party, he finally joined the KGB—now renamed the Federal Security Service, or FSB according to its Russian acronym—in 1994. He served in the Moscow economic crime task force of the FSB, investigating contraband cases. He rose to the rank of captain. But over the course of four years while he was in service, it became increasingly clear to him that the job of an FSB officer wasn't to fight crime, it was to make money.

Kabanov wanted to fight crime—if he had wanted to make a lot of money, he would have gone into business. But he felt that precisely because he wanted to fight crime rather than be a businessman, he was booted out of the FSB in 1998. Looking for another way to fight crime, he co-founded the National Anti-Corruption Committee, an NGO housed in a smoke-filled eighteenth century stone building on a quiet, central Moscow street.

Burly, with a crew cut, he would look extremely intimidating were he an acting officer. As it is, he's only a former officer, even though his work has taken him far: then-President Dmitry Medvedev, as part of his anti-corruption drive, had Kabanov join his presidential commission on civil society. Today, Kabanov frequently appears on state TV, offering brutal, expletive-ridden exposés of the world he left behind and which he continues to investigate.

Kabanov insists that he's no angel. But he also realizes that his experiences, coupled with his research after he left the force, were crucial in offering him a glimpse of a structure and way of life that he now understands is perfectly feudal.

"I had a turning point right before I left [the FSB]. There were several turning points, in fact," he recalls. "I didn't understand why our salary was the equivalent of $50 a month [circa 1995] when we handled goods worth millions of dollars. But back then the guiding principle was from the old days, to hold back, to drink cheap vodka, but not take [bribes]. We considered ourselves an elite force. 'What are we, cops, to take bribes?' we used to say."

For cops, he said, it was normal to "feed off the land"—an approximation of the ancient custom of *kormleniye*, or feeding, by which government officials in remote places got their salaries from the population they were in charge of protecting or keeping in line, rather than from the Tsar's treasury. Rank and file bribe-taking among cops was common in the Soviet era, even though it exploded in the 1990s.

But what started happening in the FSB during the 1990s was different, Kabanov said. It was coming from the top, not from the bottom.

"First we started noticing that our generals were living beyond their means." He described how they started showing up in swanky cars wearing luxurious clothes, and developed a taste for expensive imported alcohol. Details about their apartments and dachas trickled down to the lower ranks.

When these same generals started closing contraband cases that Kabanov was investigating, he began to understand that it was no coincidence. "We thought they were behaving strangely, but it turned out that they were just running businesses." It was a normal occurrence, for instance, for a shipment of cigarettes to wind up being presented as a gift to high-ranking officials of government agencies. And much of the illegal revenue his task force intercepted wasn't returned to the state treasury where it belonged, but was pocketed by the generals and colonels who felt their salaries were too small to allow such riches to pass through their hands untouched.

As much as he was revolted by what he saw, Kabanov understood that he had to make a choice. The pressure was increasing to go with the flow and become a businessman in uniform. To stay honest and fight the graft was impossible, because it was spreading too quickly.

On several occasions, he found himself tempted. Once, senior colleagues offered him money to unpack a shipment he had confiscated. He refused, and went to his boss instead. "My boss called me an idiot."

Eventually, the system itself booted him out, after his repeated refusals to play by its rules.

Officers in the Customs Service—an offshoot of the FSB—paid $300,000 to get him fired, he says. Other officers who had generously invited him to join their racket now accused him of extorting money and accepting a $100,000 bribe. His consultations with his brother, a former FSB officer who left the force to start his own private security agency, served as another pretext. Kirill Kabanov was discharged in 1998, let loose into the open.

"When I was on the force I would brandish [the FSB identification card, or badge] if someone was rude to me. I came to understand that this badge gives you a feeling of power, a feeling of being protected from the chaotic, unlimited power of the government," he explained. "And when it was taken away, I understood that I had become one of the cattle, the mindless masses. It was terrible. I felt unprotected."

It was a mere coincidence that the year Kabanov was kicked out of the FSB, Vladimir Putin became its director. Kabanov's FSB career was over, but for many of his colleagues who opted to become businessmen in uniform, it was just the beginning.

2.

In his 1973 novel, *Loyal Ruslan*, Georgy Vladimov tells the harrowing story of a guard dog of the same name. Part of a canine regiment deployed to a labor camp in Stalin's Gulag, the dog knew no other work and he was dedicated to his job.

"About twenty dogs congregated on the platform near the end of the rails, walking along the fence and barking at passing trains in unison. The animals were beautiful and well-groomed; it was nice to marvel at them from afar, but no one dared to go up on the platform, for locals knew how hard it would be to escape afterwards. The dogs awaited prisoners, but the prisoners never arrived that day, nor the following day, nor in a week, nor in two weeks."[59]

Khrushchev's de-Stalinization campaign was too humane to shoot the guard dogs after the camp was shut down, and they were left to their own devices, roaming the abandoned territory in search of food and someone to guard. A few years later, the dogs came upon a familiar picture: a procession of men with backpacks trudging towards them through the steppe. Mistaking a geological expedition for a new batch of prisoners, the dogs were overjoyed with the return of their old, habitual order of life, where there were people to patrol and herd about the territory. The fact that the geologists were not escaped prisoners simply did not fit into the dogs' understanding of how the world functioned. With the dogs relentlessly attacking them as the escapees that they believed them to be, the men could do nothing but shoot them. And the last thing that the loyal Ruslan feels before his death is an utter betrayal by his own masters, by the people who taught him to patrol prisoners in the first place.

If President Boris Yeltsin's administration left hundreds of thousands of men to their own devices after the fall of the Soviet Union and the disintegration of the holy ideology that these men had sworn to guard, then Vladimir Putin appears to have had more compassion for these wayward, leftover men. It is hard to say which approach did more damage.

In a chaotic bid to diminish the influence of the organization, Yeltsin's government began haphazardly hacking the KGB to pieces. It cut off core agencies—Kremlin security, foreign intelligence, border patrol, and electronic intelligence. It stifled funding for the new Russian Security Ministry, and, having done that, renamed it yet again in 1995, calling it the Federal Security Service. Between 1991 and 1995, the service was renamed six times. And the reshuffling would continue well into Putin's term. By 2006, Putin signed a decree to transfer control of all detention centers—including prisons operated by the FSB—to the Justice Ministry, though *de facto* the FSB, in an ongoing struggle for finance and influence, retained control of its Lefortovo Prison.[60]

A brief period of openness after 1991—with some security officers taking part in a series of public discussions out of fear that they would lose even more funding and influence if they didn't—was widely mistaken, particularly in the West, for a victory over the KGB.

But the emerging evidence that former officers were increasingly occupying government posts in Vladimir Putin's administration[61] set alarm bells ringing, particularly in the light of changes that had begun long before Putin even rejoined the FSB as its director in 1998, changes that had already made the state security apparatus more powerful.

As early as 1993, the last Soviet head of the KGB, Vadim Bakatin, warned that Russia's security services had "never lost control" to begin with.[62] And by 1995, the FSB was proclaimed to be "far more powerful than the now-defunct KGB."[63]

This suggests that for all the changes forced on the organization by the government—stripping it of funds and prestige, making it directly subordinate to the president, dividing its multitude of functions—the state was still dealing with an equally powerful behemoth, numbering the same body of officers.

Hundreds of thousands of people who had sworn an oath to one country suddenly found themselves serving another, and yet a fundamental premise of its security apparatus—who they served and why—had never been addressed by the government.

Former security officers like Kirill Kabanov, who served in the FSB's counter-contraband department from 1993 through 1998, link Russia's most formidable threat—rampant, crippling corruption—to this one unanswered question.

"Ideologically, a majority of the people who came over from the KGB felt disadvantaged, felt a sense of betrayal. First their colleagues abroad were betrayed, then this humiliation of Lubyanka under siege—all this forms [inferiority] complexes," he told me.

The lack of a new value system had a disorienting effect on officers over the very identity of the government they were serving. Up until 1990, businessmen, speculators, and dissidents were clear foes to be sought out and persecuted, at least in theory. Suddenly after 1991, these former foes were in the government, and security officers found themselves serving the very people they had been supposed to persecute under the Soviet system.

"Earning $50 a month, they were pushed into business. And they were provoked into certain hidden relations," Kabanov explained. "Okay, so I'll be a security guard for hire. I will serve my boss, and whatever my boss tells me to do I will do it. But if there's an additional service, like protection from criminals, then please be so kind as to add to my salary. And the business structure builds up this system."

Every former security officer that I have interviewed sooner or later came to this key problem of betrayal—not betrayal of the motherland, but betrayal by the government. Each of them complained of the lack of a higher purpose that was an integral part of the job. That higher purpose was identified in different ways: most described it as ideology, some spoke of patriotism, others of laws. In Russian, one of the words for treason and betrayal is *izmena*—a word that also connotes change. The idea that one could change masters or change a set of values that he had previously sworn an oath to is deeply unsettling and unforgiveable for any officer.

And yet this was precisely what most officers were forced to do during the 1990s.

Despite a slew of departments embroiled in a perpetual conflict between each other for resources, influence, and the favor of the sovereign, and despite Yeltsin's attempts to separate intelligence from counterintelligence, officers from domestic as well as foreign departments pointed to a single problem—the lack of a system of coordinates and a unified *raison d'etre*.

Yuri Gervis, a KGB officer who, like Kabanov, worked in the anti-contraband department, went on to serve another five years in the FSB, only to quit in 1996 to go into law practice. For him, the very "idea of government" had been a crucial stimulus without which he could not serve.

"When I started working in the FSB, the difference was that we didn't mix [personal gain with legal responsibility]. People went there—and I know this about myself and my colleagues—for the sake of an idea. The idea of the government," he said, "of government interests, of law and order. But now, there is no central idea in Russia. However bad the idea that Russia used to have, it was still there. Now there is nothing. What is it that we are trying to attain? Personal profit? But then where are the boundaries? In America you are supposed to have a house, a television set, and a car. Nothing has been formulated for us. Are we all supposed to be like Berezovsky? What is our idea? Is it to hold the 2014 Winter Olympics?"

For the domestic corps, these problems pushed officers into the private sphere, with many retaining their connections to the power structures, now in the service of business. The Soviet era concept of active reserve—a quasi-legal scheme by which KGB officers would work for another organization while retaining their title and salary with the KGB—returned, with a new, powerful incentive to use one's FSB connections for private gain rather than necessarily serving the FSB.[64] Virtually practicing corporate espionage, these officers started insisting on "double-dipping" at both places of work. As one officer described to security expert Andrei Soldatov, "I was forced to do my official job and then the job for the FSB, having meetings with agents at night, so why am I refused a second salary?"[65]

While the foreign intelligence wing of the former KGB was not nearly as debilitated by corruption as the domestic corps, its officers were plagued by the same questions. The Foreign Intelligence Service (SVR) had to grapple with a new understanding of the very concept of friend and foe as it built a new *modus operandi* after the Cold War was over.

Oleg Nechiporenko, a KGB general who served under legal cover in Mexico during the 1970s, described a dangerous dissonance where the goals of the officers and the goals of the particular government they were serving were beginning to diverge.

"When the Soviet Union ceased to exist, … the country entered a new dimension. The head of intelligence said then, 'we have no friends and enemies, we have national interests,'" he said. But those national interests, as he and other former spies have pointed out, were not clearly defined.

"I don't know. I have my own views about the role of the enemy, the role of the friend, and the role of the victim. If there is an army, shouldn't they have enemies to fight, rather than 'interests'? These roles are integral to any conflict. An army imagines a foe, they imagine their motherland in the role of a potential victim, and they imagine themselves as protectors of that victim. Those who have been delegated by society with the legitimate right to wield force—and those are all power structures of the executive government in any society—don't they need those roles to be motivated?"

When I posed the same question of ideology to Gennady Yevstafiev, a retired SVR general who followed the same career ladder once ascended by Vladimir Putin, serving in the KGB's notorious First Main Directorate (PGU) as an intelligence officer under legal cover, he described a lacuna that he went to great lengths to fill.

"Many people asked themselves this question. We weren't the first to be faced with it. When I was faced with this question, I started reading, looking for an answer," he explained. Having been attracted to the service by its aura of an intellectual elite, Yevstafiyev had naturally turned to historic literature, and found the motto of the seventeenth century French statesman, Jean-Baptiste Colbert: *Pro rege saepe, pro patria semper*. "'For king—often, for country—always.' It's a brilliant formula, and it often helped me reconcile myself to what was happening in the country."

If the motto presumed that sometimes the interests of the king differed from the interests of the country, did Yevstafiyev always find that he could distinguish between the two?

He laughed in response. "It's completely obvious! Didn't you see that the interests of [Boris] Yeltsin and the country were diametrically opposed?"

For educated, principled officers like Yevstafiyev and Nechiporenko, with careers spanning nearly half a century and decades served abroad, it was possible to find an inner justification for their service that was only moderately at odds with the interests of their government, if it diverged at all.

But for a vast majority of servicemen in the domestic corps, who joined the force for a mix of "ideological and material" stimuli, as Yevstafiyev put it, the lack of a clear-cut set of instructions or a mission that they could follow to their death revived an inherently feudal network of organization based on an explosive, often contradictory mix of loyalty and profit.

"Everyone turns into a vassal," Kirill Kabanov told me of the state of his former colleagues towards the end of the 1990s. "Because there were no new rules of the game, and to this day they don't exist."

Kabanov grasped the importance that divine right had for such a chaotic, archaic system.

"The difference is that in the classical system the chief feudal lord is anointed by God," Kabanov said. "And by serving him you serve God."

3.

There is no shortage of divine right delusions among Russia's security structures. A senior Russian official once described Viktor Cherkesov, the one-time head of Putin's drug-fighting agency and an offshoot of the KGB, as being convinced that the security forces were "like the masons, given tasks by God." During the height of his influence Cherkesov, who went on to lose Putin's favor after blowing the whistle on a pre-election clan war within the forces in 2007, had said that the *siloviki*, the term referring to security personnel and literally connoting "those of force," were viewed as "demigods... doing something that will either save Russia or badly damage it."[66] For Gennady Gudkov, a former KGB officer who became a prominent parliamentarian, the services also constituted something of a "Masonic" brotherhood.[67]

These divine allusions predate the ideological zeal of the Soviet era. A regiment of the White Army wore black tunics and called itself a "brotherhood of monastic knights,"[68] while Putin's 2006 decree to change the security services' uniform from green to black in a bid to distinguish it from the military was interpreted as historically symbolic.

There was another secret society that wore black monk's tunics in the more brutal recesses of Russia's history; a regiment instructed to don pauper's rags to cover gold-embroidered brocades and mink furs when they rode out on black horses to slaughter unrepentant boyars and confiscate their property; a brotherhood that forswore breaking bread with outsiders and jealously served a sovereign who believed himself to be Christ come back to lead the true chosen people to salvation.

Ivan the Terrible instigated the *oprichnina* in 1565, when he divided Muscovy into the lands of the sovereign (the *oprichnina*) and the lands of the aristocracy (the *zemshchina*), singling himself out not only as the head of the church but as a living god. The *oprichnina* essentially constituted a holy land—boyars who had lived on it were forcefully relocated and given new lands in the *zemshchina*. Noblemen who were suspected of treason had their property confiscated—as well as their lives, and, in Ivan's understanding, their very souls.

The separation of lands, in other words, launched a seven-year reign of terror that would only be matched by Joseph Stalin's mass purges in the 1930s.

Historians are still divided over whether the *oprichnina* was an act of policy that was taken too far or merely the product of Ivan's deranged mind. But the chief function of the secret police—also called the *oprichnina*—was not policing the people or protecting the sovereign but rather confiscating on behalf of the sovereign as part of a holy crusade. Thus Russia's first secret police emerges both as a religious phenomenon and an economic one. A large part of what happened between 1565 and 1572 was, essentially, a vast redistribution of property as Ivan IV, who had just proclaimed himself the first Tsar of Russia, sought to consolidate the elites.

The fall of Constantinople to the Turks in 1453 amounted to a turning point for the way that Russian rulers would see their autocracy for the next several centuries. Muscovy, which had nominally considered the Byzantine emperor its suzerain, would go beyond merely adopting the Byzantine model to make its Tsar the head of the Orthodox Church; its sacralization of the monarch would mean that he was not just god-like—he was "understood to be a supernatural being."[69] The very ceremony of anointment, meanwhile, likened the Russian monarch to Christ himself.[70]

This circumstance was well noted by foreign travelers during the period, who marvelled at the Russians treating their Tsar "as a higher god."[71]

When applied by Ivan the Terrible, the entire mystical explanation for his *oprichnina* actually served to justify and legitimize another dimension: property ownership not just by the landed aristocracy, but by those deemed worthy of it by the sovereign. The elaborate praying rituals, the black rags cast over tunics embroidered in gold and fur, the monastic order, all masked a very simple process: Ivan was confiscating land and property from the old nobles, the boyars, and creating a new nobility of *oprichniki*—his loyal soldiers, in the service of a demigod. Their closeness to this God-anointed sovereign gave them the right to confiscate, elevating their pillage to the level of a holy crusade.

4.

When Kirill Kabanov was booted out of the FSB in 1998, he suffered a brief period of anxiety over losing his badge, that coveted symbol that separated officers into a higher caste which was immune to the brutality of the government because it was the government itself. Kabanov got over the shock relatively quickly because he soon joined forces with Georgy Satarov, a political expert and a former aide to President Boris Yeltsin, and created the National Anti-Corruption Committee.

But for his former colleagues, building their careers years before Putin would come to power, it was already clear that the lure of newly-available luxury goods and properties—be they real estate or businesses—enhanced the existing, Soviet-era mystique of their badge.

"I got over it rather quickly," Kabanov said of the days after he quit the FSB—and in no small part he owed it to the success of his NGO. "[But] our officers… became like drug addicts to power. It is part of the psychology. If you don't represent the law, then anyone who does can walk all over you. And people are afraid to be in that category where people can walk all over you."

By the time Vladimir Putin, himself a former KGB officer, returned to the organization as its director in 1998, the system was already firmly in place. When he became Russian president in 2000, he integrated himself into the quasi-feudal relationships that were already forming between business and power, and tried to make the best of them.

"Putin is part of this system," Kabanov said. "Did he have a choice to change it?"

Putin's mere appearance at the apex of the government, his KGB background, the familiar, cold, expressionless mask worn by a fellow member of the elite, served to legitimize a pattern of behavior that had already re-emerged and was firmly entrenched.

Thousands of officers disenfranchised during the Yeltsin era breathed a sigh of relief when, by his mere appearance, they seemed to be given unspoken permission to find ways to enrich themselves to compensate for what the state salaries lacked. And they were heartened by this unspoken permission. Kabanov watched as many of his former colleagues started capitalizing on the virtually unlimited powers that their status acquired with the appearance of new property. He saw their lifestyles transformed as they bragged about their expensive watches, their new Mercedes SUVs, the furs that they started wearing in winter, and the exclusive nightclubs they talked of visiting the night before.

They started treating their jobs as a sort of divine right, a mandate to extort first hundreds of thousands, then millions of dollars from opponents who crossed their interests. "It was a life of glamor," Kabanov said.

As early as 2003, he recalled meeting a banker who wore a sword and shield in white and yellow gold on the lapel of his jacket. "'What are you doing walking around like that,' I ask him. 'Don't you understand,' he says, 'it's the symbol of the new nobility! Vladimir Vladimirovich is creating a new nobility!'"[72]

These attitudes didn't limit themselves to the FSB—they corresponded with lower-tier bribery in other law enforcement agencies and even civilian bodies like the Tax Inspectorate. But because the practice itself was not new, the officials involved seemed to be searching for a justification for a way of life that they were not able to change. The idea of belonging to a government that no longer looked like the disgrace it had become during the Yeltsin period offered them that justification.

But many seemed to adopt the lifestyle out of a sense of inertia.

Kabanov described another acquaintance, a colonel in the Investigative Committee of the Interior Ministry (one of two Investigative Committees with functions similar to those of the US Federal Bureau of Investigation), who took to smoking $85 cigars (despite an official salary of less than $1200 a month). He had a special golden knife to clip the cigars—and he also bought himself a coat lined with jaguar fur. When Kabanov confronted him about his lifestyle, he got an honest response: "I want to live a little," the colonel said. "What if they arrest me tomorrow?"

Vladimir Putin, himself born of the KGB, appeared to be the perfect candidate for someone these people could trust, obey, and manipulate all at once. Citing Gennady Gudkov, journalists Peter Baker and Susan Glasser described Putin as presiding over a highly cohesive "brotherhood" that believed it had a "monopoly on upholding the integrity of the Russian state."[73]

The reality, however, has proven far more complex.

Led by Putin, the rise of the *siloviki* by 2000 may indeed have had as its objective the reining in of a corrupt bureaucracy, as it did under Putin's mentor, Soviet KGB head Yuri Andropov. Putin's pledge to establish a "dictatorship of the law" seemed to herald nothing short of a restoration of the kind of "law and order" widely associated with the KGB. In fact, not only was there a yearning for a perceived "rigid law and order of the past"[74] among the general populace, the business elite also proved eager to embrace former security men for their efficiency, their connections, and their sense of order.

But the now notorious "snowball effect" of *siloviki* rising to the top echelons of government—with Putin inviting former KGB friends into the Kremlin, and each bringing his own clique of St. Petersburg associates[75]—hardly countered the rampant corruption left over from the Yeltsin era that Putin purportedly sought to quell. Instead it entrenched it, with the *siloviki* themselves becoming that corrupt bureaucracy.

A better illustration of this point is the remarkable transformation of legislation pertaining to private property during Perestroika. If business and speculation was a crime sometimes punishable by death in the Soviet Union, then it would have been naïve to expect that the criminal code and the legislation regulating business and trade would be miraculously reformed overnight. Instead, reforms often appeared to be layered onto existing laws. The resulting muddled legislation regulating this sphere turned into a powerful weapon of both the *siloviki*, pursuing their own commercial ends, and Putin's administration as a whole. What Putin was referring to when he spoke of "law" was so incomprehensible that the implementation of that "law" was theoretically enough for him to imprison every individual in the country.

It was this weapon, after all, that was used to imprison Yukos founder Mikhail Khodorkovsky when he began posing a political threat, and to confiscate his oil empire, and to convict opposition activist Alexei Navalny of embezzlement in 2013.

The very idea of government, the sought-after ideology, the "idea of Russia," should have been a set of coherent, viable laws that could serve as an objective for these men—a group of values that they could share with their leader.

But those values did not exist.

Instead, the loyalty of many of the security officers to Putin was cemented by economics—a set of values that was, in many respects, feudal.

"These were people who'd already been disillusioned and betrayed once," Kirill Kabanov spoke of his colleagues. "And they formed something of an ideology—one that was understood by the people. And that ideology was—if you control the chief economic assets, then you are essentially holding everyone by the balls. You have unlimited power. Was it the initiative of Vladimir Vladimirovich? Not exactly. It was their initiative. They came to him and said, 'You're our boss.'"

The balance was such that those who were inside the system benefitted and had little incentive to criticize—while those on the outside were vulnerable to the chaos of "the law," applied by many officers eager to take advantage of this system to their own enrichment.

But precisely because it was a system that pre-dated Putin—a system of organizing relations that officers had to "remember" from the past—it came with its own set of limitations and regulations. Once those unspoken regulations, remembered from centuries past, were internalized, the result was a system that benefitted far too many people—both the rulers and the ruled—to be easily discarded.

Mark Galeotti, a British scholar who has extensively studied Russia's security and organized crime groups, is one of the few who has identified the positive factors of corruption which explain its resilience. This may be explained by comparing it to the ancient feudal practice of *kormleniye*, or tax farming.

Literally "feeding," *kormleniye* was a system of supporting a prince's administration at the expense of the local population. A cheaper form of administration, it allowed the prince to dispatch a viceregent to a remote area, where he would be "fed" exclusively by the locals. Widely used in the fourteenth and fifteenth centuries, it was believed to be formally abolished under reforms of Tsar Ivan the Terrible in favor of direct taxes to the treasury.[76] But despite its formal abolition, the term has frequently appeared to describe various forms of corruption in Russia and across the Soviet Union that continue to this day. British anthropologists Caroline Humphrey and David Sneath noted that many of their respondents in former Soviet republics and Russia would equate various forms of bribery "not with 'market relations' but with the very different patrimonial institutions of earlier times, such as 'feeding' (*kormleniye*), 'feudalism,' and 'serfdom.'"[77]

Despite its moral shortcomings, tax farming was efficient enough for Russia's emperors to keep coming back to it again and again simply because it worked to ensure management and the loyalty of state officials operating from remote places.

"Corruption was a useful tool in that you didn't have to pay everyone a high salary. *Kormleniye* is absolutely nothing new. In the nineteenth century, a small bribe to an official wasn't even considered a bribe," Galeotti explained. "Putin is certainly heir to that tradition. But he's interested in effectiveness as well as control."

The practice whereby officers shaved money off enterprises and ran their own businesses, whether in benign or not so benign protection rackets, or *kryshas*, came with a catch.

"As long as you do your job, as long as you're loyal, whatever else you happen to do, up to a certain level, is permissible. Individuals are going to get sacked, get demoted. But for that to happen, you have to screw up. You have to take a bribe higher than the accepted level. Or you have to pick a turf war at the wrong time with the wrong person. Or you just have to be really bad at your job," Galeotti said. "There is still a sense that you have to be doing your core job, and you have to be good at it, or at least at a certain level. You can't just not bother turning up to work. You still have to earn that freedom of entrepreneurialism."

The spate of high-profile sackings in 2006—when Putin fired a handful of FSB generals and replaced Prosecutor General Vladimir Ustinov over alleged links to what, for all purposes, was a protection racket—signalled that there were limits to how officers could use their jobs for self-enrichment.

Still, within the haphazard system of feudal bonds that tied Putin to his security apparatus and his bureaucracy, his power was deeply limited. He could sack officers who abused their *kormleniye* privileges by taking more than their rank allowed. But by having promoted these officers to the highest echelons of power in the first place, by allowing them to make money, he tied himself down and curtailed his own maneuvering space in the economic reforms that he clearly sought to pursue.

These extra-legal forms of management entangled a critical mass of people to the point that made fighting corruption from the top nearly impossible.

As Kirill Kabanov struggled to expose and punish graft case by case, he began to realize that Putin was just as dependent on his officers and the bureaucracy he had recreated as they were on him.

"Because so many things are done outside the law, you broke the law, they broke the law. Your reputation becomes dependent on them," Kabanov explained.

These bonds are reflected in Putin's personnel policy both as president and as prime minister, where he is wont to avoid high-profile sackings. When officials are rotated, they are often given lower-profile posts with a high potential for rent-seeking activity, to keep them quiet and loyal—a practice that has been compared to traditions of the Soviet nomenclature, "in which elites were circulated within, but rarely expelled from, the ruling class."[78]

In September 2006, for instance, Putin fired nineteen senior law enforcement officials suspected of corruption. In fact, it later emerged that they were still coming to work months later. "What does this tell you?" Kabanov said.

"That they went to him and said, 'Vladimir Vladimirovich, what is this? We did all this for you! We're your flesh and blood!'"

By allowing them to extract rent from the fiefdoms he had given them as part of their government posts—for that, in the absence of ideology or law, was the only bond strong enough to tie them to him and ensure his power—he severely limited his own leverage over these people; now they answered only to him, and not to the law.

Putin's return to a third term as president in 2012 certainly heartened a large part of the higher-tier corps within the FSB. Although he had never truly left and ran the country from his post as prime minister between 2008 and 2012, the FSB still nominally answered to the president even if *de facto* they took their orders from Putin.

"As long as Putin is there, we have our *krysha* (protection racket)," Galeotti said, explaining why many officers were relieved to hear that Putin would replace Dmitry Medvedev as president in 2012. "The basic element is that Putin espouses the beliefs that they all share, gut-level nationalism, that sense of technocratic order of society, that sense that the masses just ought to let the elites run the country. He speaks their language in a way that Medvedev never did."

But the FSB, like any structure, is not uniformly content—just as not all of its members practice tax farming. There is evidence that the factors that helped enrichment spread and cemented the FSB's loyalty to Putin are the same ones undermining the very stability of his control. Andrei Soldatov, the Moscow-based security expert, noted growing unhappiness due to funding disparities within the FSB.[79] And the disparity of "extracurricular" enrichment opportunities between lower-ranking officials and senior officers is a dangerous imbalance rife with conflict. Loyalty, in other words, is directly proportional to financial well-being—and for those many officers who struggle to do their job without engaging in extracurricular enrichment schemes, seeing their bosses brag about expensive watches only aggravates their discontent.

"They do not harbor a sense of reverence [for Putin]," Yuri Gervis told me of the attitudes of his former colleagues in the FSB, in an obvious understatement.

It was a vicious circle: many officers contented themselves with the *status quo*, provided that it allowed for enrichment, as they hung on every word of the sovereign. But those who believed in the law and lived on their salaries alone were powerless to change the behavior of their colleagues and bosses. And they too looked to the top, blaming Putin.

Kirill Kabanov insisted that corruption could be fought only when a critical mass of officers internalized norms of behavior that had no room for tax farming. But in frustration, he once told a small group of journalists: "Everyone in this room knows the name of the person from whom this corruption is coming."[80]

Chapter 6
The Audience

In Russia only he is great whom I am talking to—and only while I am talking to him.
—**Emperor Paul I**

1.

COLONEL PAVEL ZAITSEV of the Investigative Committee, Russia's equivalent of the FBI, had many contraband cases under his belt—one nearly got him sent to jail. But none stupefied him more than a mysterious shipment of Chinese goods he discovered during a routine check of a Chinese vendor in Moscow in spring 2005.

It wasn't that someone was importing cheap, Chinese-manufactured shoes and underwear without paying customs duties—the out-of-control consumer market that hit Russia in the 1990s meant that tons of the stuff was unloaded at outdoor venues without the police so much as batting an eyelid as long as protection was paid. But this particular shipment indicated a magnitude and regularity that Zaitsev had not encountered before.

"It was as though someone had lifted the border like a curtain and let a hundred train wagons pass, and then let it down again," Zaitsev told me years later, when, like many whistleblowers, he had left the Investigative Committee to become a lawyer.

At first, according to the documents he obtained from the Chinese vendor, it seemed that the importer was using a military unit designated with the number 6302 as cover. But his colleagues in the Defence Ministry weren't able to locate a military unit with that number anywhere in Moscow.

And as he investigated further, the facts continued to defy logic. He learned that each year, 5,000 train wagons of cheap Chinese goods were delivered to the same recipient, evading customs. Each wagon, according to various estimates, including Zaitsev's, contained goods with a retail value between $340,000 and $600,000.

"I go back to my office, trying to wrap my brain around it. Five thousand wagons a year. That's ten to twenty wagons a day. It took them two weeks to get to Moscow. And while I was sitting there, more were on their way."

Each day, at least a dozen train wagons carrying goods that had not passed customs were traveling across Russia from the Far Eastern port town of Nakhodka. And each day for the last year they had traveled thousands of kilometers without anyone detecting them.

He dug further in search of the mysterious military unit while his team gathered more documents about the shipment. And soon the answer hit him, obvious as daylight: there was no importer trying to hide behind a non-existent military unit. Instead, the military unit in question turned out to be none other than the central headquarters of the Federal Security Service (FSB) on Lubyanka Square, right in the heart of Moscow. It was the FSB that was importing thousands of tons of cheap Chinese shoes and underwear—and facilitating an off-the-books retail turnover that exceeded $1 billion a year.

"Just like that!" Zaitsev added for emphasis, grinning mischievously. Invoices gathered in the investigation suggested the FSB wasn't even hiding the fact: each shipment was paid through FSB accounts, and the identification number of the FSB officer receiving the shipment was indicated in every invoice. It was the same person each time.

Indeed, having the FSB mentioned in the accompanying documents was the whole point: no one at customs would dare question a shipment of goods being imported by the FSB—with that kind of authority, the shipment didn't even need to pass customs. Any law enforcement officer who dared to stop the trainload over its two-week course through the Siberian steppes would cease asking questions as soon as he saw those three ominous letters.

Zaitsev went to the FSB's internal affairs department, where he had close contacts. They told him only that they had known about the case all along—but hadn't bothered informing him because they knew he "wouldn't agree to reach a deal."

But having started the investigation, Zaitsev was determined to move it further. In April 2005 he had police intercept 130 wagons of the shipment and hold it at a sorting station just outside of Moscow, deploying an armed Rapid Response Unit (SORB) to guard the wagons. That was when the trouble began.

Learning of the interception, the Federal Customs Service, which had close ties with the FSB, launched its own criminal investigation and sent its own Rapid Response Unit to take custody of the shipment.

"They tried to take the shipment from us by force. The police Rapid Response Unit against the Customs Rapid Response Unit," Zaitsev explained. When I asked why, he was incredulous: no one was concealing the commercial interest that the shipment presented.

"That was money standing there! I was glad that a war didn't break out. They could have started shooting."

It was due to an amazing coincidence that the standoff between two armed units representing the same government didn't lead to bloodshed: as the officers pointed their rifles at each other, they recognized their comrades from the battles they had fought side by side trying to quell separatist unrest in Chechnya. But in the murky world where they operated, the vassal of your vassal was not your vassal. Your well-being and your success depended solely on the strength of your *krysha*, or protection—and whether that particular protection was favored at court at that particular moment.

The totality of what was happening made little sense—as though Zaitsev and the officers he was investigating lived in two parallel worlds, and the world of law and order he had sworn to uphold was negligible by comparison. One had to simply mention the FSB to any law enforcement officer who stopped you—and, if your connection was convincing enough, the officer would suddenly behave differently, either negotiating for a piece of the action or quietly turning away as he swallowed his pride.

In other words, it wasn't that some unsavory importer was using the name of the FSB to intimidate customs and police—it was the FSB itself leasing out its very mystique for a large share of the retail profits. The distinction between that share of profits going to the state as customs duties or as kickbacks to individual FSB officers didn't seem to matter. The FSB officers were the government as much as the treasury was.

No, there was no use in going against the FSB, and Zaitsev, who had already nearly gone to jail for doing just that, was taken off the case.

2.

In what would become Vladimir Putin's largest purge of his security agencies, some nineteen officials—including senior generals of the FSB and the Interior Ministry—were sacked in the course of a week in September 2006.[81] Outwardly, the purge was said to be tied to the so-called *Tri Kita* (Three Whales) scandal—an earlier FSB-linked furniture contraband fiasco that went public in 2000 thanks to Pavel Zaitsev's ill-fated investigation.

But according to Pavel Zaitsev, something else had to have caused heads to roll in the fall of 2006. That something appeared to be the far larger contraband racket being run right out of the FSB's Moscow headquarters: the real trigger for the purge, Zaitsev and several government officials alleged, was the disgrace of a near-shoot-out between police and customs Rapid Response Units over the shipment of Chinese shoes and underwear. The subsequent purge opened the door for Putin's hand-picked investigator, Vladimir Loskutov to eventually solve *Tri Kita*, one of the longest running criminal investigations in Russia's recent history, and lead to the accused being brought to justice.

But for nearly six years, there was a standoff over *Tri Kita*—a case where a furniture store was alleged to be protected by no less than the deputy head of the FSB. The case would involve a tangle of counter-allegations from three different law enforcement agencies deliberating whether one Pavel Zaitsev could be permitted to investigate a well-connected businessman. In that turf war, Zaitsev, who didn't have many patrons other than the law, clearly lost out. Two people connected to the case would die—one of them a journalist and a parliamentarian.

Why it took Vladimir Putin's personal involvement and a high-profile purge to untangle the knot can be explained by a winding chain of personal connections that went up to the very top—for the case involved the interests of those in direct proximity to Putin.

The case that would fundamentally shake up Putin's court—and perhaps even sway his very decision about a successor—started small, and it started just a few months after Putin himself was inaugurated as president in 2000.

Two customs officials—Alexander Volkov and Marat Faizulin—first noticed that something was amiss at a string of Moscow furniture stores in the summer of 2000. Some 400 tons of high-quality Italian furniture was bypassing customs and arriving—via a shady firm called Liga Mars—at a chain of high-end furniture stores called *Tri Kita*. The chain and the firm were owned and operated by furniture magnate Sergei Zuyev. The amount of money was small—just $2 million worth of contraband furniture, costing the Russian budget about $600,000 in unpaid customs duties.[82] But Volkov and Faizulin—whether out of ambition or commercial interest of their own—were intent on doing their job, and on August 25 they led a raid of fifteen armed men on the furniture center.[83] On September 7 they launched a criminal case.

The investigation landed on Zaitsev's desk in October 2000, and his routine checks started unearthing what amounted to a whole conspiracy—judging by the colossal pressure to put a stop to the case, Zuyev was an untouchable.

"On November 22, one of the investigators in [my unit] questioned a witness who testified that resistance to the investigation was coming from someone by the name of Zhukov—an officer of the FSB's central apparatus," Zaitsev later said.[84]

Just hours after the witness was questioned, an officer from the Prosecutor General's Office—an agency that rivalled the Investigative Committee—arrived demanding that the case be transferred to his agency. Zaitsev and his unit were taken off the case, and the investigation was taken up by the Prosecutor General's Office. After letting it sit for a few months, it closed the case in May 2001, absolving Sergei Zuyev of any crime.

And in another indication that Volkov, Faizulin and Zaitsev had clearly messed with the wrong man—a man protected by no ordinary superior—the officers were to face retribution. Faizulin and Volkov would be charged with abuse of authority, while Zaitsev would face two years in prison for an unauthorized search and arrest. All three would manage to avoid jail time, but the defence witness for Faizulin and Volkov, would be murdered. The murder has not been solved.

Who was Sergei Zuyev, and who, most of all, were his patrons, that the men who investigated his alleged crimes would be hounded for the next half a decade?

On November 22, 2000, just hours after prosecutors had removed the *Tri Kita* case from Pavel Zaitsev's jurisdiction, he continued digging into the origins of the pressure. Who, exactly, were the FSB officers that figured in the witness's testimony, and why were they resisting the investigation?

Having a name, it was easy to connect the dots. The Zhukov who figured in the testimony turned out to be Colonel Yevgeny Zhukov, who served as an aide to the chief of the FSB's economic crimes department, Yuri Zaostrovtsev. Zaostrovtsev was the deputy chief of the FSB.

There was more, however.

Zaitsev learned that Zaostrovtsev's father, Yevgeny Zaostrovtsev, was closely connected to Zuyev's furniture empire. By some accounts, he owned firms that were among the official founders of *Tri Kita*. By other accounts, Yevgeny Zaostrovtsev ran a private security agency that worked for *Tri Kita*.[85] The formal association, however, meant little: what really mattered was that Zaostrovtsev Sr., himself reportedly a former KGB officer, was a direct associate of Sergei Zuyev.

"With a *krysha* like that," Zaitsev told me years later, "why pay anyone?"

Nor was Sergei Zuyev a small fish. While not exactly an oligarch, he had quickly managed to amass a fortune after opening the Soviet Union's first furniture cooperative in 1988. By 1995, he used that money to build *Grant*, one of Russia's first large shopping malls. By 2000, he had expanded his empire to include *Tri Kita*, which the Guinness Book of World Records listed as the largest furniture store in Europe. There was a reason for that: according to Zuyev himself, 99 percent of *Tri Kita*'s investment capital came from foreign companies including a number of German firms.[86] It would be alleged later that those firms were distantly connected to Vladimir Putin, and his pre-presidential business interests.[87]

All this could not have failed to play a role in another tantalizing detail that Zaitsev unearthed while he was investigating Zuyev: with his furniture empire under investigation, Zuyev was promised an audience with Vladimir Putin. According to telephone taps conducted by Zaitsev's unit, in one conversation in November of 2000 Zuyev was told that such a meeting had already been arranged.

"I know that he was promised such a meeting over the telephone," Zaitsev told me. "Whether it took place or not, whether they lied to him, or whether the meeting indeed happened and what was discussed, I do not know."

There was no way to verify where those promises led, for the audio recording was among the evidence confiscated from the police by the FSB in February 2001. But it is not difficult to imagine that Zuyev's higher-placed patrons were indeed in a position to organize such an audience: FSB deputy chief Yuri Zaostrovtsev had been acquainted with Putin during their days in the KGB directorate in St. Petersburg in the early 1990s.[88]

For someone facing investigation, an audience with the president would solve all his problems, and judging by the number of such promised audiences, Zuyev was not the only businessman who saw them as a panacea.

"I've come across so many promises that you could fill a book," Zaitsev told me with dismay. "There's lots of swindlers in Moscow. They can say, 'We've arranged a meeting,' and take money. This is a common occurrence—whether among law enforcement authorities or people with family connections."

Where there is a market, there is a demand. That businessmen would seek a personal meeting with a high-placed official—or better yet with Putin himself—suggests that they themselves recognize the utter powerlessness of the law to solve their problems. In the world of Russian business, where entrepreneurs could not trust legislative protection or institutional mechanisms of conducting business, who you knew wasn't just a valuable asset, it was your chief capital.[89] And a connection to Vladimir Putin was priceless.

3.

As a teenager, years before he would go on to start a successful company in the financial services sector, Ivan Narinsky[90] once found himself approached by a gang of neighborhood thugs who tried to take his money. Being a bit of a nerd, a good student, and coming from a "good family," as he said, Ivan knew he was no match for them. So he tried something he'd seen in the movies, and it saved him from a beating. "I know Kostyan," he told the thugs. Kostyan, of course, did not exist, but the confidence with which Ivan mentioned his name had its effect. "The guys whispered something among themselves and gave me my money back."

Ivan recalled this anecdote after I had asked him about his attitude towards Vladimir Putin. It was December 2011, and the ancient idea that security organs in Russia existed first for their own enrichment and only afterwards for your protection was so ingrained that even arguing about it had become useless. The primary job of the security services, journalists openly wrote by that time, was protecting the sovereign and his interests.[91]

Ten years after starting his own business, weary of the perpetual FSB officers he had to deal with, the meetings in Lubyanka, the sweet-talk with the investigators to ensure that they didn't go after him, and the dismay of watching two of his friends wind up in the dreaded pretrial detention centers for vague economic crimes, Ivan Narinsky had sold part of his business and was trying to move what remained of it to Europe. He was in his early thirties, and he was already exhausted.

"Putin is just another Kostyan," he concluded. An imaginary force to be used as a talisman to ward off those who were in his service and after your money.

Ivan had tried to model his business on what he imagined an ideal American start-up should look like. Instead, he found himself adopting habits similar to those of the corrupt law enforcement officers trying to feed off his profits.

"No one knows the law because it does not apply to anything," he told me. "There is only the law of the criminal world, which has replaced the non-existent state law." The law of the real world— the street-wise law, the law of *ponyatiya*, or, literally, "that which is understood"—was more "ethical," Ivan said, than the non-existent law of the state.

"That which is understood" governed his relations with his business partners and with the state officials whom he inevitably had to deal with. "When I go to an official, he will judge me based on whether I am right by *ponyatiya* or not."

What, after all, was the alternative? It wasn't that Ivan had adhered to every letter of the law in starting his business—because the law was impossible to adhere to in the first place, it had become irrelevant. Business structures were not determined by who owned what stock, but by personal relations, power plays, and trust.

"My former partner was the owner of the business," he explained. "How was it that he was the owner of the business? He had no stock, no shares, no official deed. He was just the owner, and everyone accepted that."

And that was just the way things were.

Ivan seemed to recognize that there was something deeply wrong about acting in such a system—and that may have pushed him to seek another place of residence. But he had also internalized an ethical maneuver to justify your actions when you had no other choice.

"When people do something immoral, they come up with a [rote justification]—it's either believing that the other person's worse than you, or that everyone's doing it, and you vindicate your behavior. These are the instruments we have, and they are all that we can use."

Ivan himself had come to this understanding through his extensive experiences dealing with various law enforcement authorities in a number of capacities. A pivotal incident taught him not to judge them or to position himself against "them"—but to understand that just as there were different businessmen, there were different officers—even among those whose job it was to shake him down. Ultimately, they were all part of that system.

"I was once called in to the Investigative Committee for questioning," he described. "I come in, and they tell me, 'you're done for.'" It turned out that he had fallen victim to a group of extortionists who worked together with investigators, prosecutors, and judges. Both he and his investigators understood that any business owner with a modicum of success was vulnerable to persecution because somewhere, somehow, he had broken the law. And if he had come to their attention, investigators were obliged to launch a case—whether the motives were wholesome or not.

"After a long and difficult talk, the investigator—she was a smart woman—told me, 'I see that you're a good man. Go.'" The investigator offered some advice on the glaring vulnerabilities of his case, and pointed out weak spots in his activity that could be used against him. But she also told him what exactly he would need to write, and how to frame his argument, if he were to get into a fix.

"I walked out of her office feeling relieved that there were decent people out there," he said. "But then it becomes clear that she's not free. She has a boss. It is not possible to have people within this system that do not obey its rules."

For Ivan, it was easy to understand how an officer who went ahead with a commercially-motivated case could easily justify his actions. "'Morally, I am right,' he would say, 'because I gave him a much lighter punishment than he deserved.'"

Everyone, it seemed, was both a victim and an executioner in the system at the same time, and each one used the instruments at his disposal because he had no choice. This was an honest outlook, but understanding the reality of how things worked and how you were involved in it took a psychological toll.

"It's not that it's the Stockholm syndrome," he said as he mentioned the FSB officers he has had to deal with. "It's just that when you're talking to them, you realize that they're normal, decent, even charming people. But I've also had to deal with thirty-year-old jerks in the Lubyanka. For them everything is for show."

Whoever you were, you used the instruments at your disposal to get what you wanted and get ahead. You used your connections, because if you didn't, then someone else would use them against you. In order for your connections in authority to work, you had to believe in their power—you had to convince everyone around you of their power.

Ivan, who lived in a gated suburban settlement outside Moscow, among million-dollar mansions, described a neighbor who was a general in the FSB. Not only did he run a private security agency on the side and use his authority to raid businesses, but he also bragged about it, as though it was a logical result of his authority.

"Everyone brags about how many generals they know," he said.

The bitter irony that Ivan had discovered, however, was that paying such people to protect you didn't normally work. "You develop a relationship with someone—the higher up he is, the better. The FSB is considered the most coveted. But if something happens, they won't help you. They can only start a criminal case against your rival. They are not the instruments. They are the bosses."

Paying an FSB "handler" to protect you could backfire. "He starts intimidating you, you become scared. Then he asks for more money. But when it comes to actually protecting you, it turns out that everyone has his fiefdom, and whoever you pay for protection will not go against the interests of his colleagues."

That too was part of the system—one that Ivan had learned to take for granted as if it was a force of nature that was at times brutal, at times convenient.

One other factor explained his humility: as an Orthodox Christian, he was deeply religious. And he applied his faith to his idea of what a government should be. "We delegate to him [the sovereign] the right to be a god. But Putin is no Tsar, not even a little bit. Because a Tsar is God-given."

It wasn't that Putin had enabled the murky, extra-legal world of "understandings" that Ivan, like law enforcement officers and fellow businessmen, found themselves obeying. That world had always existed in Russia. It was that Putin, having come from it himself, had failed to transcend it.

"Putin?" he concluded. "He's not even interesting. He won't even make history."

4.

In 2000, the law had proved useless in the clash of interests between a furniture magnate, the FSB, and the Prosecutor General's Office on the one hand, and the Investigative Committee on the other. It was similarly useless in 2005, when the Investigative Committee tried to put a stop to the FSB's million-dollar Chinese import business. The trial of Pavel Zaitsev demonstrated just how superfluous this paper law was in the face of the "understandings" reached between powerful groups with fiefdoms to mind.

Having closed the case against furniture magnate Sergei Zuyev in 2001, the Prosecutor General's Office went ahead and launched criminal cases against Zaitsev and the two customs officials who had investigated Zuyev in the first place.

Zaitsev was acquitted by the Moscow City Court in September 2002, but on the appeal of the Prosecutor General's Office, the Supreme Court called for a retrial in February 2003. During that retrial, the judge, Olga Kudeshkina, blew the whistle. She dismissed herself from the case, claiming that she was being pressured to hand down a guilty verdict not just by Deputy Prosecutor General Yuri Biryukov, but also by the presiding judge of the Moscow City Court, Olga Yegorova.[92] Another judge then sentenced Zaitsev to a two-year suspended sentence, but to sweeten the pill, he was allowed to keep his job.

Judging by the widespread evidence of how guilty verdicts are passed, not only is this easy to imagine, but it is surprising that Zaitsev wasn't jailed outright. An experienced criminal defence lawyer once described this process to me: in a trial, the prosecutor often simply passes his flash card to the judge. The judge, to save time, copies the prosecution's statement onto his computer, changes the title, prints it and reads it out in the courtroom as a verdict.

Yevgeny Arkhipov, representing Sergei Magnitsky, the lawyer for the Hermitage Capital investment fund who died in pretrial detention in 2009, explained part of the reason why this was so easy. Just because the concept of presumption of innocence was spelled out in the Russian Constitution did not mean the idea was accepted by all of its citizens.

"Most laymen have absolutely no understanding of the presumption of innocence or human rights," he said. "Judges, investigators, and prosecutors are also laymen."[93]

Extra-legal "understandings" better fitted the concept of fairness and justice for a large number of judges, investigators and prosecutors. But what happened when their "understandings" clashed with the understandings of another, equally powerful group?

Much like in the court of an absolute monarchy, it was up to the chief arbiter—the sovereign—to pass judgment.

Vladimir Putin officially announced in 2002 during a meeting with security officials that he would be taking the *Tri Kita* investigation under his personal control.[94] Having to keep up the appearances of a legal framework, there was a delicate balance to maintain—his role as arbiter had to be kept hidden, he had to remain impartial and mind the interests of all parties involved in order to keep their loyalty, and he had to make sure that, at least publicly, his words were not influencing what was still supposed to be an independent investigation.

The problem had been officially brought up before the president in 2002. That February, an investigative journalist from *Novaya Gazeta* (New Newspaper), Yuri Shchekochikhin, had raised the issue at the State Duma security committee, in his capacity as a parliamentarian. (After repeated telephone threats, Shchekochikhin died in 2003 from an extremely rare, and lethal, allergic reaction that some evidence suggests could be linked to a poisoning. Investigators have launched several probes into his death, but they were all closed. Zaitsev, as many others, believe that Shchekochikhin was murdered.)[95]

That March, Putin appointed Vladimir Loskutov, a senior investigator from the Leningrad region and reputedly a close acquaintance, to the case. The appointment was significant since Loskutov did not answer to Prosecutor General Vladimir Ustinov—whose interests were reportedly affected by the case. While Putin, as was his wont, would not voice any opinion on the case, his later comment about Loskutov's appointment suggested he could only trust an outsider to investigate it: "I was forced to bring an investigator from the Leningrad region because he needed to be a person unconnected to law enforcement bodies."[96]

But four more years would pass before any arrests were made. Two things apparently made that possible: in spring 2006, Putin involved another agency, the Federal Drug Control Service, headed by his close ally, former KGB officer Viktor Cherkesov, in the case. And in May 2006, he sacked Prosecutor General Vladimir Ustinov.[97] The road, it seemed, was clear for the first arrests. Those followed that summer: Sergei Zuyev and five of his accomplices were taken into custody in June. Their trial would drag out for four more years. In 2010, Zuyev would be found guilty and sentenced to eight years in prison. His other accomplices would be given lighter terms.[98]

Three months later, reports appeared about a massive purge in the FSB and the Interior Ministry. And while on the surface they seemed a direct result of the *Tri Kita* investigation, evidence suggested that the extent of their involvement in rent-seeking activities went far beyond *Tri Kita*. Moreover, those officials directly named in the *Tri Kita* scandal, like Zhukov and Zaostrovtsev, would be quietly transferred to other posts later on.

When the purges were leaked to the press, sources close to Putin's administration, within the FSB and from other law enforcement bodies specifically linked the firings not to *Tri Kita*, but the Chinese contraband scandal that Pavel Zaitsev uncovered the previous year.[99]

More unsettling still is evidence that a number of the FSB officers announced in the purge continued showing up to work as if nothing had happened.[100] They would quietly be removed months later, when the scandal was forgotten. Kirill Kabanov believes this is the direct result of Putin's close ties with these people.

But even the purges, quiet and incomplete as they were, could not prevent the case from escalating into an all-out clan war. In the autumn of 2007, the FSB arrested Viktor Cherkesov's deputy at the Federal Drug Control Agency, Alexander Bulbov, for unauthorized wire taps in the *Tri Kita* investigation. The move was a clear retaliation for the purges, which were interpreted as a blow to the FSB and the Prosecutor General's Office. That it was indeed a clan war within Putin's court was stated by none other than Viktor Cherkesov himself, who penned an open letter calling on security organs to avoid a battle and reconcile—especially since a transfer of power from Putin to a successor was about to take place. Not only was Cherkesov warning against a clan war; his letter was an unprecedented statement by a senior security official that commerce among officers was unacceptable.[101]

All these processes coincided with a momentous shift in Putin's course. With just months left until his second term as president expired, in the autumn of 2007 all of Russia was holding its breath about which course Putin would take: either sidestep the Constitution barring him from a third term and run again, or pick from one of two potential successors. The first and likeliest candidate was long-time Defence Minister and former KGB officer Sergei Ivanov, a hardliner who had recently been promoted. The other was a soft-spoken lawyer, Dmitry Medvedev, who had once headed Putin's campaign staff in 2000.

In the first days of December, just ahead of the parliamentary elections, the choice unexpectedly fell on Medvedev. Aside from the *Tri Kita* scandal, the clan war alleged by Cherkesov was widely believed to stem from anxiety about who Putin would eventually pick as his successor, as factions vied for superiority in the leader's eyes. But the reverse could also have been true: a clan war within the security forces of the magnitude described may have been taken into account in the decision to pick a successor. Perhaps Putin felt threatened by a chagrined FSB; perhaps Ivanov presented more of an independent, less manageable figure than Medvedev—who would docilely step aside in 2011 and make way for Putin to return to the presidency. Political decisions were taken by weighing courtly factions and their commercial interests, much as they were for hundreds of years.

Could Putin have acted in any other way? It is an enticing, but ultimately useless, question. However, it would be helpful to return to the origins and remember that the *Tri Kita* case exploded just months after Putin was inaugurated in May of 2000. The young president was already facing competing clans, which included men like Yuri Zaostrovtsev, who had arrived at his post long before Putin rose through the ranks to the top office. And however much he was compared to a Tsar from the beginning, he could not transcend the system that had brought him to power. For even a Tsar was made by his courtiers.

Pavel Zaitsev did not believe the entire FSB corps to be corrupt. Honest people worked there, he said, but "you don't hear anything about them." He still does not know whether the meeting between Putin and businessman Sergei Zuyev ever took place. But he harbors a hope that it did—and that what Putin heard during that audience made him resolved to untangle the mess that that he had inherited.

Chapter 7

Agent Loyal and his Little Racket

*One method was particularly common: when an oprichnik
and a zemets who have regular interactions with one
another meet, the oprichnik grabs the zemets by the neck,
drags him to court, and claims that the man defamed him
and the Oprichnina in general; and though the Grand
Prince [Tsar Ivan the Terrible] knows that this is not the
case, the plaintiff is proclaimed an honest man, and he
is given the estate of the defendant, and the defendant is
beaten and taken through the streets, and then beheaded or
thrown into prison for life.*
—**Livonian officials Johann Taube** and **Elbert
Kruse**, in their 1582 treatise on Tsar Ivan the
Terrible, whom they had served as oprichniki for
several years before fleeing Muscovy

*And the system replicates itself. The main principle through
which you come to power is the principle of loyalty….*
—**Kirill Kabanov**, FSB colonel turned anti-
corruption crusader

What we protect is what we possess.
—A cynical Russian proverb

1.

ON THE NIGHT of April 27, 2009, Major Denis Yevsyukov, a cold-eyed, thirty-one-year-old police precinct head in the southern Moscow neighborhood of Tsaritsino, walked into his local supermarket. He was a regular there, and like many modern cops, he had developed a habit of piling groceries into his cart and walking out without bothering to pay. And because he was a cop, no one bothered to say anything about it to him.

But on that night, moderately drunk, he walked in with his gun in his hand. He casually shot the first person he came across, and lazily motioned for a woman to get down on the floor. But then he picked her up and held her at gunpoint as he walked down the aisles looking for other victims. The woman managed to free herself, but Major Yevsyukov did not go after her. He calmly reloaded his gun and continued shooting. And though he killed two people and wounded seven that night, he didn't remember firing a single shot.

He would also never recall the three hours prior to the incident, when he and his wife, Karine, celebrated his birthday at a nearby café called Golden Time. He did not remember the stranger who drove up to the café to talk to him, nor the fact that, as evidenced by his wife in court, he had turned silent, "green," and catatonic after that conversation. He didn't remember going home, changing into his uniform, and taking a cab to the supermarket.

Jailed for life in a rush trial, Yevsyukov insisted that he had had a memory lapse, and no motive for what he did has since been uncovered, generating a string of vague conspiracy theories hinting at everything from hypnosis to a vast plot to take down Russia's long-time Interior Minister, Rashid Nurgaliyev.

But nearly a year later, the exiled telecoms tycoon Yevgeny Chichvarkin, sitting without work in London after being hounded out of Russia by a whole slew of corrupt Interior Ministry officers, revealed what he thought was almost certainly part of the motive for what Yevsyukov did that night. Chichvarkin claimed that Yevsyukov was inadvertently woven into his own case. Unravelling the thread of this complex story reveals the all-pervasive nature of a protection racket philosophy that runs from the bottom to the top of Russian officialdom. And the story of a cop who went on a shooting spree turned out to be a major footnote in one of the biggest contraband scandals of the decade.

Yevsyukov's lethal meltdown occurred amid the mounting social frustration over Russia's criminalized law enforcement, with President Dmitry Medvedev launching a momentous reform campaign to civilize the police force. Just a day after the shooting, Medvedev sacked Moscow's chief of police Vladimir Pronin; four more heads would roll in Yevsyukov's own district as institutions were given a signal to brace for a major show trial. A swift investigation ensued, and by February 2010 a quick trial jailed Yevsyukov for life, an unprecedented sentence for a cop in a system where uniformed assailants, rapists, and murderers were frequently given only a few years in prison, often suspended.

The hype that accompanied the launch of Medvedev's reform campaign masked a very important circumstance: Yevsyukov, in carrying out his casual thefts at the supermarket, was not unusual. In 2009 alone, some 2,500 official crimes were attributed to police officers. Throughout the decade, not a year would go by without a criminal ring of police officers getting implicated in everything from extortion to kidnapping and rape.

Yevsyukov himself, his colleagues alleged, rose through the ranks using the renowned "envelope" method. Engaging two rookies to collect protection cash from a series of kiosks and stores, he would also earn an additional $5,000 from the families of suspected criminals, offering to close the case for a fee by registering the suspect as a cadaver.

Former police operative Andrei Romanov, one of several who was fired by Yevsyukov after his promotion, alleged that Yevsyukov would generously share the loot with their bosses—Southern District Chief Viktor Ageyev and his deputy, Oleg Baryshnikov.[102] (Ageyev, who would go on to resign, neither confirmed nor denied these printed allegations.) By sending envelopes higher up within the ranks, he generated impressive revenue for his police department, and thus was not passed up for promotions.

Police officers running protection rackets were so widespread in Russia by 2010 that they didn't even raise eyebrows anymore. The practice had emerged sporadically throughout Russian history; it was not unheard of in Soviet Russia. During the early 1990s, as businesses starting hiring cops to protect them from racketeers, the police and FSB replaced criminal protection groups.

"It's much easier for a firm to use police officers to put pressure on competitors than private security," Andrei, a retired police colonel who went into private security, described. "They virtually have a price list for this type of service. In the past, it was done more through relatives or friends of friends. Now it's enough to just show up and ask for whatever it is you need. Say a cop checked you for something. You resolved the issue [assuming through a bribe]. And after that you can come back to the cop because he knows you and you've given him money. You just go up to him and say, 'Hey, you want to earn some more money?'"

But it was Yevsyukov's treatment of his local supermarket, located under his precinct's jurisdiction, or domain, that was most striking. Store employees tried to stop him once, but he threatened them. "Since he identified himself as a police officer, no one dared to stop him," one of the store's employees, identified as Svetlana Alexandrovna P., said in her witness statement to investigators.[103]

And if running a protection racket was common, so was acquiring the objects you were charged with protecting. "It's a common phenomenon, with precinct heads casually looting stores and shops on their territory," Igor Trunov, a lawyer who represented victims of the shooting, recalled from previous cases. "The higher the rank, the bigger the 'loot.'"[104]

Looting, in fact, was only part of a far more complicated system, which bore all the hallmarks of medieval Russian *kormleniye,* that precinct cops practiced on their territory.

"We have two markets in our town," a police major from a provincial Russian town who asked not to be identified told me. "Two cops worked the markets. They were responsible for fruit shipment. Every month, they would receive a levy of fruit."

Responsible, in this case, meant that the cops were protecting the market. But protecting from whom? From the law, it turns out. Russia's Criminal Code is full of ambiguities, particularly the section regulating private entrepreneurship and licensing. Cops would shake down local residents trying to sell produce off their land plot, and even if the sellers had a licence, any cop who wanted to find a minor violation could do so. For the smallholders, paying off the police would be impossible, but it was usually difficult to produce a licence that a cop would accept as error-free.

That left more well-established fruit traders, often from southern ethnic republics or former Soviet states, being faced with: "Don't have the right documentation for the watermelons? That'll be one hundred kilos of watermelons, or we'll have to shut you down," as the police major said, explaining the shake-down process. Larger sellers already took account of these expenses in their budgets.

The police major doubted that Yevsyukov had randomly walked off without paying. Set-ups like these were common, but they meant that there had to have been some form of mutual agreement between the supermarket director and the police precinct.

These routine violations, however, didn't explain what pushed a successful police officer like Denis Yevsyukov, building his career as a resourceful, up-and-coming racketeer, over the edge.

And the mysterious three hours that disappeared from his memory on April 26 had a peculiar effect on his show trial legacy. Yes, a cop was finally behind bars for his brutality. But both Yevsyukov's defence and his victims seemed to agree that real closure could only come from a motive—and the investigators had failed utterly in uncovering one.

"We don't have a single opinion about the motive of the crime," Trunov told me. "It's clear that there was a motive. Experts have reported that he was sane, that he wasn't drunk, and that he wasn't under the influence of drugs. Attempts to blame hypnosis are unrealistic, because it is impossible for someone to be in a state of hypnosis for so long. In light of this information vacuum, anything is possible."

Yevsyukov's lawyer, Tatyana Bushuyeva, would go on to appeal the court ruling precisely because she was dissatisfied with the investigators' failure to produce a motive.

"The investigators were not interested in this at all," she said. "Those three hours were a black hole. But the investigators did not even try to reconstruct the events in that interval."

2.

On the evening of December 22, 2008, Yevgeny Chichvarkin, the boyish telecoms billionaire, a one-time favorite at the Kremlin court, and a man on whose behalf Vladimir Putin himself had once ordered a shake-up of the Federal Customs Service back in 2006, realized that his time in Russia was up.

Sitting in the offices of Altimo, which had just purchased his debt-ridden Yevroset retailer, he could see a car with police operatives holding vigil outside, waiting for him to come out. Just five days ago, it had become clear that Chichvarkin was no longer a witness but a suspect in a long-expired kidnapping case that police investigators pulled out from the archives just for that occasion. In September, police had already arrested Chichvarkin's vice president and head of security at Yevroset, Boris Levin, and had been interrogating him throughout the autumn. There was no question that the operatives waiting for Chichvarkin in the parking lot weren't just there for a chat.

So, with the help of Altimo's vice president, Oleg Malis, Chichvarkin quietly walked out of the back entrance of the offices towards a car provided by the company. He got in the back seat and lay down on the floor as the driver sped off towards Domodedovo Airport.[105] In a few hours, he would join a growing diaspora of rich Russians living in self-imposed exile in London.

Except that there was one catch: in contrast with the political exiles who chose to avoid the fate of Mikhail Khodorkovsky and flee while they could, there was absolutely nothing political in the pressure that finally forced Chichvarkin to jump in the car and head for the airport.

By the end of the first decade of the twenty-first century, Russia had one of the fastest-growing telecoms markets in the world, with a turnover of $4.5 billion in 2004.[106] Mobile phones, flash cards, smart phones, and laptops could be purchased on virtually every street corner of Moscow—one had to only look around for the familiar yellow band of Yevroset to find the top mobile retailer.

In 1997, Yevgeny Chichvarkin was just twenty-two when he invested $2,500 in what would become one of Russia's leading mobile phone retailers. But while mobile phones had become widely available in Russia, they became truly legal only in 2005, thanks to efforts of officials and businessmen that included Chichvarkin. Until then, they had constituted one of the largest siphoning scams under the auspices of the Federal Customs Service—which, in turn, generated the largest share of budget revenue for the Russian government. A combination of murky laws and bribe-hungry officials created a situation where businessmen like Chichvarkin functioned in a semi-legal gray area.

To understand how the customs racket worked—and what changed in 2005 to cause a few enraged police officials to go after Chichvarkin—we should go back to the Soviet Union.

"There was nothing new in the contraband criminal cases that started appearing, as society adopted market practices," said Yuri Gervis, a former FSB officer who investigated contraband cases in the early 1990s. He went into private law practice and then represented Yevgeny Chichvarkin precisely because his case was connected to customs. "Contraband is simply the transportation of objects without declaring them with the intent of hiding them from customs" to avoid paying duties, Gervis said.

Starting in the period under Leonid Brezhnev, by the 1980s contraband became rampant. Diplomats and officials who had access to foreign travel would transport currency, furniture, jewelry, and rare art, buying antiques in the Soviet Union and selling them abroad. Gervis recalled a particular oak chest that wound up being confiscated at the border multiple times in 1990. After each confiscation, it would wind up in a Soviet shop, where different people would purchase it and try to ship it out again. Well-connected people sent out valuables to relatives through traveling officials. In turn, deficit commodities like tobacco, jeans, and Western cosmetics would be secretly brought in from across the border—a shipment of Philip Morris cigarettes was once hidden in a load of toilet paper.

But then in 1991, Communist rule collapsed and the ideological norms that governed the criminal code disappeared. Private commerce became legal, and so did import and export. But because a whole business had developed around the criminalization of contraband, it continued.

"The criminal code changed, and instead of being called contraband, it was called evasion of customs duties," Gervis recalled. Whatever it was called, the bribes were still being paid, and customs officials profited. And another important aspect of the customs service remained the same: besides petrodollars, customs duties provided the single largest source of income for the Russian government. And its officers, seeing themselves as servants of this government, as "men of the sovereign," saw no reason why they shouldn't profit.

"The chief role of the Federal Customs Service is to replenish the budget. That is why there is so much attention to it from the FSB and the Interior Ministry," Gervis said.

And as these officers watched new, up and coming businessmen getting rich with no new system of values and an entirely dysfunctional network of legal norms, there was nothing wrong, in the eyes of the officers, with profiting from those businessmen.

"For a businessman, it makes no difference how this regulation is carried out," Gervis said. "Either way it is a tax, an *obrok*. Just like in the days of the Tartar-Mongolian yoke."

By 2005, an informal system of duties that both customs officials and businessmen seemed to benefit from crystallized at Moscow's Sheremetyevo Airport, the largest import hub for mobile telephones in Russia. In return for kickbacks from mobile phone importers, the head of airport customs created a simplified system of customs duties based on price range: phones costing up to $100 were all registered as costing just $20, between $100 and $200 as just $30, and so forth. For a $4.5 billion market, this constituted from $150 to $300 million in "duties."[107]

Protected by the Interior Ministry, the system worked, in as much as all parties felt that they were getting rich enough. Police officials would regularly "confiscate" telephones just like precinct officers getting a share of the watermelons sold at a market under their "protection." Because the phones weren't entirely legal to begin with, importers like Yevgeny Chichvarkin couldn't complain.

But then in spring 2005, the "tax burden" started getting out of hand as new Interior Ministry departments started trying to get into the racket. An officer from the newly-created Department K, which oversaw the communications sector, arrived at Sheremetyevo and demanded a bigger cut: $1 from each mobile phone. Some businesses balked at the additional "tax," which would generate an income of $20 million for Department K, and refused to pay. In response, Department K officials launched an investigation against Sheremetyevo customs, and the whole simplified scheme was taken down. Yakov Ardashnikov, the businessman who had refused to pay the additional cut, fled to Israel to escape contraband charges, while Valery Kuzmin, deputy head of Sheremetyevo customs, would go on to be sentenced to nine years in jail for involvement in the contraband shipment of mobile phones sold in Yevroset stores.[108]

The raids made a serious dent in Russia's mobile phone business, with police confiscating about $100 million worth of phones. That, and the fact that the simplified duties system was exposed and shut down, virtually paralyzed local retailers like Yevroset. It became clear that something had to be done—and that's when Economics Minister German Gref, whom Putin had appointed in 2004 to help clean up the customs business, got involved.

According to Gervis, Chichvarkin met with Gref to try to convince him to simplify the customs process.

Later that year, Gref held a two-hour meeting with top mobile phones retailers and struck a deal. Gref personally guaranteed that customs would process all their shipments on time, as long as the importers committed to paying customs duties in full. According to one retailer at the meeting, Gref went as far as urging them to call his office directly if there was the slightest delay.[109]

Chichvarkin had a further incentive for transparency—his company was planning an IPO, a sale of shares to the public, in 2006. And though it was about twice as expensive to pay full duties legally, as opposed to discounted "bribes" that went to customs officials, the importers benefited in the long term, with more foreign companies willing to do business under a legitimate import scheme.

The only party that seemed to be losing out was Department K, which lost tens of millions of dollars a year from the legalization process. And Yevgeny Chichvarkin, who played a major role in convincing Gref to simplify customs legally, became a top enemy.

"All of Chichvarkin's problems began precisely when he tried to move his company towards more transparency," Gervis said. And though he was now legally declaring all his shipments and paying full duties, it didn't prevent Department K officers from trying to shake him down.

In spring 2006, after legally passing through customs, a shipment of 167,500 Motorola phones was impounded by Department K officials. "Fuck you and your IPO," an officer reportedly said then.[110] A Department K representative then went to Yevroset and demanded $10 million to stop the harassment. But since Yevroset had moved to a fully legal scheme, the shake-down proved more difficult. Attempts by Department K to prove the shipment was contraband failed—Yevroset had declared it in full and paid all duties legally. And an attempt to declare the phones fake backfired—Motorola officially vouched for the shipment, and then reportedly complained to the US State Department.

For security officers, there's possibly nothing worse than having your own private racket get so out of control that the top boss learns of it. In the centuries-old norms that governed bribery in Russia, the key rule was *brat' po chinu*—to take according to your rank. No matter what formal, legal norms governed administrative relations, the system of *kormleniye* was still very much in place, by virtue of the impossibility of administering such vast territories with their endless webs of clashing interests. From the widespread bribery in the administration of Nicholas I to rent-seeking former KGB officers of the early 1990s, using their connections to clinch lucrative deals with foreign capital entering the market, that one rule worked in a country where all others kept changing. Take according to your rank, and make sure to remain loyal to and share with your patron. If you happened to take too much, or fail to share accordingly, then you had better make sure that your little racket did not reach the ears of the sovereign.

In the case of the Yevroset shakedown, Vladimir Putin did apparently learn of it. According to unnamed Yevroset sources cited in leading Russian publications, Putin learned of this from none other than US President George W. Bush—and, of all places, at the G8 Summit in St. Petersburg—the one venue where he could successfully nurture the illusion that his country was a civilized nation with rule of law.

Putin was reportedly enraged.[111]

That very summer, Putin already had the *Tri Kita* case on his mind. And now here was another contraband scandal that was jeopardizing hopes of Russia ever joining the WTO. Putin met immediately with Motorola officials, and then called in Interior Minister Rashid Nurgaliyev and German Gref, ordering them to sort out the mess.[112]

The mess was sorted, but it had to be done with the stealth and caution that was crucial to keeping the peace among restive *siloviki* factions constantly struggling for revenue—for Putin, as we have seen, is severely limited in the punishment he can levy on security officers. Just four rank and file investigators involved in the attempted shakedown of Yevroset were charged; one is still at large, and the other three were soon released on parole.

Still, for disgruntled Department K officials, it was a slap in the face from the government that added insult to injury. Not only was a young entrepreneur who wore weird clothes getting rich at their expense (for the legal route that allowed Chichvarkin to import more phones had severely restricted their customs income), he was clearly basking in the favor of the sovereign, or at least thought he was. And Chichvarkin's slight overestimation of that favor—and of Putin's willingness and ability to protect him from the *siloviki*—may have contributed to his undoing.

As a weapon against Chichvarkin, officials dug up the case of a former Yevroset employee who claimed to have been kidnapped and roughed up by Yevroset's security service in 2003. And that was where an ambitious young cop named Denis Yevsyukov came in: turning up in the wrong place at the wrong time.

3.

The "connection" with Denis Yevsyukov should not be overestimated. He played no pivotal role in the developing Chichvarkin scandal. His precinct got caught in the crossfire between Department K and Yevroset—but that was no reason, after all, for him to go on a supermarket shooting spree. However, the mounting checks on his precinct—and how with such checks, coming from rival law enforcement structures, the roof tends to cave in on you if you are the weaker clan—illustrates the resilient complexity of Russian corruption, its all-pervasiveness, and its sprawling domino effect on all spheres of life.

There is, of course, no way to get inside Yevsyukov's head to gauge what role, if any, the checks on his precinct in spring 2009 played in his growing psychosis. Igor Trunov, the lawyer representing Yevsyukov's victims, called the connection tenuous and far-fetched, saying that though he'd received Chichvarkin's report before it was published, he decided not to pursue it. One of Yevsyukov's lawyers,

Tatyana Bushuyeva, told me the connection was intriguing for lack of other motives. Yevsyukov's other lawyer, Mikhail Vokin, was reticent and warned me sternly against asking too many questions. He did, however, pass on my own questions to Yevsyukov in his jail cell, and relayed his one-word answer: "Nonsense."

Nevertheless, it is a fact that just months before Yevsyukov's shooting spree, there was growing interest in his police precinct from investigators, police officers, and even the FSB. And while Viktor Ageyev, Yevsyukov's boss and key patron, resigned the day after the shooting, he had actually submitted his resignation on April 22—less than a week before the shooting incident. In other words, an important resignation that appeared to be the direct result of Yevsyukov's shooting spree was in fact anything but.

The reasons for the growing interest in Yevsyukov's police precinct have very much to do with Chichvarkin, Yevroset, and the small incident in 2003.

In 2002, Yevroset had started having problems with one of its couriers, Andrei Vlaskin. That year, Vlaskin, according to Yevroset, started stealing telephones from Yevroset and selling them on the side, making about $34,000 a month—a racket he kept up for at least eighteen months.[113] The reason he got away with it for so long was the same one that made any racket, on any level, possible: the phones were illegal to start out with, since no import duties had been paid. In those years, everything was contraband—for the laws regulating customs and commerce were so cumbersome and so detached from reality that adhering to them would have made business impossible. Shady, informal methods governed business relations in Russia instead.

In that messy, twilit world, it's hard to identify the line between what is acceptable and what isn't, what is criminal and what is legal. According to Yuri Gervis, Yevroset's security department filed a complaint against Vlaskin with the Southern District Police Department, where Yevsyukov then worked as a police detective. Various sources suggested[114] that Yevsyukov personally handled the complaint and initiated the case in summer 2003. Yevroset security head Boris Levin said that Yevsyukov's handling of the case was routine: the paperwork was signed by him or his underlings.[115]

But according to investigators who, as Chichvarkin claims,

were bent on building up a kidnapping case against Yevroset, the firm's security department used friendly, informal relations and some $68,000 in bribes to involve Yevsyukov's police department in Vlaskin's detention.[116]

The officers at the Southern District Police Department launched a case against Vlaskin, who went on the run. According to an investigative source, it was Yevsyukov who was responsible for the search for Vlaskin.[117] Police found him in Tambov and transferred him to the Southern District Police Department in Moscow. There, one of Yevsyukov's colleagues, Alexander Kurta, personally handed over Vlaskin to Boris Levin, Yevroset's vice president and the head of its security service.

Vlaskin claimed he was handcuffed and taken to a rented apartment in southern Moscow, where he was chained to a radiator and, according to various sources, "pressured" to pay back what he'd stolen—some $409,000 plus an additional 570,000 rubles ($16,600).[118] Chichvarkin has denied his own involvement in the kidnapping. According to Gervis, the pressure on Vlaskin was mild—and once a deal was struck to sell Vlaskin's property in Tambov, Yevroset helped him do it. They also bought him a Moscow apartment in compensation. Yevroset security head Boris Levin would later be cleared of kidnapping charges, but did not deny that he held Vlaskin and in one instance, as he put it, forced him to return stolen property using measures that were outside of the "lawful protocol."[119]

Whatever the case, an obscure complaint was made by Vlaskin and filed away. Usually, a murky kidnapping like this where there were no good or bad guys, was forgotten.

But in 2008, some five years later, officials at the Interior Ministry's K Department pulled the complaint out from the files. On September 2, armed, masked police officers raided the offices of Yevroset and arrested Boris Levin on kidnapping charges. According to Yuri Gervis, Department K officials once again came to Yevroset, demanding a sum that was half of the company's capitalization to close the case.

There are several possible reasons why they did this.

The most obvious was revenge—still smarting over their failed extortion attempt in 2006, they came across a *bona fide* kidnapping case that presented an excellent opportunity as an airtight extortion weapon. But there was another potential motive. During that time, Chichvarkin was embroiled in a bitter debt dispute with MTS, one of the big three cellular providers in Russia, which was making overtures to buy out Yevroset on the cheap. Some media commentators have pointed to a connection between the kidnapping charges and a takeover attempt by MTS,[120] but there is no proof of this.

Whatever their motives, in order to make a more damning case against Yevroset, Department K officials worked through the Investigative Committee of the Prosecutor's Office to try to prove not only that Vlaskin was kidnapped, but that the original case against him, for stealing phones, had been fabricated. And that the police department that fabricated the case was none other than Yevsyukov's.

In January 2009, investigators started confiscating criminal cases from the Southern District Police Department. Many of the cases had been instigated but never pursued—and among them was Vlaskin's. On February 2, 2009, investigators arrived at the department for another batch of documents, only to find that the hundreds of folders they were looking for were dumped in the rubbish bins behind the building. When the investigators tried to take the folders, they themselves were removed—practically by force— from the premises.[121]

After the rubbish incident, investigators called in the head of the department—Viktor Ageyev—for interrogation. Most of Yevsyukov's colleagues were interrogated over the Vlaskin case as well during that period, and it seemed that Yevsyukov might be next.

Indeed, Yevsyukov was eventually questioned in connection with the Vlaskin case—but only after his arrest for the shooting spree, in July 2009.[122] Yevsyukov's lawyer, Tatyana Bushuyeva, told me she knew of this questioning. She also said that Yevsyukov was held in a cell with someone she said was the "former head of security of Yevroset"—apparently part of a common practice where acquaintances were placed in the same cell to get them to talk about each other's case.

But lawyer Mikhail Vokin, asked about the reports that Yevsyukov had been questioned, denied them, saying he was under oath to keep the investigation secret.

"In March, two FSB agents were attached to investigators conducting a probe of the Southern Police District department,"

Gervis told me. "There was pressure, and there were demands to hand [over] their superiors."

On April 22, Viktor Ageyev filed his resignation papers, apparently in connection with the investigations at his department. Four days later, on the evening of April 26, his subordinate, Denis Yevsyukov, by that time the head of the Tsaritsino Precinct, snapped and shot nine people in a supermarket.

4.

At the end of the day, it is immaterial whether or not the chain of events described above went to Yevsyukov's head and caused him to snap—it cannot be proven either way.

Instead, it demonstrates something more interesting—an environment where there are no good guys among the players. A whole network of warring power factions, who, from top to bottom, from police generals to FSB colonels to investigators of the prosecutor's office, down to the rookies in the local police precincts getting their *obrok* in watermelons, are all functioning according to the same pattern: the protection racket. Instead of protecting the confusing, constantly changing laws, they are protecting the interests of their patrons.

Who are those patrons?

That is the biggest question. In a classical, absolutist monarchy, their chief patron would have been the sovereign, their king and country—which would have been the same thing. But Putin's Russia, which has many of the trappings of an absolutist monarchy, refuses to see itself as such. The scholar Lilia Shevtsova has underlined the contradictions that this presents: Putin has preserved personified and undivided power, she writes. However, describing Yeltsin's rule as "elected monarchy," she applies the same metaphor to Putin's rule, "accenting the contradictions between personified power and the elective method of legitimizing it."[123]

A maddening dissonance ensues: Putin had a theoretical option of "building a responsible system of governance based not on the irrational and mystic power embodied in the leader but on the rule of law."[124]

But he either could not, or would not do so.

Those words were written in 2004; by 2013 that dissonance has only grown, amid contradictory laws that fail to work and Putin's constant calls to fight corruption. Why, despite yearly orders from Putin—his personal orders, harsh, determined, and ominous—does corruption only grow?

Given the messy framework of laws, the instructions given to the *siloviki* must be interpreted on a completely different level. What, from their perspective, is corrupt, and what is untouchable? Studying people's attitudes towards bribery in post-Soviet Russia, sociologists Caroline Humphrey and David Sneath came across that same idea of sacredness that Russian political scholars are all too aware of: "The Soviet State... had a quasi-sacred character of invincibility and unquestionability, underpinned by harsh, numerous, and well-organized internal security services."[125]

What follows from this is a rationalization of corruption not as the violation of rule of law (which doesn't exist), but as the whole sphere of private commerce in itself. Private commerce becomes corruption by definition. Given the concept of the government as "the all-encompassing domain of power and control, and the generator of legitimacy... any activities beyond the purview of the state [are] slotted into an opposed and subversive category of the spontaneous, uncontrolled, self-interested, and morally dubious."[126]

But state power in Putin's Russia was only sacred when it wanted to see itself as such—in all other cases, it was a "democracy" with "rule of law." And amid that dissonance, feudal relationships dictated to what extent commercial activities were balanced with their service to the state: the vassal of your vassal is not your vassal.

Order, in this case, pertains to the interests of state power—all else, whether it's a businessman or a rival agency taking more bribes than they're worth, is fair game.

The "all-encompassing" aspect of the Russian government isn't just a mystical concept. It is primarily an economic one—especially if we remember that oil, gas, and customs duties, not individual income taxes, constitute the bulk of federal revenue.

Seeing themselves as part of that all-encompassing economic entity, the milch cow for an enormous, chaotic, and poverty-stricken country, security officers cannot help but see businessmen like Chichvarkin as sources of their own private income.

And this brings us once again to that unverified incident in 2006 when Putin called in Interior Minister Rashid Nurgaliyev and Economics Minister German Gref and told them to sort out the Department K racket.

There is no documented proof of this incident—and it may well never have happened, since we only have unnamed Yevroset sources speaking about it. But we know of similarly undocumented meetings which bore all the marks of behind the door instructions to clean up one of an endless multitude of extrajudicial messes. If this meeting indeed happened, then by its chaotic result we can only surmise that the initial instructions were utterly distorted on their way from Putin to Rashid Nurgaliyev, from Rashid Nurgaliyev to his deputies, and from those deputies to the head of Department K, Boris Miroshnichenko.

Whatever instructions were issued, corruption was fought selectively—and only against those that were fair game, outside the protective sphere of the government.

For that is what happens when, as Humphrey and Sneath put it, a "sacred" state "crumbles from the center, when its leaders become mere fallible humans, and its parts are left largely to fend for themselves."[127]

Given these ongoing transformations, it is no wonder that corruption becomes a security threat, and that security officers themselves begin to recoil from it—and it is wrong to believe that Putin has always had the loyal support of his security officers. The *siloviki* understand that Putin is a mere mortal, but something in their behavior, in the structure of the relationships that they build with one another in the service of the state, automatically assumes that he is not.

They recognize this contradiction and they direct at Putin all their love and all their hatred: a love that is patrimonial and therefore purely economical (for he is their ultimate protector), and a hatred that is mystical—they cannot forgive him for being a fallible human, for extolling commerce as the chief ideology, and disgracing the very idea of state power.

Chapter 8

The Police Major

If anyone is behind Dymovsky, it's God Himself.
—**Alexei**, a retired police colonel and an associate
of Dymovsky

*We are told, "don't be afraid, nothing will happen to you,
the System won't betray you." This started in 2000, and it
came from a person we all know, a man who will not betray
his own kind. Vladimir Putin. Ever heard of him?*
—**Marat Rumyantsev**, reserve officer

1.

FRESH OUT OF prison, with a police tail following him every-
where he went, Major Alexei Dymovsky poured me a glass of cheap
wine at a provincial café and became apocalyptic.

"I know the structure of the police, I know how it works from
the inside," he said after I asked him what brought him to town.
"Right now, someone is artificially creating tensions between the
people and the police. Once the first shot is fired, it will all sweep
over Russia. People will die. A civil war will begin."

It was spring 2010, and Dymovksy was a media personality.
Six months earlier, he had recorded a video address to Vladimir
Putin complaining of rampant corruption that went viral. Within
weeks of the video, he was jailed on charges of fraud. Once he was

released from jail in January, he began giving press conferences in Moscow and was eager to join a cause, whether it was standing up for whistleblowers or for the working man.

He'd just arrived in the Siberian mining town of Mezhdurechensk on the back of a mine blast that was sparking region-wide unrest.

"There will be blood here tomorrow," he said as his eyes filled with tears, looking away from me with an expression of genuine fear and dismay.

There was no blood the next day, for the tensions had petered out after Prime Minister Putin raised base salaries and ordered the firing of a scapegoat. But even on his own, Dymovsky, this fumbling, sentimental cop who believed in conspiracy theories, for a moment emerged as an uncanny oppositionist force from the one place no one expected: the police. And while he would fade into obscurity by the time protests gripped the Moscow capital for real in 2011, he exposed a growing dissatisfaction not among the middle class oppositionists, but among officers serving the state.

The brutality, corruption, and depravity of the police force had become something of a backdrop by 2009, an environment that many no longer even noticed. Bribery was seen by political critics of Putin's regime as the result of the very mindset of "these people" and their low salaries, as though it was hard for them to imagine that these wielders of force, the beneficiaries of what had *de facto* become a protection racket extending into all spheres of commerce, would ever rebel against a system that was seen as deliberately working in their favor to keep them loyal to the regime.

But that November, seven months after Major Denis Yevsyukov shot nine people in a Moscow supermarket, Alexei Dymovsky, another police major, from the southern Russian port town of Novorossiysk, shocked the whole country with a mere YouTube video.

Part of the shock element resulted from the exploding of a persistent Moscow stereotype, that of an enlightened elite of internet users versus the backwards masses who only watched television. The police force, for the most part, was seen as falling into the latter category, so the fact that a precinct officer from a provincial town would use the internet instead of his gun to try to prove a point turned prevailing views on the relationship between the regime and its executioners upside down.

On November 5, 2009, Dymovsky, on the suggestion of a friend, created a personal website and posted two videos—one addressed to fellow officers,[128] and one directly to the man he perceived as the boss of his bosses—Vladimir Putin. (Technically, the Interior Ministry answered directly to the president, but Dymovsky admitted to me that he had so little interest or knowledge of politics at the time that he "hardly knew what Medvedev's name was.") He was so nervous about the video address that he drank a glass of vodka before recording.

The videos showed a chubby, depressed-looking man in uniform baldly describing his grievances—stumbling over every other word. And the key complaints directed to Putin primarily focused on his working conditions—Dymovsky's bosses were refusing to extend his sick leave and threatening to fire him.

"Vladimir Vladimirovich, I'm appealing to you as an officer of the police. Dymovsky, Alexei Alexandrovich. I'm currently not working, but I'm a senior operative. I'm appealing to you with the following request. Maybe you don't know, maybe you're not being told, but I want you to know how we live. Simple officers, simple police officers who solve cases, detain suspects, write up complaints, who work. I appeal to you. I live on 14,000 rubles (about $400) a month. I work 30 days out of 31 days in a month. I get no overtime. On Saturdays at 2 PM, we're told that since we don't have any cases solved, we have to work until 8 PM. I asked, 'are we being paid for this?' And I was told 'no, this is the personal wish of the head of police.' Recently I applied to a clinic because my arm was going numb. And I was told that I have to leave the clinic because they had an order from the head of police not to treat any officer."

He went on to detail routine violations at his department—including orders to falsify evidence against suspects to boost statistics, and outright jailings of innocent homeless people.

To fellow officers, he said:

"I ask you to join us. There are a lot of us who want to work honestly. I ask the pensioners to join us. You've already worked, you have nothing to fear. Look at the young people who join the police! They say they are not daunted by salaries of 12,000 rubles ($350) because they can rely on a generous *kalym*." (Dymovsky seems to have confused *kalym*—which is a bride price in some ethnic republics in Russia—with *obrok,* or a tribute paid by a peasant to his lord.)

Not a single word of what he said was news to anyone, but the monotonous, jargon-ridden voice of a cop, the lowest cog in the Interior Ministry, detailing those petty abuses punctured the uneasy tolerance of police corruption for the second time that year.

Despite Dymovsky's request to meet with Putin "eye to eye," the prime minister responded to the video address and to the ensuing scandal with an icy silence. His press secretary, Dmitry Peskov, said that while the prime minister was informed of the address, he had not bothered to watch it.[129] Putin would never utter the word "Dymovsky," and never bring up the issue of his complaint. For apart from complaining about low salaries and general corruption, Dymovsky broke every unspoken rule in the book: addressing the Tsar, he named his boss, Novorossiysk police chief Vladimir Chernositov, and accused him of giving orders to imprison an innocent person in exchange for being given the rank of major.

"Dymovsky did not say anything new. It's all happened before," Mikhail Pashkin, chairman of the Moscow Police Union and an avid critic of Interior Minister Rashid Nurgaliyev, told me. "We've been talking about this kind of stuff for the last ten years. It's just that he found a new medium, video."[130]

Police whistleblowers frequently faced retribution. Grigory Chekalin, a former deputy prosecutor of the Chita region, fought criminal allegations after he refused to fabricate charges against two people he believed were innocent. He fled to Moscow, virtually exiled from his home city. In Moscow, officers who complain might just lose their jobs.

"If an officer wants to live by the law, they try to get rid of him," said Pashkin. "Or if an Interior Ministry officer is facing someone who has more money than he does—then he will get prosecuted for bribe-taking. They jailed a [certain] officer for eleven years over $400 that they found in the corridor. He spent six years in prison. The problem was, he [started investigating] a store that was [protected] by a different structure. He's a lawyer now, and a member of our union. We tried to defend him."

Dymovsky became an instant celebrity; whisked to Moscow, he gave a press conference where he laid out vague plans to organize efforts to fight corruption in the bottom rungs of power. And as Dymovsky had promised, heartened by his example, more cops followed, recounting the medieval hell of police departments across the country in their monotonous voices.

The dozens of new video revelations posted on his site, *Dymovskiy.name*, bore a single common pattern: these cops had already complained to their superiors about being given orders to break the law, and their complaints earned them nothing but ostracism. Desperate, they tried to channel the wave of public indignation to get their cases across to the government, seeking protection to practice what they saw as honest police work. But most of these attempts went nowhere; and Dymovsky's, in the end, would be no exception—exiled from the force, they were lucky if they were not in jail.

President Dmitry Medvedev's epic overhaul of the Interior Ministry—beginning with a plan to cut 20 percent of the work force and raise salaries, going through a series of high profile purges, and culminating in renaming the *militsia* into the *politsia* for a more Western-sounding corps—did nothing to reinstate these dozens of police officers, who, like Major Dymovsky, blew the whistle on the dirty work they were being forced to do.

2.

The Russian language doesn't have a term for whistleblowing, but it does have a word for a snitch. And like any military organization structure, the Interior Ministry did not tolerate subordinates ratting publicly on their bosses. Despite feeble gestures from the Kremlin to fire a few police commanders in the Krasnodar Region where Dymovsky's home town of Novorossiysk was located, local structures came down hard on the hapless police major—using every means in their arsenal to discredit his name.

Almost the day after the video address was picked up by the media, the Krasnodar region Interior Ministry head Sergei Kucheruk fired Dymovsky for slander, while his bosses, Valery Medvedev and Vladimir Chernositov, filed a slander suit against him. But that was only the beginning.

The Interior Ministry immediately unleashed a powerful campaign against Dymovsky. Sources leaked quotes to the press that orders had been given to "bury" the whistleblower.[131] Spokesmen for the ministry publicly called him insane; an ex-wife posted a video statement accusing him of being a dirty cop.

Under the unspoken laws that enforced loyalty in power structures that had no viable written code to adhere to, the punishment for accusing one's superiors of a crime was to be discredited and slapped with one's own crimes. In a system where everyone broke the rules, these crimes did not have to be fabricated.

Even as the Interior Ministry's security department began checking the validity of his claims, local police also started digging for dirt against Dymovsky. All that investigators could actually find were allegations of embezzling about $850 in the course of eighteen months. Given the scope of police racketeering that Dymovsky and other officers described to me, this was a laughable sum.

Within a month, Dymovsky was presented with charges of fraud and abuse of office. In January 2010, he was taken into custody and locked up in a pretrial detention center.

What was interesting was that investigators made little effort to deny that the persecution was a direct retaliation for snitching to Putin. Inna Biryukova, a spokeswoman for the Krasnodar regional Investigative Committee, said the fraud checks were not connected to his video. But when I asked her when exactly those checks were initiated—before or after the video was posted—she said, "After."

But the Kremlin's anti-corruption drive, which started gaining momentum soon after the outcry sparked by the videos, acted in Dymovsky's favor. In December 2009, Medvedev decreed that the Interior Ministry should be reformed by 2012; in February, he sacked sixteen interior ministry officials—one of them Boris Martynov, head of the Krasnodar Regional Police, which had Dymovsky's department in its jurisdiction.

In that context, the media attention given to Dymovsky's imprisonment only vindicated his claims and his own status as a new type of dissident. Politically, a police whistleblower in prison threatened to make a laughing stock of President Dmitry Medvedev's reform campaign. In that light, Dymovsky's release from prison six weeks later on March 7, 2010, made perfect sense. And the prosecutors who approved the decision gave a perfectly Soviet explanation. "The decision to release him was made because the necessity to keep him in custody has passed," Inna Biryukova told me when I asked whether the media attention reflected on the decision to release him on bail.[132]

The investigation into fraud allegations against Dymovsky never went to court and seemed to be filed away as a potential weapon for further use. As for the slander case, a court ordered Dymovsky to pay 50,000 rubles ($1,500) each to Chernositov and Medvedev for spreading false rumors against them.

Instead, the regional Interior Ministry took on a more localised approach and started waging a "softer" war: officials connected Dymovsky's *Belaya Lenta* movement, which staged a series of protests in Novorossiysk during his imprisonment, to the US Agency for International Development in a bid to portray the Dymovsky scandal as a Western intervention attempt. One of *Belaya Lenta*'s leaders, Vadim Karastelyov, was arrested once while handing out flyers; on another occasion he was severely beaten by unidentified attackers.

Karastelyov told me that Valery Medvedev—who was behind the slander suit—detained him personally in Novorossiysk as he was handing out flyers.[133] The behavior of Dymovsky's bosses, if not backed by Interior Ministry officials in Moscow, was clearly tolerated because Dymovsky had violated the unspoken rules of the game.

Less easy to understand is the reaction of the federal government. In the context of its police reform campaign, simply ignoring Dymovsky was certainly an option, and on the surface this appeared to be precisely what both Medvedev's Kremlin and Putin's White House were doing. But the noticeable silence with which it was treating the case raised even more questions. Putin's press secretary, Dmitry Peskov, could go on at great lengths about human rights activists and oppositionists; but on Dymovsky everyone was silent.

When reports appeared in the media that winter asking "Who is behind Dymovsky?" and when I got to know Dymovsky and his friends better, I started to understand part of the reason for the silence.

3.

Dymovsky's video address sparked more than a wave of solidarity from lower-rank cops across the country. It brought a general neurosis to the fore: calls for the entire Interior Ministry to be reformed played into a collective horror that some powerful force was out to destroy the Ministry in an attempt to undermine the government. Even Moscow's gypsy cabbies—the ones who boasted of friends and relatives in the "power structures"—suddenly started claiming there was a "vast plot" to take down Interior Minister Rashid Nurgaliyev.

The very fact that an inarticulate police major like Dymovsky was on the evening news was so unheard of that it started fueling rumors that someone was out to transform and destroy the entire Ministry. Because transformation and destruction never benefitted the average subject, all camps agreed that someone was out to shake things up to gain power. The only question that they differed on was who.

Following the beating to death of a student by three policemen, a senior United Russia deputy, Andrei Makarov, weighed in with his own apocalyptic vision. The Interior Ministry, he said at a November press conference, "is impossible to reform, therefore it must be liquidated."[134] It was corrupt, depraved, and, to boot, was struggling to "discredit" a bill to decriminalize tax violations—a bill that was supported from up on high by Vladimir Putin himself. One did not have to be a lawyer to understand why the Interior Ministry spoke out against the decriminalization: charges of tax violations were the most common mechanism used to apply pressure on businessmen to shake them down.

Depending on one's position and source of income, the increasing changes that were gaining momentum in the second year of Medvedev's term were interpreted as either legitimate reforms, spearheaded by the president, or a shadowy bid by a hardliner group to destroy the Interior Ministry, gain hold of its financial positions, and use it to fortify their power.

And Dymovsky—or whoever was behind him—was automatically categorized as part of a shadowy plot.

"My experience tells me that Dymovsky's questionable moral

qualities are written on his forehead in capital letters," Valery Zorkin, the powerful chairman of no less than Russia's Constitutional Court, penned in a column in the official *Rossiyskaya Gazeta (Russia's Newspaper)* that December. "Not even a brilliant PR team, attached by someone to put the spin on Dymovsky, could erase those letters. And that someone deliberately attached this PR team to Dymovsky is pretty clear.... It is important to understand that there is a [anti-police] campaign under way."[135]

To understand all this talk of a shadowy plot, I went to Kirill Kabanov, the former FSB colonel, who still carried a gun when he went to work in the National Anti-Corruption Committee, an NGO with apparently friendly links to the Presidential Administration.

Yes, he said, there were ulterior motives in the reform campaign—rather, a hardliner group, as he saw it, was taking advantage of the presidential reform campaign to strengthen its position.

"The Interior Ministry has a problem. There's a group, sometimes called the 'smaller politburo.' A hardliner group. It believes that Nurgaliyev's position is not supportive enough of the *siloviki*. This group is trying to shake up the system, to get better control of the president and the prime minister."

This "smaller politburo," he told me, was connected to a former KGB associate of Putin's, the current drug tsar Viktor Ivanov, head of the Federal Service for Drug Control.

And it was very possible that this hardliner, FSB-backed group was using Dymovsky, without his knowledge, for its own purposes.

"These people are starting to put the spin on him. I have one question about Dymovsky. Here he is in Moscow, here he is at a press conference. He gets out of the building and gets into a brand new Audi A8 with a Moscow license plate."

"Did that mean Dymovsky had a patron?" I asked.

"No, he's being used."

It was not difficult to find who was "behind" Dymovsky. One was a tall, blond, weather-beaten man in his early forties named Marat Rumyantsev—a contractor for the security services. Another was a former police colonel who identified himself only as Alexei. And like many who had flocked to Dymovsky, they appeared genuinely dismayed at just how commonplace the violations described in his video had become.

They agreed to meet at a Moscow restaurant—and arrived in an Audi minivan.

"When you read about the people behind Dymovsky, these terrifying PR technologists with millions of dollars, that's us," Marat Rumyantsev told me. "On the third day they announced that America was behind Dymovsky. We were on the floor laughing. My wife was asking me, 'When are they going to start paying you?'"

It was Marat and Alexei who picked up Dymovsky in Moscow, where he ran from Novorossiysk after posting his video, fearing retribution from his bosses.

"I was one of the first people that called him. I told him, you did something I've always wanted to do, but I didn't have the guts," Alexei said. "He came to Moscow in a t-shirt when it was -5°C (23°F) outside. I bought him a sweater and some clothes so he could look decent at a press conference. I got him settled in a hotel. All with my own money. My wife was upset."

Alexei was a fifteen-year veteran of the Moscow police force, a colonel who retired after getting fed up with being rapped on the knuckles for tracking criminals with friends in high places.

But just who, exactly, was Marat Rumyantsev? And though he was clearly sincere, what stopped him from being used, unknowingly, in the interests of more powerful officials?

Kabanov described to me how security structures often co-opted public initiative groups to work to their advantage. It was very possible, he said, that Vadim Karastelyov's *Belaya Lenta*, which Dymovsky joined as a leader, could have been approached without even knowing who that patron was. "Let's say there's a NGO or a protest group. This *siloviki* group moves in and says, 'We'll help you.'"

While Alexei said that he started his own private security agency after leaving the force, Marat Rumyantsev was slightly more evasive about his background. In the late 1980s, he had served in the army, then the Special Forces of the Defence Ministry's Chief Intelligence Directorate (GRU). He even tried to join Alfa Group—the elite forces of the KGB—but his first and last day on the job was August 19, 1991, the day of the coup that put an end to everything.

In 1992, he did a six-month stint in the police organized crime unit, but left the force after being forbidden to go after a protected drug dealer.

"Then I went back where I came from," he said. "The Special Forces. Reserve officer."

Before I had time to bring up the issue of being used, Marat brought it up himself. "I've had this feeling several times—what if this is some kind of project, and we're being used in it without our knowledge?"

Alexei said he was convinced that they were being used, but said he was certain that Dymovsky himself was too unmanageable. "If anyone is behind Dymovsky, it's God himself."

It was becoming clear that whether or not these officers were part of a higher-up plot to take control of the Interior Ministry was immaterial. Or, to be more precise, whether or not there was a plot, they did not knowingly play a role in it. Instead, they presented a different kind of threat entirely: if a plot were to materialize, they could be used as formidable fodder. For, as foes of the government, they felt far more desperate, more betrayed, and more disenfranchised than any so-called "liberal opposition" could claim—nor did they want anything to do with the liberal human rights activists who, Marat said, were also trying to use Dymovsky to promote themselves.

"As a citizen of this country, I'm certain that everything that's being done right now is a diversion to destroy the Russian Federation," Marat Rumyantsev told me.

What had turned the police profession into a money-making operation?

"An order was given at some point that there's no more money for salaries. In return, we are shown that we can do whatever we want, we are told, 'don't be afraid, nothing will happen to you, the System won't betray you.' This started in 2000, and it came from a person we all know, a man who will not betray his own kind. Vladimir Putin. Ever heard of him?"

4.

In the case of Major Alexei Dymovsky, truly, the medium was the message. Talking directly to (or at) Putin about the violations committed by one's superiors was itself an act of defiance. It was also the only thing he did to turn himself from a provincial police officer into a dissident and a celebrity.

In fact, the whole story of Dymovsky, distilled to the basics, was a one-sided conversation with his sovereign.

And it didn't begin with the video, but with an unsuccessful phone call to Putin's 2007 phone-in show. It was the last one that Putin held as president, and Dymovsky wanted to ask him when he would put an end to corruption in the police. The operators, quite obviously, did not put him through.

But Putin's silence in the wake of Dymovsky's video was also telling. A small-time provincial officer, extending a trembling hand, wanted to discuss police problems with the one man he felt was responsible for corruption, who could thus put an end to it. "Eye to eye," man to man.

And Putin utterly refused the invitation.

After that refusal was made clear, Dymovsky told a radio station—and Putin by proxy—that he no longer wanted to meet with him. "I want to officially state that I will not meet with the prime minister because I consider it to be an insult to my honor,"[136] Dymovsky announced. Since the prime minister didn't want to talk with his people—which he clearly demonstrated by ignoring Dymovsky's video—Dymovsky had no reason to talk to him either.

Subsequently, Dymovsky would refuse to meet with politicians who he said were trying to use him to promote themselves. And that too was telling—telling in the sense that Dymovsky seemed to have something to say to Putin, but not to other "elected" officials, the faces of Russia's flimsy, powerless institutions.

By the time Dymovsky arrived in Mezhdurechensk in May 2010, eager to speak out on a social conflict simmering in that mining town, the furor around his name had died down. But Dymovsky was convinced that it was just the beginning.

"Someone is artificially creating tensions between the people and the police," he told me, echoing what Marat Rumyantsev had described a few months before. "Once the first shot is fired, it will all sweep over Russia. People will die. A civil war will begin. In the ensuing conflict, those with means will take their things and run. And military troops from NATO and the European Union will enter Russia and divide it. That's what all this is for."

This was no longer the fumbling cop I'd seen in the video, as if the gloss of publicity and the deprivations of prison had chiseled his face and added a melancholy cast to his look. Dymovsky would shed tears at intervals, but he spoke clearly and with a deep sense of mission. It just wasn't clear what, exactly, that mission was.

That what he was seeing around him was the result of a deliberate plot and not of chaos and disarray seemed clear to Dymovsky. It was as though he could not reconcile himself to the notion that Putin was somehow not in control of the way security officers interacted with each other, that he was not all-powerful. And for that reason, it seemed, in Dymovsky's mind he was equated with a traitor.

"Why couldn't Putin fly out here instead of hanging out at Abramovich's dacha? Why couldn't he talk to the people? Our government is afraid of the people. And the people are afraid of lawlessness."

Clearly, though, the mechanisms for change did not seem to be in the hands of Major Dymovsky, and he admitted as much.

"There will come a time when they [the corrupt officials running Russia] will reap what they sow. I know it. It can't go on forever. It can't get any worse."

PART III
THE BOYARS

Chapter 9

Doing Business with Putin

*At that moment Boris clearly realized what he had before
surmised, that in the army, besides the subordination and
discipline prescribed in the military code... there was
another, more important, subordination.... More than ever
was Boris resolved to serve in future not according to the
written code, but under this unwritten law.*
—**Leo Tolstoy**, *War and Peace*

*At that point I realized there was something deeply wrong
in terms of my own situation with Putin. He clearly wasn't
my friend.*
—**William Browder**, CEO of Hermitage Capital

1.

BY THE TIME William Browder understood why he had fallen
from Vladimir Putin's good graces, it was far too late, and his lawyer
was dead.

The notorious death of the lawyer, Sergei Magnitsky, would set
in motion one of the biggest international scandals since the Cold
War; a scandal that would affect everything from trade relations to
the fate of hundreds of Russian orphans, and a scandal from which
no one would emerge entirely blameless.

But the story began as many did in Russia: with a businessman looking for opportunity in what many believed to be a developing economy transitioning towards democracy.

For William Browder, an astute investment analyst who founded the Hermitage Capital Management fund in Russia in 1996, getting rich on undervalued Russian stock was just one of the ways he was helping to improve the investment climate. Buying shares on the cheap from Russian companies and then exposing corruption to improve their transparency and to raise their stock prices wasn't only legal, it seemed like the right thing to do. Browder was using his Western know-how to bring better corporate practices to Russia's emerging market, and the fact that he was making millions of dollars in the process underlined the win-win confluence that only a free market could foster.

Browder was also convinced (or perhaps had convinced himself) that he had an "alignment of interests" with Vladimir Putin, who seemed eager to rein in the robber baron oligarchs and fix the fraud they left behind as a matter of policy and national interest.

Armed with that alignment, Hermitage Capital exposed real or perceived scams at major companies that could harm minority shares. Browder learned to take on powerful interests long before Putin became president. In 1997, Hermitage Capital succeeded in preventing oligarch Vladimir Potanin from issuing additional stock at the Sidanco company, stock which could have diluted Hermitage Capital's 2 percent of shares.[137] An exposé of Gazprom led to CEO Rem Vyakhirev getting fired in 2001, and after Hermitage Capital complained of asset-stripping plans at Russia's electricity giant, RAO UES, the government canceled the plans. Though there is evidence that dozens of lawsuits filed by Hermitage Capital were lost, according to Browder, between 1999 and 2003 the government would step in to fix every major fraud his company publicized.[138]

In return, Browder touted Russia's investment climate, heaping praise on the government and Vladimir Putin in particular, so much so that he came to be dubbed as a "cheerleader" and even a "Putinista."[139]

"My original feelings about Putin were based very narrowly on what he did for us in the first three years of his regime," Browder told me in October 2011.

He said he was horrified at what the oligarchs had done to the country and was glad to see Putin taking a tougher stance.

"When Putin came to power one of his big policies was to correct that. It was hard to be human and not feel some degree of relief to see someone who seemed to be focused, determined, and organized to take that on."

But Browder was also particularly thrilled to see Vladimir Putin in his corner.

"Since I was fighting with a number of these oligarchs who were stealing money from the companies I was investing in, I was delighted when Putin would step into the fight on our side," he told me.

But then things started going horribly wrong. On November 13, 2005, upon his return to Moscow, he was stopped at the border and sent back to London—declared, in a terse statement eventually issued by the Foreign Ministry, as a threat to national security.

For weeks, Hermitage Capital kept the deportation a secret, as if, much like the first random victims of the Stalinist purges, they were hoping that it was some sort of mistake, that perhaps Putin wasn't aware of the error. There was another man, a human rights activist, deported just two days later named Bill Bowring—maybe the names were confused.

On December 26, weeks after the mysterious deportation, Browder made a particularly glowing speech about Putin. In a half-hour interview with CNBC, he said that Putin had heard the investors and was eager to work with them; that the Yukos affair—in which Russia's richest and possibly most transparent oligarch, Mikhail Khodorkovsky, was jailed on fraud and tax evasion charges—was nothing to get emotional about.

But this overture of flattery—of the kind that Putin liked, because he did indeed like foreign investors—had no effect. The state of apparent disfavor that Browder suddenly found himself in would continue to spiral out of control.

By November 2009, his lawyer, Sergei Magnitsky, would be writing letters like the following to the head of the Butyrka pretrial detention center where he was being held on tax evasion charges:

"On November 12 I was deprived of the ability to take hot food for 24 hours and was deprived of an 8-hour period of sleep. This, evidently, became the reason for an acute increase in the pain in my pancreas and the appearance of some rather unpleasant pain in the area of my liver…. In connection with this I ask to be given recommendations for what kind of medications, if any, I should take….Apart from that, I ask to finally be informed of when I shall be administered an ultrasound that had been scheduled for August."

Magnitsky, in pretrial detention since November 2008 on charges of helping Hermitage Capital evade taxes, was held for four more days in a tiny cell with no hot water, his cot less than a meter away from a hole in the floor that served as a toilet.

On November 16, 2009, two doctors, who had been kept from seeing Magnitsky for well over an hour after they arrived, finally discovered him on the floor of his cell, having died from pancreatitis that prison doctors, reportedly on orders from Magnitsky's investigators, had refused to treat. There was some evidence that he was beaten shortly before his death.

Despite a national outcry over the death, the disaster that began when Browder was barred entry into Russia did not end there.

By 2013, Russian authorities were trying to get Interpol to declare Browder a wanted man. Magnitsky, in a case unprecedented in Russian history, was tried as a dead man—and found guilty.

This macabre retribution appeared to be a response to Browder's own revenge. In 2011, he had started lobbying US Congress for a bill that would bar sixty Russian officials from entering America and freeze their assets there. It would become known as the Magnitsky Act, which was passed in late 2012. Considering how members of Russia's elite had a penchant for vacationing in the US and sending their children to study there, the bill was a slap in the face for the Kremlin. Putin, who had been banking on improved trade relations resulting from the repeal of the Cold War-era Jackson-Vanik Amendment, would retaliate with an anti-Magnitsky Law. It was a tit-for-tat bill, except that it included a clause widely seen as hurting Russians more than Americans: a ban on the adoption of Russian orphans by Americans, in a country whose citizens were not particularly eager to adopt.

Why did Browder's initial "alignment" of interests with the Kremlin turn into a collision? If Browder had inadvertently stumbled into a world where dead men were tried for tax fraud, where orphans paid the price for international business feuds, what kind of world was it, and why was it so resilient?

2.

In 2007 Browder, having been barred from Russia, was living in London, watching as his once $4.5 billion investment fund struggled to survive. But he seemed to know enough about how Russian power worked to understand that only personal connections and clout could help bring him back into the country.

On January 27, Deputy Prime Minister Dmitry Medvedev, by then evidently one of two heirs apparent to Putin, made his debut at the World Economic Forum in Davos, where Browder was a perennial presence. As the future president sat quietly eating his dessert, Browder approached him to broach the subject of his visa—and ask Medvedev if he could put in a word for him.

Just at that moment, though, other journalists approached the two, and it became clear that whatever Medvedev said would be a public statement.

"Since this was his international debut it wouldn't have done it any good to say no, so he said, yes, please give me your application and I will submit it with a recommendation that your visa be approved," Browder said of the meeting.

The exchange apparently had an effect—though not exactly what Browder had been expecting.

A few weeks after the request, Browder's deputy in Moscow got a phone call from Artyom Kuznetsov, a lieutenant colonel with the Interior Ministry, saying he'd like to meet for a "face to face chat." It was unclear how—or whether—the exchange with Medvedev led to Kuznetsov contacting Hermitage Capital, but apparently the police colonel had been given Browder's visa application for consideration.

"He would have to write a report and depending on what [we] provide in the meeting and how [we] behave will determine what [he will] write in [the] report," Browder said.

Hermitage Capital refused the offer of an informal meeting, demanding questions and answers in writing.

What happened next was a bureaucratic retribution of Kafkaesque proportions, involving a whole army of prosecutors, investigators, tax officials, and judges.

In June 2007, Kuznetsov led a raid of twenty-five masked police officers on Hermitage Capital, extracting hundreds of accounting documents. A similar raid followed on the legal firm Firestone Duncan, which advised Browder, and where Sergei Magnitsky worked. The documents and seals of three Hermitage Capital shell companies obtained in the raid ended up being used in a scheme to get an unprecedented tax refund of $230 million—processed and paid out within the course of a day at a central Moscow tax inspectorate. It was believed that after pocketing a share of the refund, Kuznetsov and his colleagues then used the embezzlement to put together a criminal case against Hermitage Capital.

When Browder objected, Kuznetsov swooped down on Firestone's tireless lawyer, Sergei Magnitsky, who had exposed the fraud, and arrested him in November 2008 on charges of tax evasion. After eleven months of refusing to cave in to pressure to recant his testimony against Kuznetsov and testify against Hermitage, Magnitsky died.

If we separate the Russian spheres of *zakon* (the law as it is on paper) and the murkier *ponyatiya* (or understandings—the so-called unspoken rules which actually govern the country), it is easy to see how someone like Browder could have violated both. With regards to the law on paper, we have already seen how practically every businessman in Russia is guilty in some way. The journalist David Hoffman recounts how small businessmen would complain that according to official calculations, their total tax bill would amount to unrealistic sums—as much as 110 percent of their profits. "The laws made almost every businessman and taxpayer a lawbreaker—and thus a potential criminal and thus a willing supplicant to power and, finally, a briber," he wrote. [140]

As a minority shareholder, Browder appeared to have used these same laws against powerful company owners and profited from them—forgetting that in the process, he was also violating them himself, as all businessmen in Russia were.

The tax evasion charges leveled against Hermitage Capital stand out in particular. Russian authorities, who issued an international arrest warrant for Browder in 2013, alleged that as it bought up shares of Gazprom at the turn of the millennium, Hermitage avoided the limitation that barred foreign companies from owning shares in state-controlled energy companies like Gazprom. It did this by allegedly registering several Russian companies in the internal Republic of Kalmykia, and buying the shares in their names. To avoid the 35 percent corporate tax, these firms, according to several employee testimonials, hired disabled employees and paid the reduced tax rate of 5 percent.[141]

Browder has not denied certain financial and tax arrangements, but he insisted they were entirely legal. "If one took these accusations seriously, then every foreign investor in Russia should be under arrest," Browder told the *Financial Times* in spring 2013.[142]

Depending on the quality and expertise of one's lawyers, this scheme could either be legal or illegal. But by the time Browder fell out of favor and refused to strike a deal with Police Lieutenant Colonel Artyom Kuznetsov, the accusations were dug out and used against him and Sergei Magnitsky in particular.

But something had to happen for Browder, a loyal investor and a cheerleader for Putin, to fall out of favor so suddenly. If he had crossed the paths of companies like Gazprom and got away with it for years, whose path did he cross then, and why did his fortunes change?

It was only by the summer of 2006—after some eight months of unsuccessfully trying to get his visa reinstated—that Browder began to understand what had happened.

"What really drove the point home was Putin being asked [about me] at the press conference at the G8," Browder said.

When a journalist asked Putin specifically about Browder at the G8 Summit he was hosting in St. Petersburg in July 2006, Putin characteristically avoided mentioning him by name—as he would with Khodorkovsky and many others who had lost his favor.

"I will say honestly that I simply do not know the reason why a specific person was denied entry into the Russian Federation," Putin said. "I can imagine that this person broke the laws of our country, and if others break the laws, then we will deny [entry] to them."[143]

For Browder, the refusal to mention him by name seemed to sting, particularly as he had evidence that Putin had discussed his case at an earlier Security Council meeting. Those discussions seem to hold the key to what finally tipped the favor against Browder.

While it is impossible to verify this kind of information, Browder says that according to two different sources who attended the National Security Council meetings, certain people were arguing against letting Browder back into the country, and their arguments, apparently, prevailed with Putin.

"At that point I realized there was something deeply wrong in terms of my own situation with Putin," Browder said. "He clearly wasn't my friend."[144]

3.

Who were those "certain people," and why was it only then that they succeeded in lobbying Putin even though Browder had been making mischief for Russian oligarchs for a good part of ten years?

Finding irrefutable answers to those questions is impossible for the same reason that investigative journalism is all but absent in Russia—no one will ever go on the record with an account of what happened in backroom talks at such a high level.

But we can easily discern a pattern whereby favor at the very top and protection from above not only determines a businessman's fortune, but the extent of his chances of winding up in jail. Browder may have misread those patterns, or overestimated his own privilege with regards to Russian elites.

Browder said he believes that one of the companies he invested in, like Gazprom, Surgutneftegaz, and Transneft—though he does not know which one—was behind the move to kick him out of Russia. Indeed, Russian authorities have since accused Browder of buying Gazprom stock to "try to get access to financial and other documents that have strategic significance for Russia."[145]

"I can't tell for sure which of the companies gave the order to bar me from Russia," Browder told me. "I'm certain it was coming from one of the companies whose corruption we were exposing." If that was the case then it isn't clear why these companies—which have a hefty state presence or Browder wouldn't have invested in them—hadn't pounced sooner, as when Browder helped get the CEO of Gazprom fired in 2001.

The answer may have something to do with the cumulative effect of Browder's activities in Russia's hydrocarbons sector.

In 2003, the arrest of Yukos chief Mikhail Khodorkovsky, Russia's richest oil magnate, sent shockwaves through the business world. The jailing, as we shall see in Chapter 13, was the result of a Russian oligarch breaking the unwritten rules that governed the delicate balance of power between the realm of the businessmen and the realm of the sovereign.

At the time, Browder had believed that the arrest was an attempt by Putin to clean up corporate governance, and even praised the persecution.

"In retrospect, my appreciation of [Putin] was wrong, but at the time I thought he was cleaning up Russia," Browder said. He saw Khodorkovsky's arrest as the final coup in reining in the Yeltsin-era oligarchs. The way he understood the aftermath, oligarchs came to Putin "one by one and asked him what they needed to do not to get arrested."

But Browder's approval of Khodorkovsky's arrest may also have been influenced by Hermitage's financial losses connected with Yukos.

Browder would later recall that Hermitage had a share of Yukos stock in 1999, but that Yukos management deliberately caused those shares to plummet—losing over 99 percent in value. And even though Yukos cleaned up its act, Browder admitted that he was still angry at the company in 2005 for all the pain that it had caused Hermitage.[146]

In 2005, the Rosneft state oil company had capitalized on the partition of Khodorkovsky's Yukos empire. After the forced bankruptcy of Yukos, its chief production asset, Yuganskneftegaz, was auctioned off to a single bidder, the previously unknown Baikalfinansgrup, for $9.7 billion. Just days later, on December 22, Baikalfinansgrup was purchased by Rosneft. The chairman of Rosneft's board of directors is Igor Sechin, Putin's right-hand man, who for years has been regarded as the second most powerful man in the country. It is to him that critics credit the dismantling of the Yukos empire.

According to one version of events cited by one of Russia's most respected business dailies, in October 2005, just a month before Browder was expelled, Hermitage had interfered with the consolidation of Rosneft's subsidiaries just as it was gearing up for an initial public offering in April of 2006. According to this version, the interference was reportedly serious enough that it prompted Sechin to lobby personally for Browder's expulsion.[147]

Browder has denied any involvement in Rosneft and its subsidies; more convolutedly, so has Sechin himself.

According to Yelena Panfilova, the head of the Russian branch of Transparency International who has extensively investigated not only Magnitsky's case, but Browder's work in Russia as well, indirect involvement in Yukos assets probably contributed to Browder's eventual expulsion—but could not have been the only factor.

"The strengthening of his position in regards to these assets could have caused some degree of nervousness among the players, who saw this as their spoils alone," she told me when I asked about the Yukos connection. "I can't say that he took part directly, but that when these assets were sold, certainly some shares wound up in their portfolios."

"He got a false sense of being privy to these elites, and it was false because these elites had their own criteria about who was privy and who was not," Panfilova explained. "And this let him down him, as it let down a lot of people in history. When you think you're an insider, but it turns out that they've only let you near them, but haven't made you one of them."

When Browder started flaunting his "alignment of interests" with Putin in 2005, he crossed the line by presuming a degree of closeness and loyalty that no foreign investor could ever have. When Browder crossed the line, he lost his *krysha*, his "roof," and his presumably "favored" status. The "inner circle" of ministers that Browder had so prided himself on knowing, now cut him loose. The state, personified by Putin and by the ministers, turned away from him and left him at the mercy of the paper law. They didn't trigger the string of embezzlement, fraud, and extortion charges—that came from specific law enforcement officials—but by distancing themselves from Browder they made it clear to law enforcement predators that he was fair game.

The phone call from Lieutenant Colonel Artyom Kuznetsov, ostensibly about Browder's visa, was an overture from a new, albeit, lower level type of *krysha*—Kuznetsov was offering Hermitage his protection services. But Hermitage refused.

And given Russia's paper law, it was only a matter of time before law enforcement officials who worked the protection racket dug up enough on his company to put someone in jail.

4.

Given that the key charge levelled at Putin's regime by his opponents is corruption, understanding the peculiar advantages this system poses for millions of people helps elucidate the resilience and the *de facto* stability of Putin's rule.

As the Medvedev-backed investigation into Magnitsky's death sputtered to an end and as those who had persecuted Browder and Magnitsky were cleared of wrongdoing by Russian authorities, new evidence started emerging about about how, exactly, they had benefitted. Many of these officials, including Lieutenant Colonel Artyom Kuznetsov and Major Pavel Karpov, both of whom Magnitsky had accused of taking parts in the tax rebate scheme, would go on to be named in the US Magnitsky List of officials banned entry to America.

Documents appeared showing that Kuznetsov, who lived on an official Interior Ministry salary of $12,300 a year, had purchased a $94,000 Mercedes convertible and a $154,000 Range Rover in the name of his wife. Travel receipts showed him splurging thousands of dollars at a five-star resort in Cyprus. Many of these receipts were dated before the June 2007 raids on Hermitage offices that enabled the fraudulent tax refunds to take place.

Karpov, meanwhile, is documented as owning a $85,000 Mercedes Benz and a $48,000 Porsche registered in his wife's name—all despite an official salary of just $6,800 a year. Far from casting a shadow on his prospects, over a year after Magnitsky's death Karpov was promoted.[148]

Not only law enforcement officials were getting rich. Olga Stepanova, the head of the Moscow Tax Office who authorized a whole string of fraudulent tax refunds between 2006 and 2008 (including the $230 million transaction with Kuznetsov), allegedly acquired over $38 million of assets—including a villa and two apartments in Dubai, a $12 million estate in the Moscow region, and a seaside villa in Montenegro—with many of the assets registered in the name of her pensioner mother-in-law.[149] In autumn 2012, following the sacking and investigation against her former patron, Defence Minister Anatoly Serdyukov, Russian authorities would launch a probe of Stepanova on allegations that she stole 8 billion rubles ($232 million) through tax fraud.[150]

The Magnitsky affair and the officials who got rich from Hermitage's refusal to accept Kuznetsov's protection services is no isolated case—because a death was involved, it publicized a mechanism that is replicated in thousands of cases. In fact, in 2006 another major investment fund—Renaissance Capital—fell victim to a nearly identical tax refund scam involving $107 million. But even RenCap, which had links to government agencies, understood that little good would come of publicizing the fraud and chose to ignore it.[151]

As for extortion and protection rackets in law enforcement, we have seen earlier just how pervasive the practice is. For every high-profile scandal involving the death of a sick person in pretrial detention, there are dozens of routine stories of police and prosecutors protecting illegal gambling establishments—and then celebrating such business partnerships with expensive vacations.[152]

The critical mass of people from a variety of government and even non-government posts involved in what has been given the blanket term of "corruption" may hold the key to why it is impossible to overcome—because we are in fact dealing with a problem of terminology and social values. Take, for instance, a widely accepted definition of corruption, proposed by Samuel Huntington, as "behavior of public officials which deviates from accepted norms to serve private ends."[153] But when a fifth of the economy consists of bribes, kickbacks, and other forms of off the books enrichment—totalling some $300 billion[154]—it is hard to see this as a "deviation." When nine out of ten economic crime cases are fabrications,[155] the "law" is merely an instrument for the enrichment of those entitled to apply it. And however bad it is, it is in fact an indelible part of the norm by virtue of its sheer pervasiveness. In other words, "corruption" is the norm for a sizable—20 percent—minority of businessmen and state officials.

And so the process that Magnitsky ultimately became a victim of was actually a way of life for millions of people—an entire social stratum that includes civil servants, tax officials, investigators, police and security officers, and even businessmen. And for every Hermitage that refused Kuznetsov's protection services, ten firms probably acquiesced. After being allowed to function this way on such small salaries for so long, a decisive denial of this kind of lifestyle could have seriously undermined the very functions of the law enforcement system. In other words, if President Dmitry Medvedev's anti-corruption campaign had actually stopped corruption, millions of police officers would suddenly be forced to live on less than $600 a month. And that on its own would have presented an acute national security problem, threatening the very foundations of Putin's hold on power.

Mark Galeotti is one of the few scholars to have recognized some of the advantageous aspects of corruption and tax farming in Russia—not just as a way of governing, but even for some parts of the population. Describing tax farming as officials being "granted areas of responsibility and revenue targets and cut loose to raise all they could without igniting rebellion," Galeotti enumerated several benefits to the state and the populace, such as low start-up costs, political loyalty from a vast swath of enriched officials whose loyalty mattered, and simply "getting the job done."[156]

It is getting the job done—making things happen—in particular that may help explain Putin's popularity among a large number of foreign investors like William Browder. Though they recognize the need for more transparency, they also see Putin as someone strong enough to balance the best of both worlds.

What this may suggest is that norms and practices termed as "corrupt" are not accepted as corrupt by everyone—only by those who suffer from them. In other words, certain norms may actually be accepted by large parts of a society, but outlawed on paper—it is this gap, in fact, that may account for many of the problems. One Western fund manager, who spoke on conditions of anonymity, described this collision: "In the Middle East, a company can't get a contract without a local partner. You end up with a contract price that should be $100 million, but it ends up being $200 million because the local partner needs 50 percent. Is there a difference between that and bribery? There isn't a difference in cost, but there is a difference in how you go about it. One is upfront and clear, the other is untransparent and shady."

As Galeotti argued, in many cases "corruption" winds up "humanizing" what is otherwise an enormously intimidating political system.[157] It is significant that Galeotti was writing this in 1998, even as then President Boris Yeltsin was rhetorically decrying corruption in his country—with corruption already rampant. By the time Putin arrived in the Kremlin, being himself part of that corrupt system, he took a problem that he had no ability to eradicate and co-opted it for the benefit of the state.

For a large part of the population, the unspoken rules that he was quietly offering, the possibility of private enrichment based on one's government caste, even as he spoke publicly about "the dictatorship of the law," was like an unexpected, endearing smile that flickered on a man at once cold, threatening, and faceless. To succeed, you had to understand where you stood with regards to the inner circle.

Chapter 10
The Inner Circle

That power which broke our own in fragments
Binds us together, alone can bind us still:
When strength is out, the body falls to dust.
Our only chance of safety, Boyars, lies
In going now, the whole assembled Council,
To the Tzar at once, in falling at his knees,
There to entreat him yet he give not up
His throne, aye, that he yet save Russia.
—**Boris Godunov**, from *The Death of Ivan the Terrible*, by Alexei Konstantinovich Tolstoy[158]

1.

ONE HUMID AUGUST evening in 2009, during the peak of the economic crisis, Andrei Kolesnikov, *Kommersant's* star reporter and one of the only journalists in Russia who had exclusive access to Vladimir Putin's ear, gathered his friends and colleagues in a fashionable Moscow gallery to muse on the meaning of life over champagne and caviar sandwiches.

The featured guests, who included oligarchs like Alfa-Group chief Mikhail Fridman, former *Kommersant* editor Andrei Vasilyev, and President Dmitry Medvedev's diminutive economic advisor Arkady Dvorkovich, all had one thing in common: they had written essays for the current issue of Kolesnikov's quarterly glossy, *Russian Pioneer*.

The essays were loosely focused on a topic of Kolesnikov's choosing, which happened to be "the meaning of life."

As the guests read out their pieces, they kept getting off the subject and talking, inadvertently, about the prime minister.

There was at least one reason for the digressions. In the previous issue, in May, Kolesnikov outdid himself by talking Vladimir Putin into contributing a column to the magazine. The prime minister, in a text that read remarkably much like the way he spoke, revealed no sensational secrets about his private life nor gave any opinions on pet policy issues. Instead, Putin explained "Why it is difficult to fire a person." The topic, Kolesnikov explained to me later, had been agreed together with the prime minister in a private conversation—as a veteran pool reporter and co-author of Putin's 2000 biography, Kolesnikov had that privilege, even though he admitted he was loath to take advantage of it.

Received by the public as a supposed glimpse into Putin's inner world, the column didn't really reveal anything the public did not already know from his nine years in the Kremlin—including the fact that Putin found it difficult to fire people. Instead, it was an artefact of stardom in the same way that any handiwork of the prime minister—whether an amateur painting (which was auctioned just that May), or a doodle in a notebook—attracted curiosity by virtue of simply having come out of his mind. At least, it was presented that way by the media—so much so that Kolesnikov found it difficult to enjoy his subsequent holiday in Venice because of the continuous pestering from journalists.

Indeed, that was the whole principle of *Russian Pioneer*. Funded by billionaire Mikhail Prokhorov's Onexim holding,[159] it was written for and by the affluent elite (the Kremlin ideologist, Vladislav Surkov, was one of its authors) to give the hip and savvy a glimpse of what the masters of the universe could compose if given a proper platform. With a hefty dose of Soviet kitsch, the magazine brandished a nostalgic name and helped revive the obscure Soviet tradition of public readings— known as pioneer readings, after the *pionery*, the Communist youth groups of Kolesnikov's childhood. Now doused in fine wine, with tuxedoed waiters with earrings in one ear, and a high concentration of oligarchs and TV celebrities, the constituents of the gallery bore little resemblance to the Soviet childhoods they were paying homage to.[160]

Except for one small thing that no one seemed to be making much of: they kept returning, in jest and mock reverence, to the topic of the prime minister—as if fearing Big Brother was a fetish of sorts, even for those who consorted with him personally on a regular basis.

Sitting in front of that inebriated audience, Kolesnikov shared a moment of doubt, as if getting Putin to contribute had served as an epiphany of sorts.

"In the last issue, having secured Vladimir Putin as a columnist, I kind of got stuck," Kolesnikov told his audience. "I mean, I reached the highest achievement any editor-in-chief could hope for. And that's why I started thinking about the meaning of life."

The remarks were not without Kolesnikov's trademark irony, for he seemed to be suggesting that when your day job involves looking over Vladimir Putin's right shoulder, you start thinking about the meaning of life a lot sooner.

Nevertheless, the continuity of that issue's topic—its indirect connection with the prime minister—inevitably colored much of what was said afterwards.

When Andrei Vasilyev, the *Kommersant* editor, read his own column out loud, he paused over the word "shit."

"I'm sorry," he joked, "But Putin isn't in this issue, so it's OK [to curse]."

"No it's not!" Kolesnikov retorted from the audience to a burst of laughter.

But the joking reached an apotheosis with the appearance of Mikhail Fridman. Closely connected to Putin and the Kremlin, Fridman's Alfa-Bank once sued *Kommersant* in 2004, alleging the newspaper exaggerated liquidity problems in the bank and provoked a massive cash flight as customers stormed ATM machines (*Kommersant*, then owned by exiled oligarch Boris Berezovsky, came out with blank pages in protest after losing the suit). Fridman was a close colleague of Pyotr Aven, who was an old friend of Putin. In July 2011, Fridman would be one of twenty-seven businessmen who sat in on a closed-door meeting with President Dmitry Medvedev, amid reports that Medvedev, sensing his own diminishing chances for a second presidential term, asked the businessmen to choose between him and Putin.[161] And so he was firmly in the inner circle of the dozen or so members of the moneyed elite whose consensus, much as it had since the sixteenth century, determined who ruled Russia.

Everyone knew this, and Kolesnikov knew that everyone knew this. As Fridman settled into the chair on the stage, Kolesnikov asked him, "Today is the tenth anniversary of Putin becoming prime minister [in 1999]. Is that, um… good?" (He sounded as if he had clearly run out of questions for comment on that illustrious fact).

But Fridman recoiled in mock insult, his plump, ever-apologetic face appearing flustered. "I should stop talking to you after this," he said, to more laughter. "You're putting me on the spot."

But from the audience, Kolesnikov pressed on.

"Of course it's good!" Fridman finally managed to say.

Was Fridman mocking his own support of Putin, or was he mocking his caution over constructive criticism, as if the imprisonment of Mikhail Khodorkovsky in 2003 (for completely different reasons from criticizing Putin, as we shall see later) hung as a Damocles sword over every oligarch in Russia? Or was he mocking the Damocles sword itself?

In fact, the conceit of Putin's sinister, Stalin-like authority was already a frequent punch-line among inside jokes for any community close to state power. And though it was not the 1930s—and the elites didn't shy of such jokes publicly (as long as they did not ridicule Putin)—Kolesnikov saw it as symptomatic of a climate of fear that, however ironic or diluted, still did exist.

"Actually, this is a pretty serious situation," he told me when we met for an interview on the following day. "In the last several years, people have grown accustomed to talking about the president and the prime minister with caution. Television has conditioned them to talk like this. Because where there is no censorship there is self-censorship. And it even pops up at *Russky Pioner* readings. We joke about it, but in reality it exists."

That an oligarch like Fridman was in on the joke—and found himself expertly wriggling out of saying anything untoward, either too flattering or too critical—can reveal just how much concepts like ownership, capital, and favor are still irrevocably determined by the same kind of relationships that existed some five hundred years ago.

2.

Identifying patrimonialism as one of the three elements of modern Russia's political culture, the historian Donald N. Jensen wrote, in 2000: "Political authority was viewed by traditional Russian elites as closely related to property ownership. The Tsar—who identified the state with himself—'owned' the nation, its vast resources, and its citizens. He concentrated in his hands the most profitable branches of commerce and industry and granted favored nobles economic privileges for their support." Jensen goes on to point out that these patrimonial attitudes continue to characterize how prominent businessmen interact with the government.

Writing in 2000, before Putin would prove just how closely his governance resembled that of his predecessor, Jensen was applying these elements to President Boris Yeltsin's "court," where the modern-day "Tsar" avoided "identifying with any single faction and instead balanced off ministers, business tycoons, and security chiefs, who in the absence of selected political rules of political competition, were in perpetual competition with one another for his favor."[162]

Two circumstances were pivotal in establishing the current balance of power and money in Russia: the loans for shares program in 1995, and the subsequent decision of a few key members of the moneyed elite—headed by the most ambitious of them all, Boris Berezovsky—to prevail on the ailing President Boris Yeltsin to anoint Vladimir Putin as his successor in 1999.

These two developments are connected because they rested on a very simple premise: an agreement (and it was possibly the only thing they would ultimately agree on) by the group of people close to President Boris Yeltsin—known as the Family—that they must maintain their assets, and hence their power, at all costs. They believed that Putin—with his respect for loyalty and his understanding of how business worked—was the best option to ensure that *status quo*.

Among the chain of events that eventually connected Vladimir Putin to Boris Yeltsin was a little-known meeting, in 1991, with the man who would become the oligarch Boris Berezovsky. Putin, then the head of the International Relations Committee under St. Petersburg mayor Anatoly Sobchak, oversaw the flourishing of private business in the city—using his connections in the KGB to facilitate business deals with foreign companies, specializing in his favorite type of enterprise, the joint venture.[163]

Berezovsky, then the head of a software company LogoVAZ, needed an official middleman to facilitate a St. Petersburg business venture. A mutual friend, Pyotr Aven, introduced the two. At the time, Aven was the chairman of the Foreign Economic Relations Committee and the all-out go-to man who was instrumental in helping Putin clinch the oil for food plan where lucrative export tenders were alleged to go to some of Putin's friends in the oil processing industry while the food wound up mysteriously disappearing.[164] Berezovsky, who would later become President Putin's staunchest foe in exile, was impressed by the former KGB colonel who helped him out and didn't even ask for a bribe.[165] And he would remember his entrepreneurialism and his loyalty years later when recommending him as a successor to Yeltsin.

By 1996, Berezovsky and Pyotr Aven would become part of what was called, as an inherently new type of power structure, the *semibankirschina*, or the Rule of the Seven Banks. Russians already recognized the parallels between how their country was ruled following the collapse of the USSR, and the leadership crisis during the Time of Troubles between 1598 and 1613. The rule of the Seven Boyars—the group of nobles who reigned in Russia for several months before inviting in the Polish King Wladislaw in 1610—was easily translated into the rule of the Seven Bankers, together with its apparent sell-out to the West. Indeed, the term appeared soon after Berezovsky publicly named seven men, predominantly bankers, who controlled 50 percent of wealth in the country: Vladimir Potanin, Vladimir Gusinsky, Mikhail Khodorkovsky, Pyotr Aven, Mikhail Fridman, Alexander Smolensky, and Berezovsky himself. It was these men, according to journalist Andrei Fadin, who "form the will of the President."[166]

The Seven Boyars also included nobles who had formed the will of Tsars from Ivan the Terrible through to Boris Godunov. But the *semibankirschina* had a very specific reason for getting the bragging rights to forming President Boris Yeltsin's "will": they had ensured, using their media assets, that he beat his Communist foe, Gennady Zyuganov, against all odds during that summer's presidential elections.

There was another reason, too. Just a year before the elections—partly because Yeltsin would need their support and partially because his government was laboring under a 50 trillion ruble debt—these seven men wound up with the choicest spoils of Russia's oil and gas industry for next to nothing.

The mechanism by which this happened—called the loans for shares program—was devised in summer 1995 by Vladimir Potanin and Alfred Kokh, another St. Petersburg acquaintance of Putin from the Leningrad Privatization Office who later became the director of the State Property Committee in Moscow. Created specifically to circumvent a State Duma ban on privatizing strategic oil assets, the plan entailed offering shares of oil refineries as collateral for loans to the state—loans that everyone knew the state would never pay back. Potanin's Onexim Bank, since he was one of the authors of the plan, was first in line. It loaned the government $100 million in return for 38 percent of Norilsk Nickel and another $130 million in return for 51 percent of the Sidanko oil company (to understand just how undervalued that was, note that British Petroleum would pay $571 million for a mere 10 percent of Sidanco shares just the following year, in 1997).[167] Mikhail Khodorkovsky's Menatep bank would get the next best thing: 45 percent of the Yukos oil company for $159 million.[168]

In all, between November and December of 1995, twelve enterprises were auctioned off to these seven bankers, who promptly sold the shares back to themselves through offshore and shell companies in a rigged privatization that few even pretended was fair.[169]

Boris Berezovsky, the most power-hungry of the seven, who would go on to help secure Yeltsin's re-election in 1996, jumped into the auction at the last minute, cornering Yeltsin's bodyguard, Alexander Korzhakov, into approving a loan for shares of the Sibneft company.[170] It was for these reasons—his loan for Sibneft and his central role in organizing the so-called Davos Pact that would bankroll Yeltsin's re-election campaign—that Berezovsky would be in a position to broker first Putin's appointment as prime minister in August 1999, and then help orchestrate his ascendency to the presidential seat.

The loans for shares auction irrevocably connected the oligarchs to the president and his successor in a vicious circle of mutual debt.

And so the involvement of the government—which, however weak, still wielded the full force of the army and security structures (as the role of Yeltsin's bodyguard, Korzhakov, demonstrates)—was far more central to the acquisition of wealth than the most corrupt robber barons of the nineteenth century West could imagine.

Much as the mutual "compromising materials," or *kompromat*, in the security structures bound its members into complaisance in case loyalty failed, the loans for shares scheme bound the Seven Bankers and the president through an extraordinary and unprecedented exchange of favors. The oligarchs had bailed out a cash-strapped president who was desperately struggling to pay pensioners, teachers, doctors, and army officers to keep the country from collapsing. But they had also acquired strategic assets on the cheap—benefitting from what everyone, including the president, understood to be a rip-off. By both taking part in this rip-off, the government and the oligarchs were bound to one another in what the Australian Ambassador Glenn Waller called an "incestuous" relationship.[171]

After such an exchange, devoid of either moral legitimacy or legality, the sovereign exercised the option of taking back the property he had temporarily given to a vassal:[172] not as a matter of policy, but solely at his pleasure.

The Seven Bankers understood this long before Putin came to power—though not all of them would adhere to this ancient wisdom. Soon after his acquisition of Yukos, Mikhail Khodorkovsky demonstrated his grasp of this feudal relationship with the state. Referring to the prime minister as his "boss," he would joke that "I don't own anything, I rent it."[173] He would explain that he would even step down as head of his own bank if the prime minister asked him—because the "state is the dominant force in the economy."[174]

When, as president, Vladimir Putin did just that (first with Gusinsky, then with Berezovsky, and then with Khodorkovsky), many feigned shock, as though they had forgotten in what "incestuous" circumstances this wealth had been acquired in the first place. Those who lauded the move, like William Browder, mistakenly thought of it as part of a policy of renationalization and an attempt to implement justice, rather than the Tsar exercising his right based on the unspoken rules that had been established between him and his boyars in the absence of the rule of law.

Those rules have evolved, under Putin, into a curious mix of the ancient and the new, where the favor of the sovereign is jealously guarded and where capital is built with his approval—but where everyone wears Brioni business suits and despises cheap flattery, opting for a staunchly postmodern demeanor to attract investors.

3.

After standing for hours in the rain outside their factory on June 4, 2009, the workers of Pikalevo heard Vladimir Putin shout to them, "Don't worry, your factories will start working, I promise," and went home to their television sets, relieved. It was there that they saw the public thrashing of Oleg Deripaska, the oligarch who owned the plant where they worked. Despite Putin's soothing wrath (for they were unabashedly delighted to see a baron getting what they felt he deserved), many of the workers who had taken part in the protest later described the pen-throwing incident as "just a game."

Even without knowing the details, the workers of Pikalevo seemed to sense that Putin was lying as he referred to plant managers as "cockroaches," because they saw Deripaska's wealth, much like that of any oligarch in Russia, not as something earned by hard work, but merely a token of the favor of the Tsar.

Deripaska has prided himself on not taking part in the shameful loans for shares auctions. After founding an investment company in 1990, when he was just twenty-two, he started buying up shares in Siberian aluminium plants, gradually building up his RusAl aluminium empire and his Basic Element minerals holding. Slightly younger than the members of the Seven Bankers and untainted by the loans for shares auction, Deripaska has enjoyed a somewhat favored status in Putin's circle, and the residents of Pikalevo, who understood the structural relationship and the unspoken rules that governed this favor, clearly sensed this.

In October 2008, when the global financial meltdown reached Russia, Deripaska had already become the beneficiary of an unprecedented $4.5 billion state loan by the VEB (Vneshekonombank, the state economic development bank)—part of a $10 billion government bailout to several companies, including $2 billion for Mikhail Fridman's Alfa Group. But the handout to Deripaska exceeded VEB's $2.5 billion limit on loans to a single company by nearly two-fold.[175] And while analysts attributed the favor to Rus-Al's aggressive lobbying, "lobbying" doesn't appear to be the right word for the interaction between RusAl and the government, for an exceedingly simple reason: the chairman of the supervisory board of the VEB who approved the loan happens to be Vladimir Putin.[176] Deripaska did not need to hire lobbyists to remind legislators in Parliament of their constituency or the sources of their campaign funds. He just needed to bring up the issue with Putin directly at one of their many public (and private) meetings.

Letters published by Russian media later in 2009 evidenced what the residents of Pikalevo knew all too well: that, Deripaska's televised shaming notwithstanding, the minerals magnate was receiving not one, but a series of bailouts that were brokered by Putin personally.

It is informative to take a close look at how Deripaska went about asking Putin to extend the VEB loan into 2013. Addressing Putin in his capacity as the chairman of the VEB's supervisory board, Deripaska first pointed out how the August 2009 explosion at the Sayano-Shushenskaya Hydro-Electric Plant—which claimed over fifty lives and paralyzed energy supplies in Western Siberia—was taking its toll on RusAl's aluminium factories in the area.

"Despite the difficult situation," Deripaska wrote, "RusAl has not withdrawn from the responsibilities taken on together with RusHydro to complete the building of the Boguchanskya Hydroelectric Plant and the Boguchansk Aluminium Factory in the Irkutsk region." He added later that "the building and subsequent functioning of these factories carries enormous socio-economic importance for the development of Western Siberia,"[177] as if Putin was not already aware of this importance.

In light of these "circumstances," Deripaska requested the bank to extend the loan into 2013, concluding, "I ask you as the Chairman of the Supervisory Board of VEB to support RusAl's appeal to VEB and other government banks."

Across the top of the letter, in large, spidery script, is Putin's inscription: "To I. I. Sechin. Consider and report back."

The loan was not extended, but several of more than a dozen similar requests addressed either to Putin or to senior members of his cabinet that year were fulfilled—including a request to apply leverage on the government of Guinea, which was suing Deripaska over his aluminium interests there. Putin approved an additional handout of nearly $1 billion to Deripaska's struggling GAZ auto production sector, and an $8.3 million to BaselCement Pikalevo.

In that light, the eventual fate of the Pikalevo factories themselves is also revealing of the mechanisms Putin uses to ensure that key assets go to the people of his choosing.

The public spectacle of Deripaska's humiliation in Pikalevo was followed by revelations of a whole slew of monetary favors from Putin. But even this ambivalence wound up concealing a more complicated process by which, gradually, Putin was in fact trying to unify the three factories of Pikalevo.

There were at least two reasons why this was happening. On the surface, it was clear that Putin had to recognize, as did the workers themselves, that a production process built around three joined units could not function efficiently as long as those units belonged to different owners.

But as often happens in Russian business, an ulterior motive may have played a role in the public spectacle of Pikalevo—and in a quieter development that occurred long after the town drifted out of the public eye.

In the summer of 2011, the PhosAgro chemicals holding moved in to take control of the Pikalyovskaya Soda plant in Pikalevo—the potash production unit that was one of the three connected factories in the town. No one paid much notice of the takeover, because it was hardly representative of the bigger picture.

But according to a source in BaselCement Pikalevo, the June 2011 purchase of Pikalyovskaya Soda by PhosAgro from Alexander Bronshtein was actually part of a longer-term project to eventually unify the plants. That summer, the source said, speaking on conditions of anonymity, negotiations were already underway for PhosAgro to buy out the two other plants as well—including the Pikalevo Alumina Factory, which was still part of Deripaska's Basel empire. By that autumn, PhosAgro was in talks with BaselCement to form a joint venture that would control the alumina production plant.[178]

The company's role in unifying the three factories is significant for another reason: the chairman of the board of one of its subsidiaries is a senior official in Putin's government.

It was no accident, after all, that Putin handpicked Denis Manturov, Deputy Minister for Industry and Trade, to head a crisis committee on Pikalevo immediately after his own visit to the town—as chairman of the board at Apatit, Manturov had a vested interest in expanding the company. Far from posing a risk as a conflict of interest, from Putin's perspective Manturov's position as a state official and a financial beneficiary served only to cement his loyalty on both fronts.

How an association that would appear to be conflicting by many Western standards turns out to be not only acceptable but even necessary has less to do with Putin's preference for personal trust and more to do with historical and geographical necessity—a necessity that went far beyond the Soviet planned economy.

In fact, the very idea of managed capitalism—applied normally as a critique of Putin's regime and seen as a vestige of Soviet rule—was integral to the very creation and survival of the Russian empire's expansion.

In 1558, when Ivan the Terrible gave Anika Stroganov and his three sons a mandate to build a salt mine in the Urals, he had to sweeten the deal with a degree of autonomy unheard of in Europe at the time. Too far away to ensure security for Stroganov's enterprise, Ivan mandated that Stroganov keep his own army and establish customs, and entrusted foreign trade to him alone, creating what was, for all purposes, a state within a state. It was a level of trust that only a minister could equal, and by giving so much, the collateral was raised as well—not just the land and property of the vassal, but his very life, if not his soul.

Carried over into the modern sense, the fiefdoms are not regulated by laws, which carry little weight in distant realms where local customs and geography render them obsolete. But to ensure that these "states within states" do not break away and trigger the disintegration of the country itself, they must be regulated through personal trust and favor—not just by state officials, but by businessmen close to state power.

Chapter 11

In Favor

*If you plan to lie down under the Kremlin, then be
prepared to have the organ of your personal worth
amputated. If you want to be free, do not get involved with
the Kremlin.*
—**Stanislav Belkovsky**

*In the past, whenever I had the need to meet with the
president or the prime minister, I would get in within seven
or ten days. So I hope nothing has changed.*
—**Mikhail Prokhorov**

1.

IN SPRING 2011, billionaire Mikhail Prokhorov, a young oligarch
who earned his fortune as a partner of one of the original Seven
Bankers, Vladimir Potanin, was shown clear signs of favor for his
loyalty, his efficiency, and his penchant for saying all the right things
during President Medvedev's liberal regency: he was given a small,
personal fiefdom in the form of a pro-business political party—and
an apparent green light to campaign for a parliamentary mandate.

Jailed oil tycoon Mikhail Khodorkovsky showed the world
what happens when a Russian oligarch falls out of favor. But the
story of Mikhail Prokhorov showed an oligarch who dabbled in
politics with the Kremlin's blessing—and managed to retain his favor

despite a scandal that shook the political establishment.

Less than three months after it was given to him, Prokhorov's little fiefdom would be snatched away. But the pill would be sweetened later with the apparent permission to run for president against Putin, albeit as a candidate unlikely to get more than a few percentage points.

In summer 2011, Prokhorov's ascension to the leadership of *Pravoye Delo*, or Right Cause—which the Kremlin had covertly (it was an open secret) cobbled together from the ruins of Russia's fractured, perennially leaderless liberal opposition—raised eyebrows and hope. Over the last decade, the liberals had proved that they couldn't even unite around their opposition to the Kremlin. That their newly chosen leader was a businessman with a modicum of charisma and, most of all, had the apparent blessing of the Kremlin, suggested there was the chance of a liberal party for the first time since 2003.

But that one hopeful signal in the 2011 political season ultimately turned into a disgrace for everyone involved: during a convention in September, Prokhorov was ousted from his own party by what he described as "raiders from the Presidential Administration."[179]

It was a practice he knew well from his business days, he said when he called a snap press conference on September 14, the day he learned that party delegates were being barred from their own convention by strange men with ties to the Kremlin. An experienced businessman who knew what "raids" were and how to fight them, he was not about to kowtow to bureaucrats in the Presidential Administration.

"I'm disbanding the executive committee," he said, ostentatiously picking up a pen and signing the dismissal to the cheers and applause of the journalists.

The gesture—made to a frenzy of camera shots—heartened the supporters crowded in his oval office on the top floors of his Onexim Group building. But if there were any illusions that Prokhorov was about to become a genuine opposition force, they were utterly shattered by one question from the barrage that cut through to the heart of the matter.

"Does Putin know?" someone asked.

2.

It took less than five days for Prokhorov, who had set his sights on the post of prime minister and who was dubbed by supporters as "the Tsar and god" of his party, to temporarily disappear from the media amid whispers of another Khodorkovsky affair. For two months, he remained in the shadows, as if his fate was being decided and his usefulness analysed amid growing dissent from that same middle class the Kremlin was coveting so much. When he re-emerged in early December as a presidential candidate, the news was welcomed by whatever constituents he had—and it was clear that he had remained in favor. The real effect of the Prokhorov scandal in September 2011 was to lift the curtain and demonstrate, for all to see, the "kitchen" of how politics is really played, the strings that were attached to the players on the stage, and the small group of people—no more—who were privy to take turns holding the strings.

The key director of that drama wasn't Prokhorov at all. It was an official that Prokhorov had at one point mistakenly identified as a bureaucrat executing someone else's will. Vladislav Surkov, the first deputy chief of staff and Vladimir Putin's ideologist, was no mere official. In a power structure where Putin's ministers and aides were delegated the task of allotting assets to the right vassals, the realm of political fiefdoms was overseen by that strange dark bird, a master manipulator, and a one-man PR machine who was credited with standing behind every major and minor mystification in modern Russia.

Transferred to the Kremlin in 1999 after a series of executive PR posts in Mikhail Khodorkovsky's Yukos empire, Alfa Bank, and Channel 1 television, by 2004 Vladislav Surkov had successfully positioned himself as the Kremlin's gray cardinal, a role vacated first by the disgraced Boris Berezovsky in 2000, and then by one of Berezovsky's protégés, chief of staff Alexander Voloshin in 2004. Surkov did this from the quiet post of first deputy chief of staff, a position he occupied without change for more than a decade, until he was reassigned following the tumult of the December 2011 parliamentary elections.

A pale, dark-haired, dark-eyed half-Chechen once described as cherubic and demonic all at once,[180] Surkov stayed in the background even as he dabbled in avant-garde literature (there is a recording of him reading Allen Ginsberg in English, while in 2009 he wrote a fairly decent novel, maddeningly switching from denying to accepting and then denying again its authorship). Early on he revived the Soviet Communist Youth tradition by creating an army of young Kremlin supporters—postmodern acolytes of Putin's personality cult with a darker side that allegedly included outright thugs (who may or may not have been the ones who beat journalist Oleg Kashin nearly to death in 2010).

Surkov saw straight through to the heart of power, grasping early on that there were only two instruments of ruling Russia—the mystical and the economic. Putin, he repeated in several interviews, was sent to Russia by God to save its people.[181] As for political parties, Surkov seemed to view them as businesses to be efficiently managed and the masses as mindless, slavish, and ultimately ungrateful bioresources in the government's grand mission to better their lot. As the invisible hand that helped create the pro-Kremlin United Russia, he once harangued party functionaries in 2002 as too old and bureaucratic, instructing them to treat their posts as "a job in a firm. If you have been invested in, then bring profit!"[182]

As the organizing force behind President Medvedev's Skolkovo innovation hub (an attempt to create a Russian Silicon Valley from the top), Surkov summed up exquisitely the spiritually edifying role in which state power saw itself in relation to both its people and its natural resources: "We need positive creative energy. Extracting it from society is the aim of the new policy."[183] Poet Alexander Pushkin once called the government Russia's "only European," a government that assumed a mission to civilize and Westernize the unwilling masses. Surkov seemed happy to assume that divine arrogance as a matter of policy. Russia must be "like Sweden," he once said in response to one of my questions about building Skolkovo,[184] but the top-down attempt to modernize such a huge country meant that everything and everyone had to be kept under control. To that end, he held regular (weekly, some say) meetings not just with members of his pro-Kremlin youth group, but with the heads of federal television stations and newspapers. If Putin's propaganda ever had a name, it was Surkov.

Like Putin, he was deeply committed to maintaining the façade of democratic institutions that had existed as mere props in the

Soviet era, only to get refurbished with a more realistic gloss under Yeltsin. Whether or not they would ever develop into the real thing, for now they were an important component of Russia's PR policy to present itself as a vibrant, investor-friendly developing market that had a place in all the right international clubs (like the G8 and, eventually, the World Trade Organization).

Armed with that understanding, Surkov went about forging his "sovereign democracy" doctrine: a curiously cynical, eclectic ideology of empire-building based on money, the exploitation of resources (human and hydrocarbon), and the contemptuous haughtiness that has historically characterized the Russian government.

Through it all, however, he managed his political sphere—the "democratic" façade of Russian power—very much in accordance with how Putin ruled the country: as a patrimonial dominion to be partitioned at the pleasure of the sovereign, and only among those who could be entrusted with "managing" the assets.

"You talk about democracy while [eyeing] our hydrocarbon resources,"[185] he once told journalists in 2006, describing his managed democracy doctrine.

One of the tasks that this modern-day Machiavelli had been charged with by Putin was the successful implementation of a two-party system (managed, albeit, in the only way that Putin could understand "efficient" political parties—from the top). There had been several attempts to create a successful, managed opposition party: prior to the 2003 parliamentary elections, Surkov brought in a clever firebrand nationalist, Dmitry Rogozin, to head the *Rodina* (Motherland) party. When Rogozin grew too outspoken and ambitious, he was quietly removed to the distant, albeit respected post of Russia's envoy to NATO in Brussels. His party was co-opted and absorbed into the moderately socialist *Spravedlivaya Rossia* (Just Russia) for the 2007 parliamentary elections.

Creating a successful opposition party was still very much on the Kremlin's agenda during the presidency of Dmitry Mevdevev, when Vladimir Putin nominally moved out of the Kremlin and into the White House, the home of his cabinet.

By 2010, parliament still failed to represent the one group that Putin and Medvedev were increasingly keen on courting: the entrepreneurial middle class, liberal, innovative, and pragmatic.

United Russia—an army of pro-Putin functionaries who made up the constitutional majority—had never managed to live up to Surkov's vision of an efficient, modern political force and was increasingly failing at adequately representing the coveted middle class. The two nominal opposition parties—Gennady Zyuganov's Communist Party and Vladimir Zhirinovsky's nationalist LDPR—were there to absorb the anti-Kremlin sentiment among the working class, provide perfunctory criticism, and then cast a few token dissenting votes. And the increasingly confused Just Russia, serving an important function of drawing votes away from the Communists, was doing too poorly in the regional elections to be taken seriously.

There was another reason why the government was in need of a liberal party. Ever since taking the presidential seat in May 2008, Putin's anointed successor, Dmitry Medvedev, had exhibited a consistent pro-Western, liberal rhetoric, exhorting law enforcement to "stop scaring business," promoting innovation, and passing laws easing criminal persecution of economic crimes. The pro-business elites that were now gravitating towards Medvedev included some powerful figures from Yeltsin's "Family"—such as his daughter Tatyana Yumasheva, and the former chief of staff, Alexander Voloshin, now a businessman on the board of directors of Norilsk Nickel. If they couldn't have a liberal president to represent their interests, then they at least needed a liberal prime minister, or an influential political party.

What to do?

The Kremlin administration had already co-opted the liberal Union of Right Forces, joining it to two other politically cleansed oppositionist parties—the Democratic Party, which was snatched from under former prime minister turned Kremlin critic Mikhail Kasyanov in 2005 in a similar "takeover," and the obscure pro-business Civil Force. The party included all the prominent liberals—people who had initially supported Putin in 1999 but turned staunchly against him when their interests diverged. But it also included more pragmatic and powerful members, like the Yeltsin-era reformer Anatoly Chubais—the one who apparently brokered the Kremlin-sponsored merger in 2008, and Leonid Gozman, an experienced party functionary.

The key problem, as often in Russian politics, was money. The Union of Right Forces was apparently some $7 million in debt from its previous parliamentary campaign, and this circumstance ultimately convinced the core of its long-time members, including Leonid Gozman, to agree to the forced merger organized by the Kremlin administration.[186]

But if the party were to pass the 5 percent election threshold to make it into the State Duma, it also needed a leader who was charismatic, rich, and influential enough to get the vote. In other words, given Russia's realities he had to be a rich boyar well liked in court, and not just a professional politician. And he had to be trustworthy enough to build a successful opposition party without actually opposing Vladimir Putin's leadership in any real sense.

Who to pick, and how?

3.

For the members of Right Cause, now on regular speaking terms with the Presidential Administration (a fact that that has never been officially confirmed but that no serious politician on either side would dispute), the evident favor from the top was seen as a chance to finally move into Parliament.

"To have any chances of getting into the Duma, the party had to be given to someone who could serve as an alternative to United Russia," Leonid Gozman told me.

And the targets were ambitious: during the spring of 2011 the party made overtures to Finance Minister Alexei Kudrin, whose power, along with that of fellow cabinet minister Igor Sechin, was seen as rivaling that of Medvedev. When the invitations were declined, another cabinet liberal, Igor Shuvalov, was offered the job. But he too apparently refused.

The choice eventually fell on Mikhail Prokhorov, and it was easy to see why.

By the age of 46, Mikhail Prokhorov was a businessman who always seemed to find himself in the right place at the right time. Born to a high-placed sports official in the Soviet government, he had studied international economics at the Moscow Financial Institute, where he became close friends with Alexander Khloponin, who would go on to become a regional governor. In 1991, Prokhorov first met Interros founder Vladimir Potanin and went on to become his junior partner as they founded Oneximbank just two years later.[187] Potanin would become one of the authors of the loans for shares program, acquiring controlling shares of Norilsk Nickel in 1995, thanks to the deal.

Throughout Prokhorov's career, good things seemed to stick with him, while bad things hardly made a dent. He walked out unfazed from a 2007 scandal in the Alpine resort of Courchevel, where he was briefly detained in connection with a prostitution inquiry,[188] with no charges pressed and the incident merely cementing his image as a party animal. And in August 2008, just before the global financial crisis crashed Russia's stock market, he sold his stake in Norilsk Nickel to Potanin for $6.5 billion in cash and $3.5 billion in other shares.[189] After the crisis, Prokhorov was reported to be sitting on some $5 billion in cash.[190] He even purchased the New Jersey Nets (now renamed the Brooklyn Nets) basketball team in 2010 for $200 million.[191]

According to some sources, Prokhorov's candidacy was apparently suggested by two people who had each played decisive roles in the Yeltsin family: Putin's former chief of staff Alexander Voloshin and Yeltsin's chief of staff and son-in-law, Valentin Yumashev. Both were reputedly firmly entrenched in a circle of business interests keen to groom Medvedev for the 2012 presidency. Showing that the feelings were mutual, Medvedev had even appointed Voloshin to head a committee to develop the International Financial Center in Moscow.

Their endorsement—and the fact that Prokhorov was increasingly joining delegations of businessmen traveling abroad with Medvedev—clearly meant that Prokhorov suited Medvedev and his camp as the head of a potentially pro-Medvedev party. There was no question that he suited the career functionaries within Right Cause: with his estimated $18 billion fortune, Prokhorov would reportedly dole out some $26.5 million for the party's Duma campaign, funds which would not be returned to Prokhorov after he was ousted.[192]

But there was another reason that Prokhorov presented an ideal choice: whatever his closeness to the liberal camp, he was clearly an oligarch firmly tied to Putin.

"I have heard that Medvedev had been asking for a party for a long time, and Putin would not agree," a well-informed United Russia member, speaking on conditions of anonymity, told me after the Right Cause debacle in September. "Putin's resistance played a key role. And that was why he wouldn't allow [Finance Minister Alexei] Kudrin or [First Deputy Prime Minister Igor] Shuvalov to head it, as Medvedev wanted. Prokhorov is closer to Putin than to Medvedev. He could have played a double agent."

Mikhail Prokhorov's favor with the state was evident. In his office, he kept a photograph of himself towering over Vladimir Putin, with the prime minister looking particularly diminutive next to Prokhorov's six-foot eight-inch frame.

Like any oligarch, the ties were monetary and pragmatic. But a telling exchange between Putin and Prokhorov in early 2010 demonstrated both their informal friendliness and Prokhorov's evident loyalty and deference to Putin.

On February 24, 2010, Putin was giving one of his ubiquitous dressing-downs to a whole group of oligarchs for their failure to invest in the country's energy infrastructure. Under a deal clinched in 2008 during the partial privatization of Russia's electricity monopoly, United Energy Systems (UES), several businessmen got shares of energy companies that were part of the UES holding. The condition was that they pledged to invest sufficient funds in their renovation. And Putin, remembering the debacle of the loans for shares program, was ever keen to ensure that promises were kept. During that particular meeting, Putin threatened fines (up to 25 percent of the investment program) and even criminal prosecution. In particular, he singled out energy companies owned by Prokhorov and his former partner at Norilsk Nickel, Vladimir Potanin.

Putin's remarks about Prokhorov were not as much scathing as they were humiliating in their revelation of the oligarch's closeness to power.

"He is not feeling bad economically. As they say, he has 'cashed out.' He has money. He's visiting various offices. He dropped by to see me recently, I have very friendly relations with him," Putin said in an offhand way in the televised remarks. "He's looking for ways to apply his resources. But the responsibilities he's taken on earlier, they have to be fulfilled!"[193]

At that time, Prokhorov happened to be in Paris as part of a business delegation accompanying Medvedev. Asked about Putin's comments, he offered an unbelievable explanation: "The chairman of the government was evidently given the wrong documents about the investment program," Prokhorov was quoted as saying.[194]

But Prokhorov's explanation upon his return to Moscow left no doubt about where he stood in relation to the prime minister, and his unwillingness to jeopardize that position. When it was made public that Putin was paying attention—and that he had "all the information" he needed—the businessman, when pressed, literally took his words back. "We are in close contact with the Energy Ministry," a repentant Prokhorov said. "The prime minister is fully informed."[195]

Aside from that awkward incident, the ease with which Prokhorov could apparently "drop by" to see the prime minister continued unchanged.

On April 1, 2011, Putin "sponsored" Prokhorov's latest business initiative—a hybrid car with the unlikely name of "Yo-Mobile"—by gracing it with his very presence (much as he did with the Lada car in August 2010, when the televised image of Putin driving it through Siberia—despite outrageous ridicule on the internet—did more for its sales than any traditional ad campaign could ever hope to achieve).[196] Though Putin chided the car for its name, the fact that he was pictured driving it alongside Prokhorov sent a powerful signal advertising not just Prokhorov's product, but Prokhorov himself as a grade-A investor by virtue of his sheer closeness to Putin.

It was clear, then, that whatever effort was put into masking the Right Cause party's dependency on the Kremlin and however much they touted its independence, Prokhorov could not have headed a political party without Putin's specific approval.

There is even some evidence of when this approval took place. On April 28, just a few weeks after the "Yo-Mobile" stunt (weeks that apparently included several meetings with Putin) Prokhorov reportedly met with President Medvedev, and though the meeting was not recorded officially, Medvedev made no secret of his talks with Prokhorov. "After he formulated the idea, we talked about it with him," Medvedev said in a June 24 interview, just days before Prokhorov was elected to head the party. "And he said that he really feels the current situation isn't fair. He believes he has potential."[197]

According to various sources, Prokhorov had a private meeting with Putin immediately after his meeting with Medvedev, on the same day. "It's clear that these meetings took place back to back," Belkovsky, who maintained close ties with key members both of Right Cause and the Presidential Administration, told me. A source in Right Cause told me he knew the meeting with Putin had taken place and approval had been given by both parties.[198]

Once approval was obtained from all parties, a process coordinated, as such things normally were, by Vladislav Surkov, Right Cause was given the green light to elect Mikhail Prokhorov.

4.

By the time Prokhorov announced that he would be heading the party on June 16, the rest was a formality. He officially joined Right Cause at a convention on June 25, and just minutes later was voted its leader by 107 out of 110 delegates. Boris Nadezhdin, the party's former leader, proclaimed Prokhorov "Tsar, God, and military commander" to a general sense of relief that the habitual autocracy necessary to move anything forward in Russian politics had been restored to the party.

A massive billboard campaign followed on Moscow's streets, picturing a pensive Prokhorov over the slogan "Right is might" and emboldening hopes that a new, viable party was in the works.

Right Cause's PR strategy seemed both to flaunt its Kremlin blessing (as the only factor that would ensure its entry into Parliament) and deny it—for acknowledging it outright meant admitting that any politics that occurred in Russia did so at the bidding of the Kremlin. Thus, Prokhorov reportedly assured his supporters that he had agreed to lead the party on four conditions: unlimited access to federal television channels, guaranteed immunity for himself and his business, guaranteed immunity for everyone that he brought into the party, and even the post of prime minister if Right Cause were to garner enough votes in the parliamentary elections.[199]

It took less than two months to test whether a puppet party could turn into the real thing. It couldn't.

In August, Boris Nemtsov, who had gone on to co-chair the unregistered Parnas democratic party along with former Prime

Minister Mikhail Kasyanov after leaving Right Cause, warned Prokhorov that he was clearly underestimating Vladislav Surkov.

"I've known Prokhorov for a long time, we have good relations, and I think that he made a big mistake by agreeing to head a puppet party," Nemtsov said in public comments. He added that the party was being "handled" by Surkov—a fact that Prokhorov surely could not have ignored when he announced his conditions for heading the party, for his constant communication with Surkov about the party was later publicly confirmed.[200]

But tensions came to a head when Prokhorov apparently started interpreting the third clause of his conditions—immunity for those he brought into Right Cause—a bit too literally. One of his most controversial moves and arguably the decision that cost him his party was introducing Yevgeny Roizman, a former Duma deputy and an anti-drug crusader, as a candidate for parliament from the Right Cause party. It was a candidacy that did not have approval from the Presidential Administration, and it was easy to see why.

Roizman founded the City Without Drugs foundation in his home town of Yekaterinburg in 1999. The foundation was notorious for the brutal rehabilitation regimens used to treat drug addicts—but also for reducing deaths from overdoses in the city by 90 percent.[201] A rugged, streetwise poet, he managed to muster 40 percent of the votes to represent his region as an independent parliamentarian in the federal State Duma in 2003. As a deputy, he served on the State Duma Security Committee and advised the government on its anti-drug program. But his image as a non-conformist earned him easy enemies, and his methods made him difficult to get along with. Prosecutors even tried to have his parliamentarian immunity revoked in 2007 over a fist fight with an opponent during a live debate.[202]

For Prokhorov, who was grooming Roizman for anti-drug minister in his "shadow government," the crusader was a man of action who could draw votes. But for the Kremlin, he was clearly a liability—a man with that kind of record could not easily be managed, and a free radical in a party that had the Kremlin's blessing to be in the Duma did not mesh with the very premise of "managed democracy." Though Gozman and others inside Right Cause would tell me that Prokhorov made a number of unpopular personnel decisions and undermined his authority with a diluted ideological platform, Prokhorov's insistence on keeping Roizman on the ticket ultimately led to his standoff with the Presidential Administration.

Roizman himself attributed it to the Kremlin's concern about his popularity. "I think that with our joining, [the party] started getting more [potential votes] than they expected," he told me. "Prokhorov started surrounding himself with independent people. It is impossible to pressure him. They started fearing that it would get out of control."

By early September, rumors were circulating that Prokhorov would leave the party.

And so it was no surprise that on the first day of the party's convention on September 14, party functionaries widely seen as loyal to the Presidential Administration barred Prokhorov loyalists from the convention. A mysterious group of 25 "dead souls" that no one among Prokhorov's supporters had heard of appeared on the party tickets and were to be voted on that very day. In a desperate bid to salvage his position at the party Prokhorov called a snap press conference to remove the upstarts, insisting that he was not going anywhere despite rumors and reports that he had already been expelled.

If Prokhorov was aware that day of where the disfavor was coming from, he did not show it. As if he still hoped to strike a deal with Surkov, he blamed the takeover on a single administration official by the name of Radi Khabirov—ignoring the administrative chain of command in Russian political structures that made such bold initiative unlikely for such a low-placed official. Asked repeatedly about his negotiations with Surkov, he was forced to admit that they were taking place, but pretended to see nothing out of the ordinary about having to discuss the plans of a purportedly independent political party with the first deputy chief of staff officially responsible for managing Russia's domestic political scene.

He dodged the question the first time. But when the barrage kept coming he was forced to admit his talks, evading what exactly Surkov was getting at.

"I have not discussed this situation with Surkov. I can say that yesterday Surkov invited me and simply asked to tell him about the preparations for the convention. Nothing was being approved with anyone. Yes, I had a meeting with Surkov, and I informed him about the convention."

When I pressed Prokhorov about the party's closeness with the Presidential Administration, he continued to deny it.

"It appeared that way to you, not to me. I've always said that I made decisions in this project myself, and I dealt with the party myself."

Asked about Putin and Medvedev, Prokhorov unwittingly revealed his key miscalculation in the whole affair: that the pressure coming from the Presidential Administration was merely the arrogance of bureaucrats, that having the backing of both members of the tandem, he just needed one meeting to explain to Putin and Medvedev what was happening, and his problems would go away.

"Does Putin know?" someone asked.

"I don't know. I will try to inform all the political figures."

"What will you do if you learn that the initiative that you leave this post is coming from the country's leadership?"

"This is pretty easy to determine. And we will determine it tomorrow.... I just want to figure out what happened."

5.

The next day—September 15—everything spilled out into the open. Prokhorov quit the party and, seeing that he had nothing to lose in his dealings with the Presidential Administration, lashed out at Surkov in an attack not seen since Mikhail Khodorkovsky's fateful criticism of Vladimir Putin in 2003. If Prokhorov could not save his party, then he could at least dismantle the façade that he seemed to have been fooled into keeping in place for so long.

"I have felt with my own skin what a political monopoly is, when someone calls you every day and gives you all sorts of orders, tries to introduce his own people into the lists, pressures regional headquarters, and takes party members arriving in Moscow straight to the Presidential Administration for talks," Prokhorov told his supporters even while Kremlin loyalists were voting him out of office and approving their own party lists at a separate, breakaway convention.

"There is a puppet master in this country who has privatized the political system. His name is Vladislav Surkov. As long as people like him control the process, politics is impossible. I will do everything to get Surkov sacked."[203]

It was an emotional outburst unprecedented for an oligarch who had less than twenty-four hours ago shown the utmost deference to that very puppet master. Something had occurred on the night of September 14 that changed Prokhorov's tone.

By most accounts, after the press conference Prokhorov met with Surkov once again for talks that lasted until two in the morning. There is no official account of what was discussed, but according to the most plausible version, Prokhorov told Surkov outright that he would take up the matter with Putin and Medvedev directly. Surkov, in his casual way, indicated that he might do as he liked. But what he apparently did not say was that it would be of no use.[204]

Prokhorov tried to get an audience with Putin as early as Wednesday, September 14, but the audience was reportedly denied. After the decisive announcement on September 15, Prokhorov publicly stated that he would try to meet with Putin.

Asked how exactly he would try to get Surkov sacked, Prokhorov mentioned "public political methods." And right afterwards, he said, "I've already called the reception of the president and the prime minister and asked for a meeting. They have a busy schedule, I hope to meet within seven to ten days." In another interview, he would accuse Surkov of "misinforming"[205] Putin and Medvedev—a classic example of the idea of the Tsar being misinformed by his boyars.

This was possibly the most revealing remark in the entire Prokhorov affair. For the fact that he tried to get through to Putin and Medvedev just hours after calling Surkov a puppet master indicated that however independent Prokhorov thought himself to be, he understood exactly where the real favor was coming from, and that without it politics would be closed for him—no matter how much money or popularity he could muster.

"In the past, whenever I had the need to meet with the president or the prime minister, I would get in within seven or ten days. So I hope nothing has changed."[206]

But something evidently had. A week passed, then ten days, and Prokhorov still had not been given an audience. Medvedev never commented on the matter at all. On September 25, Putin's press secretary, Dmitry Peskov, told media that Putin had no plans to meet with Prokhorov. There was no further evidence of any meetings with

Putin or Medvedev. Russia's youngest and most promising oligarch no longer seemed to be welcome at court.

6.

It was tempting that autumn to compare Prokhorov's fate to that of Khodorkovsky—with the obvious result that where the latter utterly lost Putin's favor, Prokhorov's fall from grace was temporary. He was favored and trusted enough eventually to be allowed to run for president—and he would retain the backing of Alexei Kudrin, the former finance minister who would remain a close ally of Putin even after his resignation in September 2011.

Indeed, despite initial fears that Prokhorov would share the fate of Mikhail Khodorkovsky, no signals that the oligarch was fair game were ever given. The reason may be that Prokhorov's defiance went no further than calling Surkov a puppet master, and though he promised to stay in politics, he remained out of the limelight. For a while, he declined requests for an interview and was rarely seen speaking to the media.

Prokhorov's evident distance from the Kremlin certainly didn't help his business. By late September, the Kremlin had him kicked out of the Presidential Commission on Innovation and Modernization, where Surkov was a prominent member. In October, bureaucratic red tape that delayed road construction for his "Yo-Mobile" factory in the Leningrad region was interpreted as a possible consequence of the Kremlin's cold shoulder. Reports appeared that Prokhorov's Onexim Group might sell its shares in the Yo-Mobile venture, but these were denied by his press service.

Then, amid unprecedented public dissent that started gaining momentum after the December 4 parliamentary elections—elections where Prokhorov would have won a seat were he still head of Right Cause—he suddenly announced that he had taken "the most important decision of [his] life" and decided to run for president. Sources close to the Presidential Administration called this a Kremlin project intended to absorb disgruntled middle class voters, but Prokhorov countered cheekily that the Kremlin was a project of his instead.

The oppositionist *New Times* magazine described witnessing a dramatic scene on December 9 in which Prokhorov answered a call on his mobile, turned pale, and said it was Putin. "It's okay, he asked me to run for president. I thought I had problems," Prokhorov allegedly said.[207] But Prokhorov denied that the incident ever happened, as he would staunchly deny any interaction with Putin that winter.[208]

"Since the convention, I have not been able to get an audience," Prokhorov told me when I asked him in late January. "When I understood that I would not get an audience, well, I started acting according to my own plans."

When pressed about the rumors, he conceded that there was a stereotype that everything that happened was orchestrated by state power—and that he was trying to break out of that stereotype.

"What if we're all a project of Putin? If the mass rallies were allowed, then were they a project of Putin?"

"They were a concession," I said.

"Well, don't you think that my appearance on the political scene was yet another concession?"

His denials were logical—even if Putin had asked him to run, admitting as much would diminish the whole point of courting a middle class increasingly dissatisfied with Putin. Still, his campaign strategy too clearly shied away from direct criticism of Putin—and when I asked his campaign manager, Anton Krasovsky, directly about Prokhorov's talks with Alexei Kudrin, the self-described mediator between Putin and the opposition, he said there was nothing wrong with the connection. "I'm for continuity in state power," he told me.[209] Soon after, the Central Election Commission accepted his two million petition signatures—in an unspoken sign that Prokhorov's candidacy had the blessing of the Kremlin.

Given the approval of his presidential bid, there was clearly no retribution intended against Prokhorov. Even if there was, it did not approach the caliber of what was done to Khodorkovsky for his seeming "treason." This is interesting if we want to understand what exactly a Russian oligarch has to do to lose his sovereign's favor. For his attack on Surkov, Prokhorov was let loose, deprived of the privilege of "dropping by" to see Putin—and even that for just a short time. But Khodorkovsky was imprisoned in a Siberian jail, deprived of his multibillion-dollar oil empire, and hit with a string of impossibly arcane and mind-numbingly absurd economic charges that an international team of lawyers have been unsuccessfully fighting for a decade.

The key difference is in the extent to which Prokhorov and Khodorkovsky broke the unspoken rules.

Eight years after Khodorkovsky's arrest, there is still little consensus, really, about what exactly sent him to jail. Out of the gargantuan efforts of Khodorkovsky's defence team on the one hand and Kremlin propaganda on the other emerge two explanations, the first only slightly more accurate than the second: from the perspective of the West, Khodorkovsky went to jail because he criticized Putin, while from the Russian perspective, Khodorkovsky went to jail because he stole money from the government.

Both explanations stem from the same fallacy: Khodorkovsky's supporters focus on the illegal nature of the persecution, arguing that Putin "broke the law" to take revenge on his rival. The Kremlin, of course, argues that Khodorkovsky "broke the law" by stealing taxes.

But there were no laws to break, there were unspoken rules, the *ponyatiya*. Take, for a moment, Khodorkovsky's behavior in 2003. Feeling he had atoned for the "incestuous" acquisition of his oil assets in 1995 by making his company more legally transparent and efficient than any other in Russia, he undertook to build a transnational oil empire. Inspired by the merger of the Russian oil company TNK with British Petroleum, he made an agreement in April 2003 with Roman Abramovich's Sibneft for a merger that would create a $35 billion company that could pump more oil than a small Gulf state. The Kremlin initially backed the deal—until it became clear that Khodorkovsky was not about to defer to the government. That summer, Khodorkovsky started courting ExxonMobil and Chevron Texaco for a mega-merger that would make him the head of a transnational corporation.

And he seemed to assume that his luck in expanding his company by legal means gave him a mandate to reform the country just as he had reformed Yukos—forgetting that the country was not his to reform. Pyotr Aven, Putin's close friend from his time in St. Petersburg and later the chief of Alfa Bank, told an American journalist that Khodorkovsky was "openly going around Moscow saying they would like to buy one third of the Duma to be able to block an institutional majority."[210]

It is widely believed that two factors—Khodorkovsky's criticism of Putin for corruption during a meeting in February 2003, and his support of the Communist Party (believed, for a time, to be the only genuine oppositionist force to the Kremlin)—sealed his fate.

But Mikhail Kasyanov, who served as Putin's prime minister at that time and then fell utterly out of favor for his staunch position on Khodorkovsky—and who would never see his opposition parties allowed anywhere near the election process—suggested that the problem was not one of "opposition" *per se*, but one of agreeability.

Kasyanov told me in an earlier interview that he had asked Putin what Khodorkovsky was doing wrong, and the answer had surprised him.

"It wasn't a question of [him funding] liberal or not liberal parties. It could have been the other way around. The main problem [for Putin]—and this surprised me—was that besides the legal support that businesses could give political parties, the business had to obtain secret approval from the president for this activity. It didn't matter what parties were approved or not. What was important was that this permission be obtained."

In other words, criticizing Putin on corruption or even funding the Communist Party alone might have been enough to make him unwelcome at court, but in itself it didn't bring about the partition of Khodorkovsky's oil empire and his imprisonment. Rather, these moves were part of a whole complex of actions taken by Khodorkovsky—actions that, interpreted in the context of an eighteenth century court, amounted to an open attempt to wrest power. Khodorkovsky seemed to be making clear that he refused to compromise with Putin, refused to negotiate, and refused to be loyal because he had a better vision for Russia than Putin, and he was bent on using his capital to put that vision into motion. It was this—and not funding a particular opposition party—that ultimately spent Putin's patience. "I have eaten more dirt than I need to from that man," Putin reportedly told BP chief John Browne in a private remark shortly before Khodorkovsky's arrest.[211]

Because neither democratic institutions nor laws could guard against these kinds of attempts to wrest power, the key governing factor to ensure against revolution in Russia was personal trust. Built up with staunch displays of loyalty and agreeability, personal trust determined the extent to which a businessman could continue to extract rent from his fiefdom. There was a certain archaic logic to this that Khodorkovsky and Kasyanov, both insistent on taking Russia's constitution at face value, did not take into account: having obtained these assets from the state, the businessman was ever at the mercy of the state with regard to those assets, and given the personalized power that ruled in the absence of institutions, he was virtually at the personal whim of the ruler. Interpersonal relations and personal sympathy determined who got to own what.

"Throughout 2003 our differences with President Vladimir Putin were increasing, especially with regard to pressure on business and on Mikhail Khodorkovsky [in particular]," Kasyanov said of his own diminishing relationship with Putin. "I knew what the results of my remarks could be, and that is why I began to criticize," Kasyanov explained. Though it was more logical for a prime minister, who had to work for the president on a daily basis, to be favored based on personal agreeability with the president, the same mechanism was also at play in the relationship with businessmen.

In the case of Prokhorov, his eagerness to meet with Putin after the Right Cause debacle revealed the extent to which he had internalized this unspoken rule of agreeability. Unlike Khodorkovsky, he had made only a small miscalculation: that Surkov himself had been entrusted with managing the political realm for many years. He took pains to maintain his loyalty to Putin, and went after Surkov alone—who would be demoted from his post as deputy chief of staff amid the political unrest in December 2011.

In Khodorkovsky's case, his refusal to compromise cost him his business empire and his freedom. In Prokhorov's case, it only cost him his party.

Prokhorov, however, played his cards right, and remained in favor. He walked away from the scandal with his assets intact, and with the evident blessing to continue dabbling in politics. He would, of course, lose the presidential elections in March 2012. But he would go on to create the Civic Platform party—whose candidate, Yevgeny Roizman, would win an unprecedented mayoral election in his home city of Yekaterinburg in September 2013. With his party vocally critical of many government measures, and aiming for the federal parliamentary elections slated for 2015, it was a promising start.

But the September 2011 debacle over Right Cause—by demonstrating just how cynically managed politics in Russia were, by shattering the illusion of political theatrics—served to contribute to the protests that would spill over that winter.

Chapter 12

The Regent

1.

ON SEPTEMBER 24, 2011, President Dmitry Medvedev was struggling to say something. He looked manically, feverishly happy—and not because Prime Minister Putin had just suggested that he head the United Russia party. It was as if he had finally overcome and disposed of an inner burden weighing on him.

"Considering the offer to head the party list… and my readiness to get involved in the practical affairs of the government,"—a slight pause, for the president had made his decision and was about to speak, was about to say what so many had wanted him to say—"I believe it would be right for the convention to support the chairman of the party, Vladimir Putin, as candidate for president."[212]

There was a slight gasp among the journalists, although it would take at least a month to process and articulate the betrayal that many of them didn't yet know they felt. But just one room away the huge sports arena filled with 11,000 United Russia deputies, delegates and functionaries, reverberated not with cheers, but with a wail of relief so passive and high-pitched that one couldn't tell whether the sound issuing from these loyal members of the Duma was one of triumph or surrender.

The announcement on September 24 came earlier than expected, although it was clear that party functionaries, ministers, officials, and businessmen were struggling with the suspense.

It surprised no one, although the idea of a soft-spoken, technocratic lawyer president, Dmitry Medvedev, handpicked by Putin to hold his place as president in 2007, had filled many people, particularly the kind who would go on to demonstrate against Putin, with hope: move over, pseudo-autocrat, we are not children or lackeys to be ruled by the cold terror of your eyes; we do not want the personal rule of an alpha dog, but the institutional governance of a president as an elected guarantor of the rule of law.

That too had a sixteenth century precedent: soon after Ivan the Terrible separated Muscovy into the lands of the sovereign (the *oprichnina*) and the lands of the aristocracy (the *zemschina*), Ivan "abdicated" again in 1575 and appointed a Tartar prince, Simeon Bekbulatovich, to rule in his stead. For eleven months, Ivan the Terrible kept up the appearances of a loyal subject of Simeon even as he clearly continued to wield power. The causes of this masquerade remain a mystery to this day, but historians suggest that a vicious power struggle—between hardliners who wanted a return to the *oprichnina* and more progressive boyars in the Godunov family—pushed the increasingly paranoid Ivan to temporarily distance himself from the throne.[213]

Putin's anointment of Medvedev in 2007 was motivated only in part by a desire to install a reliable placeholder for the presidency, which Putin could not assume for a third consecutive term without changing the Constitution. The idea of a placeholder was too risky if Putin was bent only on returning to the Kremlin—it would have been much easier to hold a referendum in 2007, changing the Constitution. That suggests that the entire Medvedev project may have been partially a response to a similar, under-the-carpet struggle—albeit one that did not involve bloodshed. With Medvedev, Putin was placating the budding business and middle class, giving them a leader he thought they could identify with, and delegating the task of upholding the legal-rational state to a lawyer that he could trust.

Putin was also separating out his own *oprichnina*—establishing a realm of nominal rule of law (Medvedev) while maintaining traditional forms of rule through personalized power, shock, and awe (Putin).

By doing this, he was confusing the constituents of both realms—the cosmopolitan, educated members of the elite, the people who lived and functioned without relying on the state, remained skeptical. And the rest—particularly those millions whose government posts represented their very livelihood—were growing tired of constantly having to figure out who the boss was, and what game he was playing.

On September 24, when Putin took the stage for a second time, his party eagerly took up his speech for their campaign program without as much as a discussion, joking that it would save time on having to devise their own. Their leader had delivered his most supreme instructions and order had returned to their lives.

Speaking to journalists after the announcement, the United Russia functionaries didn't show a hint of self-consciousness concerning what they said about their leader: it occurred to no one but the journalists just how Soviet their words sounded, how reminiscent of the Communist Party.

But this wasn't mere obeisance to their leader, it really did sound like genuine relief over the key decision in their careers and their jobs having been made for them.

"Vladimir Vladimirovich's program gives us an opportunity to go calmly into the regions, it gives us a plan, a strategy to solve people's problems," Andrei Vorobyev, head of United Russia's executive committee who would go on to become governor of the Moscow region, told journalists.

When I asked him separately about the decision, he made it clear that party functionaries—the ones who by law were supposed to nominate leaders and candidates for president—had little to do with it. Like a thunderstorm after a drought, it had come from above.

"That was the decision that was made," he said with a smile. "That's life. The demand was there, this was the news [we] wanted."[214]

Delegate Alexander Nikitin, chairman of the Tambov regional parliament, didn't even try to mask his outright flattery. "Vladimir Putin is our leader. He is our guide. We orient ourselves around him. So what happened today is absolutely logical and obvious. We are happy to be his contemporaries."

I asked him if the party would have accepted the decision if it had been the other way around—with Putin as prime minister and Medvedev running for a second term. But the question seemed to stump him. "The decibels of applause were equally directed at the prime minister and the president. The party would support…" he paused, and corrected himself—"has supported the decision that was made."[215]

Just the previous day, I had probed one of the more astute United Russia members to share what her colleagues were talking about. Fresh from a meeting with Putin, she was beaming—she couldn't find the words for a moment, but then it all came out: in spite of herself, she was "amazed" by the extent of his knowledge, the "precision" of his reaction. This experienced, insightful political expert, who had criticized Putin in the past, was in awe of what she had found at the pinnacle of power—and it was hard to imagine that the awe did not color her perceptiveness.

"People in the party have a firm position on this. That Putin is the leader. He is ours. With Medvedev it's different. We respect this person, but he's not the leader," she explained, asking not to be quoted by name. "It's not that a decision [where Putin doesn't run for president] is unacceptable. It's just something they wouldn't understand. Everyone is waiting for Putin. They want him."

Just a few months earlier, at the height of the collective neurosis that the prolonged indecision had thrown the body politic into, one Konstantin Zatulin couldn't take it anymore and openly spoke out in favor of Putin against Medvedev—only to lose a key post on the State Duma CIS committee.

It would be a betrayal, he said, if Putin did not run for president.

"I didn't call Putin and his friends to consult about what I was going to say about him. Whether Putin now supports me or not, or in what form, whether he gives me a village out of generosity—that's not what I'm thinking about right now," he explained to me then. "I don't want to live in a country where the vice president of the United States dictates who should and should not run for president," he said of Joseph Biden's recent praise of Medvedev that barely went short of endorsing him for a second presidential term.[216]

These Duma deputies were easy to understand. Their careers had just been secured. And they did not see themselves as independent legislators and lawmakers, but as servants of the state charged with the impossible task of translating the most supreme instructions of the living law into a semblance of rules that could work on a local level.

But if Putin did not betray them, he had betrayed his other constituents.

2.

On November 20, Putin, as was his wont, decided to visit a martial arts match. After a close victory by Russia's Fedor Yemelyanenko, Putin, whether from his sincere love of sports or as an ill-timed PR tactic, went up on stage to congratulate the winner.

There were cheers as he appeared onstage, but then amateur videos that showed up the next day on YouTube demonstrated something very strange: as Putin started speaking, the sound was punctured by boos and whistles. It wasn't clear what, specifically, caused the jeers—whether it was Putin himself or something else about the match entirely. By the end of his speech people were cheering again, and the incident should have been forgotten.

Except that it wasn't.

The kind of jeering that most elected politicians easily brush off after sports events and even public gatherings was far more significant for an autocrat whose power rested on a mystique of fear and transcendence. Even as Putin's spokesman fumbled with unconvincing explanations that the jeers weren't directed at Putin, his denials only fed into the damage. One of Putin's most virulent opponents, the rising star of Russia's opposition, anti-corruption blogger Alexei Navalny, called the incident "the end of an era," sparking a collective neurosis that in itself was more significant than the jeering.

The jeers struck a chord with a part of society that first felt betrayed by the manipulation of the Mikhail Prokhorov scandal— when the Kremlin dangled a candidate in front of these constituents and then petulantly snatched him away—and then was humiliated by a smug Vladimir Putin telling his subjects that he and Medvedev had decided "years ago" who would rule them.

And so, when the Duma elections were predictably rigged on December 4, the routine violation, which had been largely ignored in the past, drew tens of thousands of these educated cosmopolitans onto the streets—enraged by the injustice of a leader who lived by "understandings" while forcing them to live according to the law.

Their protest against the rigging was only a pretext, for in essence their rallies were personal: they were tired of a Tsar who pretended to be a mere politician when it suited him—the Tsar who had irrevocably violated his own transcendence in their eyes; they no longer feared him, and he must be deposed.

"We are standing at a moment of critical change," Stanislav Belkovsky, a well-connected former Kremlin strategist said after a glass of whisky just days before the second mass protest rally of December 24—where tens of thousands of fledgling citizens turned up to inform Putin that he was a used condom. "The idea of the government as an overwhelming, didactic force is over."

With one foot in a tradition that did not allow for state power to admit mistakes (for a god did not make mistakes) and another in a fragile new world where a besieged politician struggled to improve his ratings, Vladimir Putin maneuvered back and forth, moving to embrace the dissenters and then turning back to scowl at them.

One of the first things he said during his last phone-in show on December 15, 2011, just five days after an unprecedented protest rally of tens of thousands of people urged him to leave power, was how pleased he was to see them.

"I really did see young people on television, mostly young, active people who have a position, who are formulating it. This makes me glad," he said. "And if it's a result of the 'Putin regime,' then that's a good thing."

But then he did an about-face, saying many demonstrators had been paid to show up and singling out opposition leaders, blaming them for trying to import Ukraine's Orange Revolution to Russia. And then he was pressured into making his most damning comment, for the moderator asked him specifically if he saw any symbolism in the white ribbons worn by demonstrators.

"To be frank, when I saw something on people's chests, I'll be honest—this is inappropriate—but I still thought that this was a promotion of the fight against HIV, that, if you'll pardon me, they had pinned contraceptives."

The comment may have been intended for others—for those still loyal to Putin, who needed the aura of fear to function and to trust power, and who needed a signal that Putin wasn't about to take a bunch of pampered Moscow hipsters seriously. And there was still that ancient Russian scapegoat, the foreign agent:

"Of course, there are those who have a Russian passport, but act in the interests of foreign states. We'll try to establish contact with them, but sometimes that's impossible." For those who did not heed reason, Putin threatened force—but with a half-baked, postmodern subtext: in part imitating the Jungle Book's dreaded Indian python, Kaa, and in part imitating a caricature of himself, he raised up his palms, looked sternly at the audience, as if pretending to hypnotize them, and said, "Come hither, Bandar-logs!"[217] referring to them as the scatter-brained monkeys in Kipling's *Jungle Book.*

Through the oprichnina he created, the realm of "understandings," and the nominal realm of the "rule of law" which he had appointed Medvedev to lead, he was destroying his own mystique. By anointing Medvedev as his successor to conform, in letter, to the Constitution, only to return for a third term in 2012, he had tried to justify the autocracy, the unaccountability of the sovereign, with the one idea it could never be justified by—the idea of democratic institutions.

Putin tried to appeal to this new middle class he had created, but his calls that they use the courts, the laws, and the institutions to get their demands met were not having their effect. They didn't just want a new election, they wanted Putin gone, personally and viscerally.

PART IV
THE SOVEREIGN AS
GOD

Chapter 13

The Cult

Imagine that the government is the husband, that state power is the husband, and that all of us—society—is the wife. In 2000, our society married Vladimir Vladimirovich Putin. Society voted for him and said: Vladimir Vladimirovich, be our husband, care for us, protect us, and give us work."
—**Vasily Yakemenko,** head of the Russian State Agency for Youth, in a seminar with the pro-Kremlin youth group, *Nashi,* December 2011

The Russian people does not want to be a masculine builder, its nature defines itself as feminine, passive, and submissive in matters of state, it always awaits a bridegroom, a man, a ruler."
—**Nicolas Berdiaev,** religious philosopher, 1915

The long-hoped-for bullet was entering his brain.... He had won the victory over himself. He loved Big Brother.
—**George Orwell,** *1984,* 1949

1.

IN THE SUMMER of 2011, Katya Obraztsova, a student from the Novgorod region, decided to put her creativity to good use. She painted her face, got on all fours at one point, and sang passionately, desperately even, about wanting to be Vladimir Putin's dog.

"I want to be your Connie, on the desk and on the balcony."

The video confused the blogosphere when it started making the YouTube rounds that summer. For the past decade, girls had been singing about their crushes on the president, displaying a personality cult that had turned overtly sexual. But this video, set to the music of a Subways song, seemed to have crossed the line: no one was quite sure whether it was just one of a multitude of Putin fan clubs getting creative, or an indirect attempt to smear the prime minister and future president.

I had the same doubts when I tracked down Katya. She turned out to be a former member of the *Stal* (Steel) youth group, a militant off-shoot of *Nashi* (Ours), a Kremlin-funded youth organization. She left the group and started her own fan club called Girls For Putin, she explained when she met me with her colleague, Maria Aleshina.

No one seemed to have told them to start the fan club or sing about Putin, but there was a high likelihood that their spontaneous efforts were rewarded. According to Katya and Maria, a bunch of girls got together and started brainstorming a video that would both support Putin and be provocative enough "hopefully" to catch his attention. While they insisted it was their own idea, they said they had sent the final product of their collaboration to Vasily Yakemenko, the head of the State Agency for Youth and the informal leader of *Nashi*. When he did not reply, they took it as his tacit approval.

"We don't deny that we're attracted to Putin," Katya said. "We don't deny that we're doing this to express our fantasies," Maria added.

But what they wound up expressing went beyond a mere crush on a powerful person. In the video, which featured several girls, there were alternate scenes of one dressed in a school uniform and an office suit. All of that came off, and at one point Katya, in case the lyrics were not suggestive enough, was shown on all fours on a desk, and then stumbling down a highway with a portrait of the prime minister and a bottle of whisky. If this was a fantasy about Vladimir Putin, then it gave off a tinge of willing self-debasement and death.

If Katya struggled to articulate the parallels she had unconsciously expressed in our conversation, history had already done it for her.

The punk group Barto, which had earned a name for its provocative, witheringly critical songs, had already taken that fantasy to its bloody conclusion with its 2011 song, "KGB":

Fucking fed up with living from salary to salary.
I'm surrounded by assholes, and they're not even rich.
It's time to change something in my life.
I want to lie down under a colonel of the KGB.
Being behind him is like being behind the Wall of China.
Order. Abundance. Eternal peace.

The video was set to graphic scenes from the 1992 film *Chekist*, about a Bolshevik secret police officer in the early days of the Revolution, who, after watching thousands of counter-revolutionaries shot in cellars on his orders, goes insane and himself pleads to be shot. As social commentary, Barto's video went beyond what girls like Katya thought they wanted Putin, a colonel of the KGB, to do to them. You can talk all you want of order, abundance, and peace, the song seemed to be saying, but what you really want is death.

And that was only natural.

In 2000, when Alisa Kharcheva was a seven-year-old girl, she had momentarily confused the name of her new president with the word *pautina*, or spider web—the abode of the *pauk*, a creature that she feared. She denied that the president's name had inadvertently imprinted an image of fear in her mind, but this random association somehow remained one of her most vivid memories of Vladimir Putin.

In September 2010, as a first year journalism student at Moscow State University, Alisa Kharcheva posed in white lingerie for an erotic calendar to be presented for Vladimir Putin's birthday. Vladimir Putin was pleased with the gift.[218]

The calendar, which appeared on bookshelves just a few days before Putin's birthday on October 7, 2010, featured twelve female journalism students wearing semi-provocative lingerie, with a dubious message to "Vladimir Vladimirovich" next to each one. The caption for February read "How about a third time?" while the March girl complained, "You put out the forest fires, but I am still aflame!" Another expressed a wish to "personally" congratulate Vladimir Vladimirovich on his birthday, and offered a mobile number (which turned out not to work). Alisa's was possibly the most innocent of the twelve: "You are the best!" her caption read. The calendar quickly became a bestseller, with over 100,000 copies distributed.

But for the educated, urban, and often oppositionist milieu that the journalism faculty belonged to, servility to a government headed by a former KGB officer was unacceptable; that this servility acquired an outright erotic dimension was enough for ostracism. Alisa got dirty looks from the university faculty; there was talk of penalizing the twelve girls who took part in the project. As if to cleanse the tarnished reputation of the student body, an oppositionist group released their own calendar, featuring girls (fully clothed) with their mouths taped to suggest that their freedom of speech was suppressed, asking Putin candid questions like "Who killed Anna Politkovskaya?"

Alisa never really understood what was wrong with expressing her support for the prime minister with an erotic calendar. For her, posing in lingerie was a perfectly natural way to demonstrate her love to a national leader who had been around almost as long as she could remember.

"I don't understand people who think it is wrong to love Putin," she confided in October 2011, just a week after Putin announced his decision to return to the presidency. "I don't understand anything about politics. I'm studying to be a journalist and hopefully someday I will understand what it is about. I like him as an image and as a personality. We have the same type of dog. He's just… charismatic. When I watched him on television, I always liked him as a man, his outward appearance… not a man as a sexual object, no, but just his appearance, as pleasing to the eye. So why not?"

Kharcheva was no mindless cog used in a Kremlin campaign to buff up the image of Russia's national leader. But nor was she self-aware enough to understand what, exactly, she was doing—and she certainly wasn't channeling a crush on the prime minister to make a political statement.

In other words, the twelve girls posing on the calendar were recruited and used—but not for a centralized campaign originating from the Kremlin.

The way Alisa Kharcheva described it, she was drawn into the project by a mutual friend of the publisher, a journalism graduate named Vladimir Tabak who had set up his own publishing business called "Faculty."

"The friend asked me, how do I feel about Vladimir Putin? I said, 'quite positively, why?' And he asked if I'd like to pose for a calendar to support him and to wish him a happy birthday. I said, 'of course I would.'"

Alisa's "of course" reveals two telling facts. On the one hand, a young, beautiful student found the opportunity to don stylish lingerie in a professional photo shoot as a fun and perfectly natural way to support a politician. At the same time, she was admittedly entirely apolitical.

For Alisa, Putin was not a politician but a leader that she regarded on a more personal level. "I think a lot of people my age feel the same way and don't get into the details," she said. She "loved" Putin, in other words, but she could not quite articulate what exactly she loved him for.

Aside from his image being "pleasing to the eye," Putin as a leader was also an inevitability. "It's not that he specifically has given me something, but if we are well off, then he must be running the country well. Among my friends, family, and acquaintances, I have not heard anyone speak badly of him."

It is quite plausible that aside from a permanent, inevitable, and unquestioningly benevolent presence, Putin had not appeared much in Alisa Kharcheva's thoughts at all—apart from being pleasing to the eye. But when she was recruited to pose in the calendar, the experience didn't seem to ascribe to her a political position—because there was nothing political to articulate. What, then, of the "friend of a friend" who came up with the idea of selling a calendar with lingerie-clad girls dedicated to the prime minister, and presenting it for his birthday? Was it his own initiative, or was he playing into a top-down personality cult crafted in the offices of the Kremlin and touched up to assume just enough trappings of postmodernism to distance the rebranded Russian national leader from his Soviet past?

2.

The first evidence of Putin's personality cult began to appear as early as 2001, a year after he was elected president. They were unusual trappings, and it was an unusual personality cult. People started hanging his portrait in their offices without anyone telling them to do so. Pictures, statuettes, and other paraphernalia were being sold in subway underpasses, not because it was obligatory, but because there was a market for it. By the end of the year, a limited edition pin-up calendar entitled "The Twelve Moods of Putin" became so sought-after that one of the two artists, Dmitry Vrubel, was getting phone calls from people begging him for a copy.[219]

It looked more like a pop fad than a cult, but it was a power cult nevertheless—for its focus was a human being who held a monopoly on the use of force. What was unusual about it was that it centered on a leader who didn't really demonstrate the kind of charisma or authoritarian traits one would normally see in a power cult—unless it was the habitual cult that upheld a monarch ruling by divine right. Most importantly, this personality cult differed from those around the Soviet leaders Lenin, Stalin, and Brezhnev in two ways: it occurred in a media culture that, however limited, still vigorously criticized the leader, and, while displays of affection were certainly encouraged from above, most of them came from below.

In fact, the most notorious artefact of the Putin cult was initially meant as a joke, until it hit the radio airwaves in 2002:

A man like Putin, full of strength
A man like Putin, who won't drink
A man like Putin, who wouldn't hurt me
A man like Putin, who won't run away!
I saw him on the news last night
He was telling us that the world has come to a
crossroads
Someone like that is easy to be with
And now I want a man like Putin.

These words were no heartfelt address at a party congress. Instead, set to a trance music dance rhythm, they constituted a hit single by the girl-group Singing Together—whose name was a nod to the Kremlin youth group, Walking Together (later to be renamed *Nashi*). Singing

Together was a project by poet and songwriter Alexander Yelin, and the project was clearly a joke—recorded for just $420, it hit Top 10 radio within four months.

As Yelin explained to me years later, he intended the song as a mockery of the cult behavior he was seeing around him, but when it was picked up by the radio, the song began fueling the cult itself, almost becoming its anthem.

Aside from the semi-official pro-Kremlin youth group *Nashi*—which engaged in flashmobs, demonstrations, book burnings, and sometimes harassment—there now appeared a number of seemingly spontaneous, unrelated fan clubs for Putin, indirectly connected to *Nashi* via social networking sites and mutual friends.

"Putin—he's one of a kind, he is ideal! In the past there was a Tsar, and now there's Putin, he's like God to me. To me he's like dad," seventeen-year-old Vika Matorina, one of the "new fetishists," gushed in June 2007[220]—to eager coverage from the oppositionist press.

Originating from below, these initiatives blended with the perpetual images of Putin on state-owned television, ostensibly generated from above: his hands-on involvement in the economy, his fishing trips, his horseback riding, his judo, and his theatrics with oligarchs like Oleg Deripaska. (A public stunt in August 2011, when Putin dived into the Black Sea to retrieve an ancient Greek amphora, backfired badly and even forced his spokesman to admit the amphora was planted.) If the latter could easily be defined as Kremlin propaganda, then the former resembled a commercial product placement campaign. Those involved in it were not marketing Putin—they were using his brand to market either their products or themselves. But not only were they unwittingly creating a cult, they were also serving as proof of its very existence across a wide enough portion of the collective psyche—if Putin didn't strike such a chord, he wouldn't have been such an effective marketing tool.

Throughout 2009, spontaneous commercial efforts to cash in on Putin's name had sprung up across several retail sectors: following the notorious Putinka vodka brand which arrived on store shelves in 2003 (and claimed, like all the others, to have nothing to do with Vladimir Putin), entrepreneurs had tried to appropriate the Putin brand for the name of a bar, a club, and even a jar of baked beans (the jar was removed from my desk by thoughtful colleagues a day before Putin's visit to our office). More surprisingly still, decades after the more fully-fledged personality cults for Soviet leaders were supposed to have inoculated the population against these seeming vestiges of a totalitarian past, the spontaneous, ironic, and often unauthorized gimmicks actually paid off, generating, in the case of a canned vegetable brand, an increase in revenue by as much as a quarter.

The Astrakhan Cannery—which produced the jar of baked beans I had on my office desk in 2009—is one example of this approach. In 2007, the company started producing canned goods under the PUIN brand. Company management insisted the name was merely an abbreviation. But in the logo, the letters PUIN appeared on a two-headed eagle—Russia's state symbol—with a sword in the middle, in the manner of a "t." So the inscription not only clearly read Putin, but the logo itself clearly resembled the sword symbol of the FSB. The company management denied the obvious Putin reference for a reason—by insisting on the meaningless PUIN abbreviation and altering the state symbol, they were getting around a law that forbade the use of such symbols for commercial purposes. One journalist described the effect: "So you buy a bottle of Putinka vodka and a jar of PUIN eggplants, sit in your kitchen, drink a shot—and suddenly your head is filled with transcendent thoughts, and you feel important all of a sudden, as if involved in state affairs."[221]

Possibly the most bizarre evidence that the cult was spontaneous was an erotic party held by the Moscow nightclub *Rai*, labelled "I want the prime minister." Despite warnings from the government that using Putin's name for advertising purposes was illegal and they would potentially be prosecuted, the party went ahead—with the nightclub's PR director, Artyom Shatrov, insisting that Putin's name was not being used for advertising purposes.

While drawing on all the traditional attributes of the power cult, the phenomenon that developed around Putin had all the trappings of a commercial brand.

"I look at Putin on television and he doesn't evoke any emotions in me," Oleg Sivun wrote in his 2007 pop-art novel, *Brands*, where Putin was named alongside Coca-Cola and Google. "He can be filled with any meaning. I try to see him as the collective unconscious, but that is too difficult and not very beautiful.... I try to see him as a shining dot, and it works. A shining dot—that is what Putin is. Putin is only that which we ourselves have imagined him to be. Putin is a product of our imagination."[222]

It was in that context of history repeating as farce, and a power cult returning as a brand, that Alisa Kharcheva found herself stripping for Putin. The friend of a friend who got her involved in the gig was a fellow student not much older than herself, named Vladimir Tabak.

By his early twenties, Tabak had graduated from the journalism department and created a successful publishing house called Faculty. Much like Katya Obraztsova, he was indirectly linked to the *Nashi* youth group—he had friends in the State Agency for Youth and had taken part in its yearly youth forum on Lake Seliger in the summer of 2010. There were even reported ties between his father and Kremlin ideologist Vladislav Surkov—but Tabak would deny this.[223]

For him, the calendar was clean, safe fun—he didn't even see it as political.

"I think a personality cult is when people kiss a leader's hand or fall on their knees in front of him," he explained to me. "Projects like these—I don't consider them a cult of personality."

The calendar, for Tabak, was a commercial endeavor that also served as a channel to express his "respect for Putin."

But Tabak also admitted, like Kharcheva, that the respect was personal rather than political.

"I'm sure Putin himself doesn't like this situation," where personality reigns in place of politics, he said. "But at this point our political system isn't developed enough."

If Tabak was trying to differentiate between Putin-themed paraphernalia and a personality cult, then he was undoubtedly referring to the one form of leader worship that occurred recently enough for at least one generation to remember it: the personality cult of Joseph Stalin.

Compare Putin's "latent" cult to Stalin's full-fledged one, and we will find one key difference, and one key similarity—the combination of which dramatically illustrates how Russians experience state power personified, and what role the media and the market play in that experience.

Tabak was wrong about hand-kissing and bowing as inherent traits of a *bona fide* personality cult, for none of those things were common around Stalin. (They were, however, common for earlier, particularly pre-Romanov, Tsars, who were venerated according to the Byzantine fashion, in the same manner as a human would worship a god: with full prostration, face to the ground—a practice that bewildered and intimidated European ambassadors who were forced to adore Russian monarchs in such a fashion. As for hand-kissing, Putin was not immune to this practice: a 2012 video caught a Macedonian monk kissing the president's hand; Putin, as was his wont, was seen flustered, trying to remove his hand with disgust.)

Stalin would be surrounded instead by worshipful speeches at party congresses, their fervour likening their object to a god:

"Thank you, Stalin. Thank you because I am joyful. Thank you because I am well. Thou who broughtest man to birth. Thou who fructifies the earth...."[224]

The key difference between the cults of Stalin and Putin is the obligatory nature of the former. While there was no controlling institution for the phenomenon that Nikita Khrushchev would go on to label as a "personality cult," party functionaries and citizens offered this kind of lip service because they had to, and the element of coercion cannot even be compared to the relative freedom enjoyed in post-Soviet Russia, even during the most repressive periods of Putin's rule.

The origins of the Stalin cult are believed to lie with his inner circle of Bolsheviks, whose group dynamics wound up spilling out beyond the Kremlin into a nationwide ideology. Stalin, historians note, distanced himself from the adulation, but that was probably only a ploy to make it more genuine.[225]

Putin, by contrast, was being marketed in the same way as a pop celebrity is—the way that a Hollywood icon helps its purveyors make money. The existence of entrepreneurs like Tabak and activists like Katya Obraztsova suggests that the Kremlin tentatively encouraged this sort of behavior even while publicly distancing itself from displays of affection. Both Tabak and Katya Obraztsova and her friends had connections with *Nashi*. They worked and spent their leisure time in the same circle—with close friends and colleagues in *Nashi*.

Tabak's activities were apparently green-lighted: he told me that he was approached by "certain people" he would not name, clearly close to the Presidential Administration, asking about his plans for the calendar. When he explained, they were satisfied and left him alone.

Another major aspect of the differences between the Stalin and Putin cults rests with the medium of expression: the power of the internet and social networking to decentralize various fan clubs and "cults"—coupled with the unprecedented criticism and hate these cults and adulation are met with in the blogosphere—make it impossible for the Putin cult to be nearly as coercive as the Stalin cult. The internet, in a way, determined the very nature of the Putin cult through viral marketing and internet trolling—rendering it voluntary, largely spontaneous, and open to derision, as the frequent hate of Putin on the internet can attest.

But what of the parallels, the common denominator that neither Tabak, nor Katya Obraztsova, nor Alisa Kharcheva would admit to, but that continue to exist?

The Bolshevik ideologues who played a role in generating adoration for their leader among the masses did not invent the cult—they channeled widespread social habits for their political ends.[226]

It would be stating the obvious to say that those social habits did not die. But what is interesting is that they have erupted with such full force despite the relatively hands-off way that the current Kremlin has channeled them. Nor has Stalin's cult, despite being officially condemned—first by Khrushchev then by post-Soviet leaders—disappeared entirely. In fact, opinion polls have reflected a positive trend in the way that Russians have viewed Stalin in the last several years. By 2012, a majority of respondents identified Stalin as the leading figure in Russia's history.[227]

But there is a more startling parallel that emerges when we return to the content of the actual messages that subjects send when they appeal to Stalin or to Putin.

"Thank you because I am joyful. Thank you because I am well," said a party functionary in 1935. In 2011, Alisa Kharcheva told me the that "we are well off" because of Putin.

The leader is good because his subjects are comfortable, not through any political or institutional affinity. And if this sounds obvious, then a far darker, more primordial element is introduced when we consider him "who fructifies the earth" and him whose mere name drives up retail sales for a completely unrelated product sold on a free market.

If food and profit emerged as one dimension of the power cult, then sex was another.

Putin's association with fertility rituals recurred on a regular basis: aside from directly calling on Russians to have more babies, he once asked a female TV anchor how many children she had and indicated she should have more. He repeated the question during a phone-in show in 2013: by that time she had three children. During an appearance at the Lake Seliger youth camp, one girl asked him how many children she would end up having—he said three. It was no wonder that girls like Kharcheva and Obraztsova found themselves expressing support for their leader primarily through a sexual channel.

The entire roster of Putin's PR "miracles"—from delivering salaries in Pikalevo, to putting out forest fires from a jet—is suggestive not so much of a populist politician, but of a sacred king who navigates the tangled, impossible universe of Russia and becomes himself an elemental force.

We first met Sir James Frazer's sacred king in Chapter 3. It is appropriate to reintroduce him now to distinguish the marketing phenomenon around Putin from those around other celebrities: in contrast to pop cults, death follows the power cult like a shadow. Katya Obraztsova's ambivalent fantasy was expressed in a mass media context where the leader is frequently accused of involvement in— or at least the tolerance of—political murders. There is no evidence linking Putin to a single political murder. But the fact that organizers of such political murders are rarely, if ever, brought to justice, and the repeated allegations against Putin, have a major effect on the popular imagination. What Putin is *believed* to be capable of doing becomes more important in the public imagination than what he actually does. The cult, thus, is both positive and negative. It is telling that when journalism students responded to the erotic, pro-Putin calendar with their own, critical one, the question "Who killed Anna Politkovskaya?" was one of the captions.

Sociologists studying the symbol of Stalin in the public imagination have noted a paradox: the percentage of people who believe Stalin to be a bloody tyrant who killed millions of people (68 percent) overlaps considerably with the percentage of people who identify him as a wise ruler who made the country thrive (50 percent). This "doublethink," as identified by political analyst Maria Lipman, points also to an irrevocable association between national greatness and violence—in the traumatized section of post-Soviet consciousness, one cannot exist without the other.[228]

In the absence of effective political mechanisms for interacting with state power, the subject or the "citizen" turned to the personal, leaving him extremely vulnerable: for in a personal capacity, the ruler could be paternal, violent, or sexual. He could "bring man to birth" or give a "knock on the head," as Putin once threatened potential troublemakers at protest rallies.

But the reverse of this is also true. In primitive societies, the office of the sacred king was dependent on one condition: when he failed to make it rain, he was slaughtered.

3.

Before returning to Katya Obraztsova, it is worth looking at how and why the Kremlin, meeting these sexual fantasies half-way, made efforts to cultivate them.

In late November 2011, as the State Youth Agency began mobilizing tens of thousands of activists of the *Nashi* pro-Kremlin youth group to demonstrate loyalty and support during the December 4 parliamentary elections, agency chief Vasily Yakemenko met with commissars of the movement to instruct them.

To motivate them, he used an ancient allegory: "In 2000, our society married Vladimir Vladimirovich Putin," he told them, according to an undercover journalist present at the closed meeting. "Society voted for him and said: Vladimir Vladimirovich, be our husband, care for us, protect us, and give us work."[229]

The words were allegedly uttered by Yakemenko, but there is evidence that he had learnt them from his *de facto* boss, first deputy chief of staff Vladislav Surkov. According to a senior *Nashi* activist close to Vasily Yakemenko, the idea of state power as the husband and the people as the wife had already appeared countless times in the regular briefings Surkov would hold with *Nashi* leaders—the activist had brought up the marriage allegory spontaneously as she described her impressions of these briefings, before I had even mentioned it myself. Clearly, it was brought up often enough and she admitted that it had made a considerable impression on her.

Surkov and Yakemenko seemed to be tapping into a powerful, pre-revolutionary myth of Russia as a bride, as Israel, and of the monarch as the sacred groom.

This should not come as a surprise in a patrimonial setting—somewhat incestuously, the patrimonial leader often combines the functions of both the father and the husband.

In Tsarist Russia, the paternal/sexual was taken to new heights. Because the Tsar was seen, essentially, as the earthly vision of God, so the country assumed the role of the church. The New Testament description of the church as the bride and Christ as the groom was applied, in Russia, to the relationship between the monarch and his subjects. This allegory persisted in odes to the Tsar and Emperor, and they reached a zenith under Nicholas I, once called "the most handsome man in Europe." The indirect idea of a marriage was obliquely referred to in the propaganda of that time, reviving the legend of how Slavic tribes called on Varangian princes to rule over them in 862, and interpreted the incident as evidence of harmony between the Russian people and their Tsar.[230] Unlike European nations, the myth went, Russians willingly called on the princes to rule over them, rather than be conquered by force.

The church allegory may have become superfluous after the Bolshevik Revolution, but the eroticized deification persisted with a new force, channeling pre-Christian cults.[231]

When I asked Katya Obraztsova about the marriage parable, it seemed to confuse her—even though her video was clearly elaborating a sexual fantasy involving Putin. "That's an unusual comparison. I would compare the people to children. [The government, Putin] is our father, and we are children. After the 1990s, the people wanted a Savior, a father, and so he appeared."

Katya Obraztsova didn't really seem to be aware of what she was tapping into. Far from a being cog in a centralized, ideological sect, she didn't seem to be getting any instructions at all. And yet she had spent three years as a teenager in an organization whose unspoken credo was to fight the opposition and support the government. How had she been recruited, and who were these girls, thousands like Katya, who were happy to offer a yearning for order and abundance to be picked up and exploited by a seemingly reluctant Kremlin? And exploited for what price?

Chapter 14
The Sect

*Surkov... is fascinating. He talks about so many
complex things. He is super well-read. But I don't always
understand what he means. Sometimes he talks about
"business angels."*
—**A member of Nashi**, 2011

1.

I REMEMBER THE girl's simple, suddenly exalted face as she stood
beating on her drum, chanting "Putin! Putin!" When she noticed
she was being watched intently, her eyes became more frenzied as
she stared directly at me, chanting with even more force as if her life
depended on it, the sound of dozens of drums both demoralizing
and strangely enchanting. She seemed to like the attention. But
when I tried to talk to her, she was told to stay silent by an older
colleague at her side.

All around me, riot police grabbed "unauthorized" anti-
government protesters, dragged them away into buses that stood
around the perimeter of central Moscow's Triumfalnaya Square, and,
once they thought no one was looking, beat them with whatever
their conscience would allow: a baton, a fist, or a boot.

It was December 6, 2011—two days into a growing revolt over
the ballot stuffing in the latest parliamentary election. The army of
pro-Kremlin *Nashi* activists stood just outside the subway, hoarse

with chanting and terrifying to behold, many of them bussed in from the nearby provinces by their Kremlin-affiliated organizers to demonstrate for a token bit of cash that the future belonged to them, and not to the more desperate-sounding protesters screaming "Down with Putin." Every time the police pounced on a dissenter and dragged him away, the *Nashi* crowd cheered. Here they were, those hypnotizing "triumphant thugs," as they were christened not just by the oppositionist bloggers, but increasingly by mainstream pundits disgusted by the rebirth of a phenomenon that had all the markings of a totalitarian youth militia. But who were they really?

Natasha Kovaleva, a chirpy, twenty-three-year-old senior assistant at the State Agency for Youth, may have felt that there was something cultist about joining a state-financed organization that got her a job, helped make friends, and was well on the way to building her life path for her. But she didn't believe it, not really. "Those are the cult members," she joked as she got off the phone with one of her colleagues.

Nor did she seem to mind the price that she was paying.

It was parliamentary election day, and Natasha, who took me to her favorite sushi chain just outside her office a few steps away from Red Square, was deliberating whether they should go to a forum where the agency's chief, Vasily Yakemenko, would instruct tens of thousands of *Nashi* activists on how to behave as they took part in demonstrations to show their support for Putin, Medvedev, and United Russia in the face of oppositionist dissent.

December 4, 2011, the day of the federal parliamentary elections, was cold, wet, dark, and bleak enough to have come out of a crime novel. Units of riot police were stationed just off Red Square, barring entry to pedestrians without an explanation, as occasional trucks filled with sleepy interior troops drove through the snowless city and groups of caped officers huddled austerely on street corners in central Moscow. It was as if a process as simple as voting held a mystical threat, as if state power, that perennial force of nature, blanketed Moscow instead of the snow that day, reminding voters of its eternal, unfeeling, and inevitable force as they pretended to take part in a democratic process.

Understanding the likelihood of tens of thousands of dissenters, the Kremlin was amassing its own force—groups deployed for their sheer numbers, crowds that would block out and dilute—and, in cases, intimidate—the protesters by their very presence.

In an organization balanced precariously between Communist Youth and the YMCA, why was a leading activist joking about how she had joined a cult?

For Natasha, a chance attendance at a speech by Vasily Yakemenko in her home town of Tula—a historical town of half a million people about 200 kilometers (120 miles) from Moscow—attracted her to the movement not so much for its promise of activism, but for its career opportunities. "There wasn't really anything cult-like about it—though I had reservations at first," she said.

Instead, like many, she had purely practical reasons to join.

The daughter of an out-of-work engineer mother who had failed to find a job after moving to Tula from Kaliningrad, Natasha found herself having to support her mother and sister from an early age. Her father, who owned an auto shop, was killed in the 1990s, when Natasha was just a child. *Nashi* didn't just offer her something to do, it set her on a career path. By autumn of 2007, she was lucky to get an internship in the Tula governor's office—all thanks to her membership in *Nashi*, she said.

The normal avenues available—local schools, clubs, or businesses, did not promise the connections necessary. But a youth organization affiliated with the state—and thus viewed with approval by local teachers and civil servants—did. At the very least, it kept young people away from drugs and gangs. And for someone like Natasha, it offered hope of Moscow. Doors would keep opening, and by 2008, she was able to come to the capital to work for Yakemenko's Youth Agency.

Once there, the confluence of work, fun, and activism that the job offered led her to stay. She didn't have to take time off to attend the Seliger youth forum, and she could count on the job's stability as she took evening classes towards a degree in economics.

It was a story that seemed to repeat itself no matter what former *Nashi* member you asked.

For Katya Obraztsova, the girl who took part in the provocative Putin video and who spent three years as a member of Steel, a militant affiliate of *Nashi*, joining the group was her only chance to get involved in activism on a local level, in a social environment where spontaneous volunteerism was rare. She had no thought of promoting a particular political movement. "I wasn't concerned about who was financing it. I liked how as an organization we were able to help war veterans. Or if there's a problem with bad roads in your town—you can do something about it through the organization."

She went further:

"It's not that the movement is doing something and I'm part of it. It's that I'm developing myself through the movement," she explained. "Say you come upon a huge forest. And the movement gives you a path through the forest. You walk that path yourself, but that path gives you direction. Otherwise you would get lost."

The direction is given by *Nashi*, by the state, and, indirectly, by Vladimir Putin.

"Putin gave us the platform for self-realization," Maria Aleshina, Katya's colleague, said.

Asked about the path in the woods, and if they felt they were being led by Putin, Katya and Maria paused. "It's not that he provides the path, it's that the movement comes from him.... I guess, then, yes, he does provide it. In the sense that it comes from him."

If the state offered them a path in the woods, it also wanted something in return.

During the pro-Kremlin, anti-opposition rally on December 6 on Triumfalnaya Square, one Sveta Kuritsina, a student at a trade school in Ivanovo, became the poster child for these activists-for-rent after she struggled to explain to a cameraman that United Russia had transformed the country because people "are dressing more better [sic]."

From the standpoint of the opposition, Sveta's fumbling, painfully naïve and badly memorized speech symbolized those "triumphant thugs" for hire: their manners, their level of education, and their non-existent political awareness. Protesters would turn up at later rallies brandishing her "dressing more better" gaffe. But then Sveta's threadbare origins emerged: her mother a textile worker, her father a driver, she lived in a meagre, hand-to-mouth world that had no room for political ideas. This explained her motivation as she chanted Putin's name in the cold for the equivalent of a few dollars in cash. And there were hundreds like her on Triumfalnaya.

Sharing a dilapidated dorm room with four girls on the outskirts of Ivanovo, she was studying to be an accountant. As she faced a bleak provincial future, she groped for every opportunity that presented itself—and when she got a chance to join Steel, she took it eagerly.[232] Sveta could be forgiven for believing that she owed what chance of social mobility she had to the state. Maybe she really did adore Putin, but that was only while she was drumming in the cold and chanting his name. As for the rest, she had to do what she had to do, and that only meant climbing a career ladder dangled in front of her by a government that, after more than a millennium, was still the dominant organizing force that "fructifies the earth."

But if the state was offering these girls a path through the woods—in exchange for beating a drum and chanting Putin's name, as Sveta and hundreds of others did that December—then where did that path lead?

2.

By 2011, *Nashi*—by sheer virtue of its affiliation and Kremlin funding—had become possibly the most reviled organization in Russia, and even some parts of the political establishment have openly criticized it. By the following year, after a spate of unprecedented protest rallies that put up the biggest challenge to Vladimir Putin's rule, the organization was all but defunct. Vladislav Surkov was replaced as chief ideologist by the more conventional Vyacheslav Volodin, while Vasily Yakemenko quit the State Agency for Youth. It seemed it was just a matter of time before something more meaningful would be concocted to take its place.

By December 2011, amid a genuinely fomenting middle class that was taking to the streets for the first time in two decades, cheerleading for the state in the manner of *Nashi*—especially for cash—symbolized, for many, the cynical, managed, and orchestrated nature of a democracy that few believed in.

But for over a decade, the group had done its thing—and subsisted on millions of dollars of government funding spent on constructing an ideology that never fully materialized.

Getting its start in 2000 as the obscure Walking Together

group, the initiative was reportedly pitched personally by its leader, Vasily Yakemenko, a former sports trainer and businessman who found himself in the Presidential Administration, to his boss, deputy chief of staff Vladislav Surkov,[233] who liked the idea of reviving a modern version of the youth groups of the Soviet Union, opening doors for its members to coveted careers in the party and the state.

But the rank and file were drawn in through much simpler means—benefits. Vasily Polovinkin, a twenty-six-year-old estate agent, described in 2012 how he was recruited as a teenager with promises of free football game tickets, discounts, and possible career options. "There wasn't any underlying idea I was aware of," he said, and he left the group because he didn't want to take part in political rallies, especially if he didn't understand the idea behind them.

Walking Together quickly became notorious for carrying out post-Soviet Russia's first book burning, as activists destroyed the novels of postmodernist writers Viktor Pelevin and Vladimir Sorokin and threatened them with legal cases. Bizarrely, the group lashed out at the writers not for their political views, but for the "depravity" and the sexual and drug-related content of their books. Touted as an independent group, from the beginning it was widely linked to Surkov, who was in turn deemed to be the only Kremlin official erudite enough and with the black sense of humor necessary to go after writers like Pelevin and Sorokin. Most *Nashi* activists had not even heard of them.

In 2005, the Kremlin reorganized the group to form a larger body called *Nashi*—still under the leadership of Walking Together's Vasily Yakemenko. In the next six years the group would target oppositionists more aggressively, with some members staging vicious flashmobs to desecrate pictures of dissenters, or hounding and harassing them with legal action. This was not a unified, top-down effort—and Natasha Kovaleva said she disapproved of many of their actions—but to what extent these moves drew on a sincere loyalist position or were more of an attempt to curry favor with higher-standing members of the team is hard to tell. Though its Kremlin sponsorship remained unofficial, most seemed to understand where the group, which would hold rallies of 50,000 each year even as oppositionist groups were being denied the right to assemble, got its protection and patronage.

During the regency of Dmitry Medvedev, the Kremlin gradually stopped denying its affiliation. *Nashi* was heavily featured at the summer career forums organized by the State Agency for Youth at Lake Seliger, which were regularly graced by Surkov and Vladimir Putin himself. In 2010, Surkov spoke at *Nashi's* national convention, and specific information about the organization's funding began to appear in the press. *Nashi* officials initially claimed that the movement was sustained by private donations from businesses—but in 2007 a defector from the group revealed that each unit had a budget of up to $12,000 a month.[234] A 2010 study of federal grant and spending records revealed that between 2007 and 2010 the government had invested well over $15 million in the group and its affiliates—the bulk of which came directly from the State Agency for Youth, which Yakemenko had come to head.[235]

But if the Soviet Union's Communist Youth rallied members around a particular ideology, in *Nashi's* case its ideology, or even a unifying idea, was hard to pinpoint. It has at various points called itself "anti-Fascist"—being initially created to fight the numerous, thuggish neo-Nazi movements in Russia. But its official title identified it as a "public organization for the development of sovereign democracy," a hazy political doctrine hatched by Vladislav Surkov. Given the fact that its most publicized activities have included the harassment of opposition figures, it is fair to call the group simply pro-government, or pro-Putin—supporting all the multifaceted, self-contradictory policies that state power in Russia can come up with.

But for the legions of its members, it was the connections, opportunities, and offers of travel that lured them into its fold.

Powerful personal connections—whether the invaluable state officials who could make anyone's career, or the friends one made from across the country—fostered a personal network that facilitated the biggest challenge for a land as large and inhospitable as Russia: forging communities. For all the notions about Russians being inherently "collectivistic," sheer distances and irreconcilable differences in value systems made effective networking and civil society hard to achieve. The very idea of organizing so many dispersed, different people was in itself so daunting that the automatic—albeit dismal—consensus was that it could only come from above—and so the Russian state occupied its traditional role in co-opting civil society. Those with a penchant for activism and no reason to be politically opposed to the state often had few easy alternatives in their communities.

But the central message one would expect from a totalitarian sect—aside from supporting the state—never materialized. Natasha, who was certainly young but not unintelligent, described being mesmerized and confused by regular meetings in the Kremlin with Vladislav Surkov.

"Surkov... is fascinating. He talks about so many complex things. He is super well-read," she described. "But I don't always understand what he means. Sometimes he talks about 'business angels.'" Natasha hadn't the foggiest idea what he could possibly mean by them, but he was apparently referring to rich people who provide start-up capital.

Nashi's lack of ideology, its pragmatic, do-whatever-you've-got-to-do-as-long-as-you're-loyal credo was no afterthought; it was a reflection of a stark, gaping and utterly postmodern lack of ideology unique to Putin's Russia as a whole.

The path in the woods had led nowhere—and a small minority was indicating to its leader that the fire of his torch had gone out—or had never been lit.

Chapter 15

The Heretics

1.

"PUTIN, I DO not want you," Olga Loseva, a journalism student proclaimed her political stance on a placard as she stood in the cold on Sakharov Prospect, at the second mass protest rally on December 24, 2011. When asked what she meant, she explained that "Putin is a bad person. [*Nashi* poster girl] Sveta [Kuritsina] from Ivanovo said she wants Putin [though Sveta Kuritsina herself said no such thing]. Well, I don't want him."

And when Artemy Troitsky, the music critic and TV host took to the stage to speak, his message, too, was personal—not political: "If a president is not doing it with his wife, he is doing it with his country!" he called to roars of applause.

They came with posters, caricatures, and hand-crafted puppets, spending all their creative energy to ridicule one man. They painted him as a tyrant, a gangster, a used condom, an orc, and a killer of children. In February, weeks before he was about to be re-elected, they came to Revolution Square to celebrate the most pagan of holidays: the welcoming of spring. To celebrate the start of Lent in Orthodox tradition, that pagan vestige was incorporated, as it was incorporated into the Catholic tradition as Fat Tuesday, as a last party before a weeks-long fast, and also as something central to the very fabric of Russian life: the burning of winter in effigy.

What they burned in effigy on Revolution Square that February wasn't just winter—it was more like the sacrifice of a sacred king.

The mass protests that erupted in December 2011 materialized like some elemental force. Every few weeks, rallied through viral Facebook posts, tens of thousands would start gathering on central Moscow squares authorised by City Hall for the staging of a protest against... what exactly?

Ostensibly, the "creative class," as those demonstrators came to be called, had been outraged by the tearing down of a democratic façade, by Putin's impudence at returning to the presidency, and by the rigged parliamentary elections that garnered a victory for his United Russia party on December 4.

But the elections were no more rigged than countless others that much of this same creative class had ignored in the past. When it immediately became clear that no amount of authorized mass protests would force the Kremlin to hold another election, they turned their attention squarely on the ruler himself. Whatever their new leaders were saying from the stage, the protest movement shared one common denominator with the pro-Kremlin activists that they called "triumphant thugs:" it was all about Putin.

On the face of it, the demographics of the protesters couldn't have differed more from the clientele that Putin was used to negotiating with. Entrepreneurs, office managers, IT specialists, students, artists, mathematicians, PR specialists, advertisers—and possibly their parents: these were the people who rarely went to the state for anything. Many of them relied on private medicine, studied abroad, sent their children to private kindergartens, and tried to stay clear of the police, unless it was to pay an unavoidable bribe to a traffic cop. They got their information over the internet, not on national television, which they despised. Each month, the money they paid in taxes amounted to the salary of a provincial teacher, doctor, or police officer. They formed co-operatives to ensure that they, and not the corrupt municipal authorities, decided how their apartment buildings were managed; outside Moscow, these first true homeowners formed land co-operatives in places where Soviet summer homes, or dachas, once stood. When they needed gas infrastructure, they had the clout and the money to work with local officials and get the job done.

And yet this active, energetic middle class constituted, by various accounts, less than 15 percent of the population of Russia. (Judging by salary alone, recent research from the Russian Academy of Science estimated that the middle class constituted no more than 8 percent of the population. At 59 percent the country boasted the largest class of the working poor, and according to the same research, just 19 percent of the population had a household computer.)[236]

The protesting segment of the middle class seemed to be projecting on to Putin everything they didn't like about Russians on the other side of the gaping divide: the perceived backwardness, xenophobia, homophobia—even hanging a rug on the wall became a symbol of entrenched backwardness. The passive acceptance of Putin was equated with ignorance, cowardice, and fear. By contrast, the protest class took to drinking wine at the increasing number of hipster venues popping up around Moscow. By the end of that winter, the hipster was the protester and the protester was the hipster; the ability to navigate (and afford) iPhones and drink French wine at Moscow's Jean Jaques café chain suddenly identified one as an opponent of Putin, for in that Manichean divide, where good was beautiful and innovative and technological and bad was corrupt and old and Putin, there was no other political program to identify with.

When Putin admitted that he had mistaken their white ribbons for condoms, the comment was taken as proof that Putin was not "with it" and never would be again.

And so they turned up for half a dozen mass demonstrations that were closer to carnival than politics: brandishing placards of Putin with condoms dangling out of his eyes, or a condom wrapped around his head, or even of Putin as a condom—stitched up and about to be used for a third time. Demonstrators handed out real condoms with large inscriptions on the wrapping warning that they could only be used once.

For the first time in Russia's history, an autocrat was tolerating the abuse, allowing tens of thousands of people to gather in the street and call him a used condom. It was a precarious balance that went against the very foundation of an autocracy: soon, either one or the other would have to go.

2.

At first, these "angry cosmopolitans," as Vladislav Surkov had dubbed them, had no formal leader. But over a few months, one emerged: Alexei Navalny, a young, charismatic political activist, anti-corruption blogger and lawyer.

On the surface, he was the prototype of a dynamic, Western-style professional politician—in a society where only power mattered, he had all the potential to bring politics into the equation.

First emerging as a talented young debater in 2006, Navalny gained notoriety by organizing a series of televised political debates. As a lawyer, he was bent on using existing mechanisms and institutions to fight what he saw as the country's chief ill—corruption. In January 2011 he launched the RosPil website—aptly named for the Russian slang word *pilit*, "to saw"—a euphemism for illicitly "sawing" or siphoning funds from a budget. A wildly successful internet fundraising campaign brought him hundreds of thousands of dollars that he would use to hire lawyers and experts to pursue each allegation case-by-case, meticulously tracking and battling government-level embezzlement.

Navalny first called United Russia a party of "crooks and thieves" in a February 2, 2011 radio interview—but in the coming months the slogan went viral. By the end of the year it had become so ubiquitously associated with the party of power that a good chunk of the credit in diminishing the number of votes that it garnered—rigging notwithstanding—should go to Navalny.

By 2013, his corruption exposés achieved something unprecedented: after being outed by Navalny as the owner of millions of dollars of foreign real estate, Vladimir Pekhtin, a member of the State Duma Ethics Commission, found himself forced to resign.

From the beginning, Navalny had come to represent what a better-developed democracy would have clearly groomed as presidential material. But it was a testament to the primitive nature of the fight for power in Russia that its most promising oppositionist—who had spent seven years in the Yabloko party—did not initially attempt to run for public office at the beginning of his political career. Only when threatened with a ten-year jail sentence, and a show trial that he could turn into a political manifestation, did

Navalny finally admit, in April 2013, that he wanted to be president. His campaign for Moscow mayor in September 2013—which he lost with a nevertheless impressive 27 percent of the vote—was fueled in part by his persecution by the state.

Was he biding his time, crafting a powerful image and a reputation as a successful anti-corruption crusader to reveal his cards when the moment was right? Or was he simply waiting for the government to make the first move? "This is not an election, it's a coronation. When we have real elections, I'll run," he told me during a protest in February 2012. But only Putin seemed powerful enough to give them those elections.

The Kremlin would give Moscow's protesting class a taste of such an election when, in September 2013, it surprised everyone by allowing Navalny, with a jail term looming over him, to run in the Moscow mayoral elections. Perceived as an aftershock of the protest movement that would eventually come to naught, the Navalny campaign demonstrated that if an opposition leader could ever come close to replacing Putin, his rise will be propelled by the Kremlin itself.

When Navalny's campaign kicked off in June, he had less than 10 percent of support. By the time Muscovites went to the polls on September 8, he had 18 percent. But when the final votes were counted, Alexei Navalny, a blogger and anti-corruption crusader who had emerged as an opposition leader on a wave of popular protest and had never run for office, garnered over 27 percent. It was no victory, of course, but it had nearly forced the incumbent Sergei Sobyanin, who had barely edged past 51 percent, to face a runoff.

On September 9, 2013, speaking before a crowd of about 10,000 people, Navalny tentatively took the microphone.

"If you want to know what a rock-star feels like, then first of all, it's really scary," he began. "They say, throw yourself into the crowd, but I can't jump that far. I am at a rally of tired people." Towards the end of his speech, he would say something very much in the vein of his foe, Vladimir Putin: "I love you all very much."

Navalny's campaign was as modern as anyone could have hoped for, built from the grass roots up. His campaign videos had matched and exceeded the sleekest political ads on American television. Through crowdsourcing, he had managed to raise $1 million, and draw over

14,000[237] volunteers, many of them activists from the region who were determined to put their newly-acquired organizational know-how to local use. Stickers, posters, and 1,000 cloth "cubes" bearing Navalny's photograph dotted the city; a red circle with Navalny's name in the middle, the mayoral candidate had become an easily recognizable brand. He had everything: the organizational skills, the door-to-door activism, the picture-perfect wife and family, and the presidential smile.

And yet, despite all that, whatever had taken place at the polling stations on September 8 still defied the spirit of elections. In the patrimonial state, power begets power, and power originates from the Kremlin.

It is possible that the people Navalny had managed to unite, not around a cause but around himself, understood this on some level, understood that he would never be mayor and that the only reason he was allowed to run was that the authorities knew he could never win.

Could these people see Navalny, who had united a splintered opposition, as their future president?

"If he doesn't make any major mistakes," said Oksana Savchenko, a doctor in her forties. "He's still young, he has yet to grow. He still needs to do a lot to be a people's president. There's a lot more people that recognize him now, but there is still a lot of distrust."

Petr Bakulov, a businessman in his thirties, said he wanted to see Navalny become mayor first. "Not yet," he said of Navalny's presidential potential.

But as the euphoria of the elections wore off, the reckoning began. If Navalny represented the future, then what kind of future was it?

"This future will come not as the result of a revolution by the creative masses," one of Navalny's prominent supporters, journalist Oleg Kashin, wrote the day after the rally. "It will be a future that results from the continuation of the Kremlin's strange game, the strangest episode of which were the Moscow elections."[238]

Kashin wasn't being pessimistic, he was simply stating a perennial truth: "when our President Navalny thanks us for our patience, it will no longer be possible to trust him." Not because he was Navalny, but because you could not trust any president.

If Kashin and many others were reconciling themselves to that kind of future, then what kind of present was it?

Who was Alexei Navalny? And was he the kind of leader that would eventually come to replace Vladimir Putin?

★ ★ ★

The story of the Moscow mayoral elections is a story in which Alexei Navalny played only a supporting role. This pragmatic, often abrasive debater, lawyer, and minority shareholder in a number of Russian companies who had rallied a following by launching a successful anti-corruption crusade, had been appropriated as a cog in a political game the government was playing as it juggled several different objectives at once.

In June 2013, Navalny was about to be handed down a sentence on embezzlement charges that would put him behind bars for five years. The investigation and trial had dragged on for well over two years—the charges, which amounted to Navalny advising Kirov regional governor Nikita Belykh on what turned out to be a money-losing lumber contract, had surfaced soon after Navalny launched his anti-corruption campaign in late 2010. As he was pushed to the helm of the popular street protests that broke out in late 2011, it seemed that the government wasn't quite sure what to do with him: jail him like Mikhail Khodorkovsky and risk galvanizing the opposition, or let him stay free in hopes that he would grow tired of the battle and be forgotten?

Whatever the decision about his fate, it could not have been unilaterally political. In 2012, Navalny had angered the powerful head of the Investigative Committee, Alexander Bastrykin, by revealing that he had founded a real estate firm in the Czech Republic. It was then that Bastrykin's agency relaunched a case against Navalny based on the old embezzlement allegations. It was widely assumed, thus, that the persecution of Navalny was based as much on Bastrykin's personal revenge as it was on political expediency. By 2013, the opposition rallies had largely dwindled and Navalny didn't seem to represent much of a political threat anymore, at least in the short term. The authorities seemed to be taking the careful approach: keep him free and let the trial take as long as possible, then, perhaps, hand down a suspended sentence that would, by law, bar him from public office but also let him stay out of jail. But in June, it was not clear what course the authorities would take.

Meanwhile, Moscow's mayor, Sergei Sobyanin, a Putin ally and an apparent liberal, suddenly called a snap election for the coming September. The move appeared baffling, but given several conflicting strategies the Kremlin was pursuing, it made political sense: that year, direct elections for governor had been reintroduced for the first time since 2004—in an apparent liberal concession to the protesting classes. Running for mayor prematurely (for Sobyanin's term wouldn't expire until 2014) and winning (for there was no doubt he would win) would help bolster Sobyanin's legitimacy and help deflate the opposition's claims that elections in Russia were rigged.

More importantly, it would play into a general drive towards democracy-building supported by many of those close to Putin, and, contrary to appearances, by Putin himself. As we have seen in previous chapters, Putin's government is not averse to democracy, in fact it has spent considerable resources building up democratic institutions—as long as those institutions function on the Kremlin's own terms.

When Navalny announced he would run for mayor, it was not clear whether this decision was the result of negotiations with Sobyanin's administration, or simply a desperate bid to make it more difficult for the authorities to jail him. But as the situation developed, it became evident that Sobyanin had an interest in keeping Navalny in the race. In an unprecedented move, the incumbent mayor publicly called on municipal deputies to endorse Navalny, helping him get the necessary 110 municipal signatures so that he could be registered as mayoral candidate.[239] Neither Navalny nor his campaign manager Leonid Volkov were keen on drawing attention to it, but it was a fact that Navalny would not have been able to gather the necessary number of signatures on his own. Not because of political pressure, but because most municipal deputies, mostly members of the pro-Kremlin United Russia party, couldn't consider endorsing anyone but the man in power.

These overtures from Sobyanin bolstered Navalny's popularity. But it would take another move from the government to really set his campaign in motion. That move came on July 18, when Navalny, against the hopes and expectations of many, was sentenced to five years in jail and taken into custody. Although a conviction barred him from public office, technically he would remain eligible until the conviction and the sentence took effect, pending appeals.

Navalny's arrest brought thousands of people to the streets to demonstrate just outside the Kremlin for his release. Whether it was due to the rally or, as some speculation had it, to Sobyanin's lobbying, or both, another spectacular thing occurred: Navalny was released the following day after prosecutors suddenly changed their minds about taking him into custody.

This evident indecisiveness on the part of the government galvanized Navalny's supporters. His campaign staff began organizing aggressive meetings with Muscovites around the city. His volunteers were all but campaigning door-to-door, in the best Western traditions.

As his popularity swelled, as the idea of a truly independent politician who could challenge the Kremlin began to seem possible, murmurings of skepticism began. Some of his more moderate supporters even began to question what, exactly, made Navalny so different from Putin. Always a fierce debater, Navalny had mostly resorted to figures and facts when fighting his opponents as he battled corruption. But suddenly, he had taken on an overly aggressive flair. At one point, when confronted about his nationalist views, he was borderline rude, retorting to a journalist's question with a sarcastic "Hello?!!"[240] The political analyst Nikolai Zlobin was rudely rebuked by Navalny's campaign manager Leonid Volkov for questioning Navalny's program. In response, Zlobin likened Navalny's style to Putin's.[241]

Some journalists, meanwhile, began noticing that Navalny would only grant interviews to friendly outlets. His mobile number, once accessible, would now only answer to the select few—so that it became easier to reach Putin's spokesman, Dmitry Peskov, than Putin's foe, Alexei Navalny. It seemed that the "love" he spoke about from the stage would be bestowed not necessarily on those who shared his views, but on those who were loyal to him personally.

More prominently, his popularity was increasingly becoming compared to a personality cult, with a number of fellow oppositionists likening his speech on September 9 to that of a Führer. Referring to Navalny as a "messianic" leader was becoming increasingly commonplace.[242]

What accounted for this kind of behavior from a leader whose entire program was built on opposing what he called a corrupt, authoritarian, and self-serving regime? Perhaps without noticing, Navalny and his closest supporters felt that the only way to challenge the Kremlin was to channel the same sense of unaccountability, brute force, and self-legitimization. But in part, it may have been an unconscious response to the fact that Navalny's growing popularity depended so much on the Kremlin itself. If Navalny wants to run for president in 2018—something he has admitted—he would not only have to maintain and increase his following, but fight the courts to get his conviction overturned. Given the dependency of the courts on the Presidential Administration, that would take careful back-door negotiations and the support of patrons close to Putin.

But it was too soon, and the Kremlin understood full well that Navalny's real strength posed only a minimal threat—albeit one that needed to be carefully contained, without overdoing it. Whatever support Navalny managed to get in the mayoral elections in September 2013, it was not enough to grant him even a modicum of immunity. Afterwards, the government would increase its pressure with yet another embezzlement investigation. Short of jailing him outright, Navalny was placed under house arrest and a court order forbade him to use the Internet (his wife would continue blogging from his Twitter account). Whether in jail or free, he may fail to garner the kind of political support that will be necessary to eventually propel him into any kind of office, and be forgotten. Or he may become the client of powerful patrons within the government and the oligarchy who may, through a number of government posts, eventually groom him into potential presidential material. The transfer of power to a person like Navalny can come quietly, from within the government, or it can come through revolution violent or bloodless, for Russia has seen both varieties.

3.

Back in the winter of 2011–2012, at the height of the protests, Navalny had represented a tiny sliver of hope, but one that flickered dimly and far away. Without a leader and a clear ideological platform, a carnival seemed all that the protesters had left as spring approached and as Putin's re-election became an inevitability. It was as though they themselves had accepted that Putin's return to the presidency was not the culmination of a logical set of events, but an elemental force that they could combat only by turning to the gods—"philosophical demands," as one activist described it.

"If someone knew what to do in this situation, then Putin would be gone. There isn't any know-how," Maria Baronova, an activist leader who was prosecuted for inciting mass protest in the repressive crackdown that eventually followed the demonstrations, told me in November 2012. "People who have a philosophical education, but who've never served in the army—what can they do? We're not hungry, we're not in poverty, and people who aren't hungry can't keep this up for long, making philosophical demands. You can't build a civil society on philosophical demands."

Throughout the winter and spring of 2012, the protesters seemed to be testing Putin: how brutal, how repressive are you going to get? The game of chicken that the standoff had become had turned passive-aggressive. If the protest movement had a strategy, it appeared to be to get its opponent to strike first, cause grievous harm, and discredit itself. Protesters appeared to be trying to outdo each other in creative ways to insult Putin, while Putin—in a move that is rather unprecedented for a true autocrat—continued to allow the protests to take place, all the while blaming them on the US Department of State.

With Putin's re-election, that strategy had disintegrated. Thousands signed up as election monitors, but their presence at the polling stations only exposed the mechanisms of rigging, rather than ensuring a clean vote. Looking behind the façade, seeing the people who were actually doing the rigging, and the votes that were being cast for Putin, only underscored the difficulty of institutional change, fueling the desperation.

May 6, 2012, the eve of Vladimir Putin's inauguration and his physical re-entry into the Kremlin, was a turning point. Between 50,000 and 100,000 people gathered for a planned demonstration on Bolotnaya Square, just across the bridge from the Kremlin, and despite their purported program, what was really on people's minds—even if not everyone spoke their thoughts—was physically preventing Putin from entering that fortress.

It wasn't exactly clear who provoked whom on that day—either police had deliberately made it difficult for protesters to enter a previously authorized demonstration area, or planted provocateurs started taunting riot police that they were going to storm the Kremlin. All of a sudden, frustrated protesters pushed through a police line, knocking down several metal detectors. And and a peaceful rally suddenly devolved into a mob. Protesters threw bricks and bottles at an equally belligerent police force. Police helmets floated in the river nearby.

On the embankment, strewn with litter and bloodied napkins, a group of enraged protesters chanting "We are the power" were confronted by an equally enraged riot police officer. "You are not the power, you are scum," he told them, visibly agitated. Another officer held him by the shoulders, as a man will hold a friend at bay when he thinks a fight is about to break out.

Police eventually dispersed the rally, but sporadic protests would erupt daily on Moscow's squares for the remainder of that month.

The protesting class, joined by writers, sympathizing journalists and beautiful people in general, took to the streets, insisting that they were merely taking a stroll. In the manner of Occupy Wall Street, they occupied a boulevard square in central Moscow, taking to the fashionable cafés that surrounded it.

But unlike Occupy Wall Street, there was far more at stake.

★ ★ ★

It was shortly after the May 6 rally that the repressions began. The Tsars of Russian history, for all their brutality, quartered their convicted traitors, but, unlike the English, did not publicly disembowel them. Yemelian Pugachev, who led an insurrection against Catherine the Great, was sentenced to be quartered on Bolotnaya Square in 1775. Nearly two and a half centuries later, Putin's charming spokesman, Dmitry Peskov, made a private remark that was nothing short of a historical Freudian slip: "The protesters who injured the police should have their livers smeared over the asphalt."[243] He was referring to Bolotnaya Square and the riots that had transpired there on May 6, 2012.

By June, police had raided the homes of a dozen activists. Dozens would be arrested in the following months, facing jail terms of up to ten years. Virtually the moment that Putin was back in the Kremlin, he introduced three bills toughening criminal penalties for inciting mass unrest, forcing NGOs with foreign financing to register as foreign agents, and setting up a registry that would have the power to shut down websites deemed extremist. Parliament rushed to pass all three bills within weeks. In an unprecedented move, the State Duma would strip one of its deputies, Gennady Gudkov, of his mandate for taking part in the protest movement—although the official pretext would be an allegedly illicit security business. And criminal proceedings would be launched against the most promising leader of the protest movement, Alexei Navalny—on the official pretext of embezzlement.

It was a crackdown so haphazard and confusing that it left oppositionist leaders disoriented—as though, on the spectrum of Russian history, they weren't harsh enough. "These are not repressions. These are spasms," Ilya Ponomaryov, one of the few parliamentarians leading the protest movement, told me that autumn. "This government only knows how to use instruments of petty harassment."

Indeed, what seemed to aggravate the protesters was the ideological confusion of the repressive apparatus—the targeted arrests of Putin's government appeared puny.

"What is happening is not totalitarianism. It's not democracy. It's simply insane," Maria Baronova said.

It was no wonder, then, that at their height, the protest rallies had regularly attracted monarchist groups—and these were not old ladies holding up pictures of Tsar Nicholas II. They were young people in anonymous masks.

One of them, a young civil worker named Alexei who said he lost his job for his political views, said that Russia needed a monarch who "has gone through military service." But hadn't Putin served in the KGB?

Putin wouldn't do for a monarch, Alexei said. "He is a sell-out. It is not his path." There is nothing holy in him, and therefore nothing that he can teach his people.

By 2013, little remained of a protest drive of the sort that Russia had not seen since 1989. The protest rallies would dwindle back to the marginal figure of a few thousand people. If, at the end of 2011, the government felt threatened enough by the movement for Putin to make overtures to the protesters, within a year the government stopped paying attention altogether. Many of the leaders were jailed or demoralized; Navalny was facing trial, and Maria Baronova was depressed.

And yet, one tiny, marginal group—feminist punks on the fringe of the radical art scene—had managed somehow to join the protest movement, split it asunder, and achieve the one thing that demonstrators had been craving, viscerally, all along: to provoke Putin into showing his true face.

They were Pussy Riot, the five girls who donned balaclavas in Russia's biggest cathedral and prayed to the Virgin Mary to banish Putin.

4.

The story of Pussy Riot and its significance wasn't so much about their protest art stunt as it was about their punishment—that, contrary to the group's own expectations, the Kremlin would be so sensitive to this sort of art stunt, and why.

Let us look closely at the series of events that led up to the Pussy Riot verdict, for they speak for themselves.

February 8, 2012. It is the height of the presidential election campaign. It is also a period of unprecedented dissent against Putin, with mass protests targeting Putin's "sacred" image.

Putin meets with Patriarch Kirill, the head of the Orthodox Church, and representatives of other religions. The Patriarch calls the years during which Putin ruled a "miracle of God." Whatever else he said, the meeting itself is perceived in the public eye as a blessing.

February 21. Five masked members of Pussy Riot perform a "punk prayer" on the altar steps of the Christ the Savior Cathedral, forbidden to laymen and especially to women. They ask the Virgin Mary to "chase Putin away." Their stunt is a direct allusion, as they would explain later, to the Patriarch's meeting with Putin. They are chased out but not arrested.

February 22. Archpriest Vsevolod Chaplin—a *de facto* mouth-piece for the church—condemns their act. "This is a sin that violates the law of God. The most important law. 'For the wages of sin is death,'" he tells news media, quoting from Romans 6:23.

February 26. Russian police announce that the Pussy Riot members are wanted on charges of hooliganism. Three of them are arrested the following month.

March 6. Two days after his election, Putin's reaction to Pussy Riot's performance is revealed to be "negative" by his spokesman, Dmitry Peskov, who called their stunt "disgusting."

Much is made of this supreme displeasure. Political scientist Marat Guelman tells Dozhd TV that there is "information" that the Patriarch asked Putin directly for "revenge." Journalist Sergei Dorenko tells news media of investigators who allegedly told him that they reported on the Pussy Riot case directly to "you know who."

April 2012. An investigator's statement on the nature of their crime (they were charged with hooliganism motivated by religious hatred) identified the consequence of their action as "diminishing the spiritual foundation of the State." Experts recruited by prosecutors stated that the women had violated canons decreed by the Church Council of Trullo held in Constantinople under Byzantine Emperor Justinian II in 692. The defence, in other words, did not have to call the trial an inquisition: the various members of the prosecuting team had inadvertently done so in their own words, revealing that power in Russia still came from God, and that Pussy Riot's true offence was not therefore just hooliganism *per se* (something that would warrant a suspended prison sentence at most).

June 25. Vsevolod Chaplin tells *The New Times* that "the church as a world view cannot be separated from the government just as the people cannot be separated from the government."

August 2. The trial has begun. During his visit to the UK, Putin is asked about the case by journalists. He says, among other things, that they should "not be judged too harshly."

August 13. Vsevolod Chaplin reveals that he has been in regular contact with Putin's chief ideologue, Vladislav Surkov. Surkov, meanwhile, is appointed to oversee relations with religious organizations within the government.

August 17. The three members of Pussy Riot are sentenced to two years in a penal colony. The lawyers refuse to recognize this as leniency, but it is one year less than the sentence demanded by the prosecution. The Russian Orthodox Church issues a statement that Putin should pardon the women.

October 2012. Yekaterina Samutsevich gets a new lawyer, who argues that since her defendant never managed to participate in the performance, she should be cleared. Samutsevich is freed during an appeals hearing—drawing accusations that she "betrayed" the cause by essentially admitting her guilt.

December 2013. With the option of a presidential pardon laid out by the Church itself, it was there at the Kremlin's disposal. Maria Alyokhina and Nadezhda Tolokonnikova had just two more months of jail when Putin suddenly moved to grant them an amnesty. With that kind of timing, it seemed clear that the point of the gesture wasn't to release the women but to use them in a demonstration of Putin's mercy. Just as the government's actions propelled Pussy Riot into international acclaim by jailing them, it showed who was directing the show by releasing them as well.

Thanks to the persecution, the Pussy Riot brand had exploded internationally, rivalling even the brand of Vladimir Putin. It managed to split the protest movement and discredit it in the eyes of many average Russians, who sincerely saw the dance as a criminal desecration of their religious values. Some Muscovites who attended the protest rallies would stop speaking to one another over their arguments about Pussy Riot. It was as though the possibility of religion as an ideological value had been forgotten, and that it took a protest stunt to remind people it was still there.

And yet, few would have heard the band's name had the government not launched a prosecution. Something had forced Vladimir Putin not only to notice what they did, but respond. If, as various sources close to the government claim off the record, Patriarch Kirill asked Putin directly for retribution over the incident, something must have forced the returning president to take heed. It was only logical, then, that the decision to release them in December 2013 was Putin's alone—a presidential amnesty, a pardon connoted by the same Russian word that signifies "grace."

Chapter 16

The Church, the Tsar, and the Holy Fool

In the nature of his body the king is on a level with all other men, but in the authority attached to his dignity he is like God.
—**Agapetus**, sixth century deacon, to Byzantine Emperor Justinian

It is impressive that they think so highly of the prime minister's work. But I would like to recall another of the main commandments: thou shalt not worship false idols.
—Putin's spokesman **Dmitry Peskov**, on a religious sect in Nizhny Novgorod that worships Putin as the reincarnation of Paul the Apostle, May 2011

1.

COLONEL IGOR GULICHEV, a Cossack, led me into the office of his boss, Ataman Sergei Shishkin. It was evening; for several hours Gulichev and I had been talking about what it meant to serve the Tsar, about Pussy Riot, and about Cossack patrols. Shishkin, who was relaxing with his comrades, many of them still in uniform, was in a jovial mood.

"Putin. A mace. An icon," he said as he motioned to the objects hanging behind him on the wall, as if telling me everything that I needed to know about the Cossack way.

The proximity of the objects, and especially the picture of Vladimir Putin and Jesus Christ hanging on an equal level startled me; I wanted to ask about it, but then remembered the mace and the sabre, both of which were fake, and thought better of it. Here were men who wanted to connect deeply to some form of tradition. Even if it was just through uniforms and decorative weapons, they were doing their best to believe that the Cossacks, that strange community with its mix of the ethnic, religious, and military, was still alive, and was ready to serve Russia's Tsar.

The previous day, Gulichev had struggled to dispel stereotypes about his community that he was unwittingly fueling.

"Maybe you want me to crack a whip, to cut some heads off?" he asked a group of journalists who had accosted his Cossack patrol. "Well, we don't need that. Cossacks aren't sadists, we don't like blood. But we want to defend the fatherland."

But the fact was, his patrol had turned out at one of Moscow's biggest train termini in a voluntary bid to uphold law and order—by chasing away unregistered street vendors and pickpockets. He and his fellow officers said they had been negotiating with city authorities and the police to give them the legal mandate single-handedly to detain people.

At first, the city government seemed eager to enlist Cossack help. Moscow's Central Prefecture gave them a bus and a police escort, and even helped call a press conference.

But when that Cossack patrol was accosted by an even bigger army of journalists, city authorities backed off and washed their hands of the matter, placing the initiative squarely with the Cossack community.

It was easy to see why reports of Cossack patrols had spun journalists into such a frenzy. Cossack regiments—with their ultra-conservativism and their brute force—had been active ever since Pussy Riot performed their punk prayer. Soon after the incident in February 2012, they pledged to protect churches from similar desecration. In September, a Cossack regiment stormed a Pussy Riot-themed exhibit at a gallery belonging to Marat Guelman. In March 2013, a similar Cossack raid interrupted a Pussy Riot-themed play at the Sakharov Center—a museum dedicated to the memory of the Soviet dissident. In fact, the Cossacks were directing their ire at anything perceived as Western: Madonna concerts and gay parades were the usual objects of their attacks.

But Cossacks weren't the only group to send out activists in defence of Orthodox values—they were merely the only one that had been doing it longer than anyone else, for hundreds of years.

The Pussy Riot case had split society, bringing out a whole array of once marginal ultra-religious groups like the Icon Bearers, with their mix of nationalism, statism, and xenophobia. Those disparate groups had long sought to fight for traditional values, what they saw as the Russian way of life—for years, joining forces with the pro-Kremlin youth group *Nashi*, they would be seen harassing controversial exhibits and performances. Following the Pussy Riot debacle, they were delighted and emboldened by the Kremlin's apparent overtures in their direction.

The government would turn out a whole slew of "traditionalist" bills: one banned gay propaganda, another criminalized insults against faith, although Russian law already included religious hatred in its criminal code. Russia's so-called anti-gay law, passed in summer 2013, riled the international community, but it was, in essence, part of a wider attempt to return to some ideal "Russian way" by rejecting what were believed to be Western imports.

Orthodox Christianity—and the ideal of church-state harmony—were integral to that "Russian way." In spring of 2012, Putin was shown on national television walking alongside Patriarch Kirill in a ritualized procession as the two accompanied the Iveron Icon of the Mother of God into Moscow's Novodevichy convent. As the procession was shown solemnly entering the church, a TV announcer narrated how Tsar Alexei had first welcomed the icon; on screen, it was like watching a Byzantine ritual transferred into the twenty-first century.

Long dormant, elements of caesaropapism, where a secular head of state also bore the sacerdotal status equal to a priest, began exposing themselves unintentionally. A Macedonian monk was forced to make an official apology to President Putin in August 2012 for spontaneously kissing his hand during a visit to the Valaam Monastery in the northern region of Karelia. Putin was captured on camera jerking his hand away, visibly irritated with the connotations of the gesture.[244]

For the leader of the Icon Bearers, Igor Miroshnichenko, a re-emerging harmony between the church and the Kremlin was all only natural. "In goals, in tendencies, the connection between the church and government is always increasing. Thank God, thank God. In Europe, I hear, the church and government are separate. We hope for the opposite tendency."[245]

If the "protest class" constituted just 15 percent, these guardians of the Russian way were part of the 15 percent at the other end of the spectrum, who thought Pussy Riot's two-year sentence was too lenient (33 percent said it was too harsh, and 31 percent said it was adequate).[246] The Kremlin was courting this social force, but unlike the all but defunct *Nashi* it had never created them. And an even more important difference between these groups and *Nashi* was the ideology they genuinely espoused, rooted, as they saw it, in Russian tradition.

Gulichev, a Cossack, seemed to speak on behalf of a tradition that carried deeper origins.

"They should have got more. Seven years," Gulichev told me of Pussy Riot. "A person does something, creates so much harm, and then says he's sorry. No. You need to suffer, accept grief and pain. And maybe then we'll forgive you. When you come, having gone through pain, then we'll think about whether we should forgive you or not. But first you have to suffer."

As for the protesters who had been rallying in the streets since late 2011, if Gulichev got the order, he would readily go and fight them, he said.

The Cossacks had never been an easily classifiable community. Several theories of their origins associated them with groups of escaped serfs who roamed in the southern steppes basking in the kind of absolute freedom that was only possible side by side with absolute autocracy.

"Everyone wanted to live freely," Gulichev said. "But the Cossacks did it!" Before the 1917 Revolution—which few Cossack communities survived—one could only consider himself a Cossack if he was born as one. But today, those boundaries are utterly blurred; Cossacks register into district cells not by birthright, but by identification. Cossack patrols were met with scepticism not least because many Muscovites didn't believe they were for real. Many of those with real Cossack roots disputed the very possibility of being genuine in the twenty-first century—how could someone be a Cossack when he spent his entire day in an office?

Gulichev, judging by his eagerness to serve the state by helping maintain law and order in the streets, didn't seem too happy about spending his day in an office either.

Still, for him, anyone could "become" a Cossack, much like being initiated into a club, or a religion.

"People who want to become Cossacks, they come to the society, we talk, if they accept our rules, our values," he said, "we let them in."

And the two crucial criteria were being Orthodox Christian and serving in the army. "There are those who don't serve in the army. But we won't pat them on the head," Gulichev said.

God and guns, he seemed to be saying, but in a completely different way. One could only serve God if one also served Caesar.

So much had made sense before 1917—or, at least, with the benefit of hindsight—when the heir of the Tsar, who was the steward of God on earth, was also honorary supreme Ataman, or Cossack chief. You served God by serving the Tsar. Now, of course, Gulichev didn't really know where the secular powers stood: his first floor office in Moscow's sleepy residential district of Lyublino thrived by the grace of the fact that the prefecture of that district just happened to be a Cossack too. But city authorities as a whole were playing all sorts of "bureaucratic tricks" with them, he said dejectedly.

Before he showed me out, he opened the door and smoked a cigarette through the crack, out into the November blizzard. "There's talk of the government setting up an all-Russian Cossack [association]," he said quietly. "There's word that Putin will head it."

"Will that be a good thing?" I asked.

"That would be…" he opened his mouth to pronounce what sounded, to me, like *okhuyenno*, an obscenity that meant "spectacular." But then he seemed to reconsider, stopped himself, and said instead, "that would be great."

2.

In March 2000, a decade after the fall of a dynasty, a collapse that left the country plundered and on the brink of civil war, in the wake of the abdication of a catastrophically unpopular ruler, Vladimir Putin celebrated his presidential victory in the offices of his campaign staff. According to one apocryphal account of that night, an elegant, dark-haired man presumed to be Vladislav Surkov poured a glass of champagne and raised a toast, "to the deification of state power."[247]

The same man would state on the record, more than a decade later, that Putin was sent by God to rule Russia.

Amid the increasing prominence of the Russian Orthodox Church during Putin's third term in the Kremlin, baffled Western observers tried to explain this resurgence of religious traditionalism by a Kremlin courting the church in a bid to shore up its own legitimacy, as a government would lean on the church in countries where there was an independent church to lean on. What they failed to see was a dynamic that defied and inverted the Western tradition of church-state relations, where a powerful, independent Pope fought with and used kings for his own political purposes. The Orthodox Church was no equal partner. It was, instead, an institution largely subjugated by the government, and had been for hundreds of years. It was part of a tradition of caesaropapism, where temporal and spiritual power converged in the head of state. That tradition is one of the most misunderstood and overlooked factors among Westerners trying to make sense of everything from Soviet rule to what is happening in Russia today.

When Surkov said that that Putin was sent by God to rule Russia, he was referring to a problem as ancient as life itself.

For the sake of flattery or personal enrichment or security or protection from one who is stronger than you, or for the sake of material or existential comfort, human beings will do this with regard to other human beings: they will give them money or food to appease them, they will hang portraits on their walls of those already deified or about to be, or speak, in the very presence of the human being they wish to deify, of a pressing need to make him more like God. Today, amid the mitigating forces of de-personified institutions, this is done with a good dose of irony, just as the modern nod of the head in greeting probably evolved from the gesture of falling on your face in complete prostration, anticipating and thus pre-empting harm at the hands of a much stronger member of your own species.

Whatever was happening in Russia in the twenty-first century was no spontaneous innovation. To understand its nature, we have to recognize it as part of an innate pattern of thinking about power dating back into ancient history.

Going back far enough into the primordial origins of human nature, the deification of a ruler, the power cult itself, presents us with a chicken and egg question. Was the king first likened to a god, or were gods merely kings that went down as legend?

★ ★ ★

Four hundred years ago, in the wake of the catastrophic collapse of another dynasty, as the Time of Troubles came to a close in 1613 with the coronation of the first Romanov Tsar Mikhail Feodorovich, a certain Ivan Timofeyevich Semyonov, a clerk in the service of the Tsar, sat down to write a chronicle on the Time of Troubles.

In that treatise, Semyonov, or Timofeyev, as he would go down in history books, found himself grappling with a pressing conundrum: which of the two natures of the Tsar, the divine or the human, predominated?

Timofeyev was not elaborating on the nature of Jesus Christ—although a similar question would bother theologians from the earliest centuries of Christianity. Nor was he referring to a specific Russian Tsar that he may or may not have served. He was trying to spell out, instead, the nature of the very idea of Tsardom, laying down a framework for the kind of Tsar that he thought Russia deserved.

Timofeyev was no original thinker in that regard, but given the scarcity of surviving Russian documents, his *Vremennik* offers an important insight into the logical process behind the deification of the Russian ruler.

"Although as a human the Tsar was in his essence, he is by his power equal to God, for he is above all, and none on this earth is above him."[248]

Although his predecessors had elaborated on the dual nature of the Tsar, divine and human, Timofeyev seemed to have placed the stress on the divine aspect. If the Tsar is equal to God, then equally, as God he must be sacred, omnipotent, and immortal.[249]

Born in either 1550 or 1560, Timofeyev had survived the reign of Ivan the Terrible. It was easy to see how Timofeyev and his contemporaries could be confused by that question during the Time of Troubles.

Just twenty years previously, Holy Rus had a tyrant who slaughtered his people in the name of God, but now, in the beginning of the seventeenth century, didn't seem to have a government at all. Given that Ivan betrayed his sacred mandate through his tyranny, and given that Boris Godunov betrayed his legal mandate through sacrilege, what made a Tsar truly legitimate enough to be the viceregent of God on earth?

As Timofeyev groped his way through that theological conundrum, he was influenced by two circumstances that possibly clashed with one another: the Byzantine legacy of the Basileus as the *de facto* head of the church, and the specific historical traumas that he and his contemporaries had stood witness to.

But his synthesis produced a Tsar whose absolute sacredness exceeded that of the Byzantine emperor, stipulating a relationship between the Tsar, the church and the subjects that went beyond the most stringent forms of caesaropapism ever known in the Byzantine or Catholic world.

The Tsar, Timofeyev wrote, can have dubious moral qualities, like Ivan and Boris; but whatever those qualities, by virtue of his position as having been enthroned by God he is to be praised and regarded "as God." Where his subjects are concerned, the bodily, human aspect of the Tsar is virtually irrelevant, it is none of their business. Since only God can judge a Tsar, and since whatever abuse and tyranny the God-ordained ruler instigates against his subjects is merely God's punishment for the sins of the people, it is also a crime against God, a heresy, to depose him.[250]

Historians have noted this paradox in Timofeyev's treatise: here he spends pages decrying the crimes of Ivan and Boris, elaborating on their betrayal of their God-given divine natures, and yet insists that the very office of the Tsar remains divine, while his subjects are not to make any distinction between their ruler and God.

If Byzantine thought drew parallels between God and the

monarch, then Russian thought in the sixteenth and seventeenth centuries went far beyond mere parallels, presupposing a sacralization of the monarch and attributing supernatural qualities to his persona.[251] "The idea that the Tsar gets his power from God was then transformed into a direct deification of the Tsar," the Russian historian Vladimir Valdenberg wrote in 1916.[252]

3.

Just as Surkov was not, essentially, saying anything new or unusual, Timofeyev was merely quoting from a sixth century Byzantine deacon, Agapetus.

In one of a series of exhortations to Emperor Justinian, Agapetus wrote, "In the nature of his body the king is on a level with all other men, but in the authority attached to his dignity he is like God."[253]

Agapetus, in turn, was drawing on the fourth century bishop, Eusebius of Caesarea. In 335 CE, standing in the presence[254] of the Roman Emperor Constantine, Eusebius delivered an oration in which he elaborated on a cosmos governed by one God, and a world governed by one ruler. "That ruler, the Roman Emperor, is the viceregent of the Christian God."

Both Agapetus and Eusebius may have been projecting onto the new tenets of Christianity a more ancient, pagan form of power worship.

Here is how Athenians in the third century BCE sang to the Macedonian king Demetrius I, as cited by the scholar Norman Russel in a telling illustration of the way the Greeks defined their relationship to royal power:

> Other gods are either far away,
> or they have no ears,
> or they do not exist, or pay no attention to
> us, not in the least;
> but you we see before us,
> not made of wood or stone but real.[255]

In an incident faintly echoed in Putin's response to the Pikalevo crisis in 2009, Emperor Nero's moves to rebuild Pompei after an earthquake in 62 CE was experienced, in the eyes of the contemporary inhabitants, as a superhuman ability. It wasn't that people believed in the literal divinity of the emperor—it was just by virtue of status and living conditions he was as far above them, and as remotely detached from the fabric of their everyday existence as the gods.[256]

After the conversion of Emperor Constantine, the transfer of the court to Constantinople and the establishment of Christianity as the state religion in the fourth century CE, the idea of the Celestial King was sublimated into the idea of the King on Earth, the Basileus, according to Mikhail Bibikov, a Russian scholar of Byzantine history. Emperors are depicted with haloes; mosaics show them walking in the company of Christ and the Apostles. The pre-Christian practice of proskynesis, the act of full prostration, becomes ritualized in the coronation ceremony: subjects, except for the patriarch, upon encountering the Basileus are to fall on their faces and kiss his feet (except, as Bibikov points out, on Sundays).[257]

Bibikov draws particular attention to the phenomenon of two thrones standing side by side, "one of them reserved for the Earthly King, who can be experienced through the proskynesis, the other for the [unseen] Celestial King."[258]

In the sixth century, Emperor Justinian would spell out the living cohesion of the government and church as one body, reflecting this new mix of ancient power worship with the emerging legal-rational state: "The two greatest gifts which God, in his love for man, has granted from on high are: the priesthood and the imperial dignity. The first serves divine things, while the latter directs and administers human affairs; both, however, proceed from the same origin and adorn the life of mankind."[259]

Here it was: the church-state *Symphonia*, or the harmony between temporal and spiritual power.

The Roman Emperor's move from Rome to Byzantium in the fourth century CE had become pivotal in the eventual East-West schism that would separate the Orthodox Church and the Catholic Church.

Leaving Rome behind for Byzantium, the Emperor helped foster an environment in the West where Roman bishops had no choice but to assume temporal authority either in the utter absence of it, or as they fought kings for influence. From the ruins of a crumbling empire, where bishops sometimes found themselves the only source of law and civil administration, the Western Papacy emerged not only as a fully independent force, but one that had the power to depose kings. It was the Pope, not the emperor, who would become the Vicar of Christ, and it was his foot, and not that of a temporal emperor, that it became the norm to kiss.

But in the East, the Orthodox Church thrived under the direct oversight of the Byzantine Emperor. The idea of church-state *Symphonia*, or harmony, was not only easier to sustain, it was necessary in order to justify, and mitigate, where necessary, the divine absolutism of the Emperor. But if harmony was the ideal, then caesaropapism was usually the reality.

4.

Consider for a moment how easy, how utterly appealing, caesaropapism can appear from a perspective of infirm faith, or simply in a situation where lack of powerful patronage meant persecution or death, where courtly flattery had turned into policy: "But you we see before us, not made of stone or wood but real." Just as there is one God governing the universe, so there is one Emperor governing the human affairs of Christians—and like a Byzantine mosaic, like the gold incrustations on the hem of the Basileus' robe, everything makes such exquisite, perfect sense.

From the Black Sea, up the River Dnieper and the Volga, through fathomless expanses of steppe and forest, all this decadent, divine splendor trickled up into a place also cursed and blessed with two essential natures: inhospitable because of its cold and its expanses, it was also lawless.

Prince Vladimir's emissaries could not tell whether they were "in heaven or on earth" when they beheld the full splendor of Byzantine Orthodox ritual, before Vladimir adopted Orthodox Christianity for himself and his subjects in 988. Brought into a frigid climate and landscape, that very splendor may have brought out the Old Testament in the new faith.

The homegrown, eleventh century idea of Russia as the New Israel would fuse with and in some ways exceed the rigid courtly and ecclesiastical rituals imported from Byzantium. This fusion may have helped emphasize the Old Testament qualities of God more as a wrathful judge than as a source of mercy and grace, according to

American historian Daniel Rowland.[260] Rituals and images of the Russian court, one historian noted, centered on an "image of the Tsar as chastising, unleashing his wrath on the wrongdoer. Like the Biblical God, the Tsar was to be feared."[261]

The practice of proskynesis too appears to have been brought in as part of Byzantine court ceremonial, partially fusing with local quasi-oriental practices. A lithograph from the reign of Tsar Alexei, the second Romanov, depicted a royal procession surrounded by peasants who were not merely kneeling, but dropping their heads to the ground in complete prostration.[262] This deep bow was made, in a gesture that struck a visiting Austrian diplomat as particularly "devout" and "poignant," just before the subjects were to cast their written petitions to the Tsar.[263]

While striving for the Byzantine ideal of church-state harmony, Russian political doctrine ended up instead incorporating outright caesopapism, leading to the church's increasingly vulnerable role.

No Russian patriarch has wielded even a modicum of the influence of the Roman Catholic popes. While popes deposed emperors and kings in the West, Russian Tsars had patriarchs deposed, arrested or killed.

When, in 1547, Metropolitan Makarii conferred upon Ivan the Terrible the title of Tsar, previously reserved for Christ, Byzantine emperors, and the Mongol khan, he did so in an attempt to instil in Ivan the conviction that he should rule as a just, Christian monarch. In a few decades, however, Ivan would sack Novgorod; aside from slaughtering thousands of civilians, his oprichniki would round up thousands of priests and beat them until they handed over their wealth.[264] And when Metropolitan Filipp, Makarii's successor, challenged the oprichnina, Ivan had him deposed and then murdered.

The Great Schism of the seventeenth century, which resulted from top-down efforts to reform the Orthodox Church, was another illustration of an influential bishop—the most powerful Russia would ever see—ultimately succumbing to the state. Patriarch Nikon joined forces with Tsar Alexei in an unprecedented attempt to overhaul church practices to bring them in line with contemporary Greek rituals, trying to bridge a divergence that he saw as threatening unity within the Orthodox Church. Nikon took advantage of the coercive powers of the state to unleash a wave of terror on those clergy who refused to break with the traditions of their forefathers in favor of what to them appeared as newfangled Greek rituals, like using three fingers to cross oneself rather than two, or having parishioners kneel instead of fully prostrate themselves. But in his growing confidence, in his attempts to transform Russia into a New Jerusalem, he crossed a line: when he insisted on the title of Great Sovereign, a title borne only by the Tsar, Alexei had him deposed. Alexei kept the reforms, however; despite the backlash from below, the Schism that would create the Old Believers, it was the only type of reform that ever succeeded in Russia: reform from above.

When Alexei's son, Peter the Great, unleashed an unprecedented campaign of Westernization by force, a campaign that would only be rivalled by Stalin, the church resisted. Peter, in a bid to sweep away the stifling patriarchy, and the exhortations of Timofeyev and Agapetus about the divinity of the Tsar, wound up only unwittingly vindicating them. When the church resisted, Peter, by the power of his own charisma, transformed the Patriarchate into a mere government body consisting of both clergy and laymen, the Most Holy Synod.

But it would be the Bolsheviks who would achieve the ultimate apotheosis in the divinization of state power, wiping out the church entirely and slaughtering hundreds of thousands of priests. Armed with the ideology of Communism, they set out to build a New Jerusalem *par excellence*, a true vision of heaven on earth; where their predecessors had failed, they would exceed both Ivan and Peter in the terror they unleashed.

We could not do justice to the story of that dynasty here; but in the context of a review of church-state relations in Russia, it is important to stress that Soviet totalitarianism owes at least as much, and probably more, to these traditions of caesaropapism as it does to the ideology of communism.

5.

In their closing arguments before the court in August 2012, the three young women arrested for performing a punk prayer in Christ the Savior Cathedral and ridiculing church-state ties, insisted that they were merely acting in the traditions of the holy fool.

Caught between stifling church ritual on the one hand and the church's subjugation by the government on the other, some members of Christian society in both sixth century Byzantium and sixteenth century Russia stumbled upon a curious loophole of absolute freedom.

They stripped naked or wore rags, they wandered about their communities throwing rocks at the nobility and the clergy, and casting insults at state officials. They danced naked and yelled in churches. They inverted social norms and etiquette; when offered wine by those coming to them in kindness, they would pour it on the ground; when approached by the Tsar they would curse at him; when the rest of the community fasted, they ate raw meat. By doing so, they invited unspeakable abuse. They were called the *yurodivy*, the fools for Christ, or, more simply, holy fools.

According to the Russian scholar Sergei Ivanov, one of the few experts on the phenomenon, it was no accident that holy fools—who differed from their European jester counterparts—emerged first in Byzantium and then in Tsarist Russia. By testing accepted norms and ethical standards, they demonstrated the impossibility of fathoming or predicting God; by testing the bounds of freedom, they made an irony of it. The holy fools thus served as a wedge between church and state: with the failure of the church to set any limitations on state power, they sought to act as a sort of spiritual control mechanism.[265] Of course, it would be wrong to speak of the success of such control mechanisms in any institutional sense, but on occasion these strange troublemakers—who were by no means necessarily opposed to the government, as we shall see in a moment—managed to achieve some curious results.

Ivanov identifies the reign of Ivan the Terrible as the peak of the phenomenon of the holy fool. It is no wonder, he writes, that Ivan himself practiced such traits: watch him weep and debase himself when facing adversaries, such as monks he suspected of treason, or in his letters to the exiled Prince Kurbksy. Ivan would in all honesty refer to himself as a "foul-smelling dog" one moment, only to strike a mercilessly regal tone in finally indicting his audience. Isn't he contradicting himself by debasing himself one moment, and then chastising his foes the next? Not in the least, Ivanov argues: "[The debasement] by no means lowers the dignity of the Tsar; on the contrary, it proves his superhuman essence, which allows him to transcend earthly laws and norms."[266]

Enter a real holy fool. In 1570, after Ivan's oprichniki slaughtered tens of thousands of civilians and clergy during the sacking of Novgorod, eyewitness accounts by at least one oprichnik and later recollections recall an extraordinary incident: a certain Nikolai, a recluse who lived alone on an estate that he did not tend, where animals roamed in their own excrement and yet continued to thrive, called out to Ivan. There are several accounts of what Nikolai said, but they all came down to this: "Ivashka [the diminutive, almost derogatory term for Ivan], why don't you get out of here and stop spilling Christian blood?"[267]

And Ivan, who had killed higher men for lesser things than that, turned around and left.

Not only would Ivan not harm the holy fools who harassed him—by sending him pieces of raw meat during Lent, for instance, in a clear reference to his butchery—he fueled their cults, eventually leading to the canonization of the most famous holy fool, St. Basil. The most easily recognizable tourist attraction in Russia, the St. Basil Cathedral on Red Square, is named after him.

According to Ivanov, there is a reason for this tolerance and respect—Ivan saw holy fools as the only human beings absolute enough to converse with. Like him, they went beyond human norms and laws. And on some level, society in general, which accepted the sacredness of the holy fool, went along with this state of affairs: Ivanov cites a legend circulating around the time that had a holy fool choose Ivan to rule as Tsar.

By 1667, the church turned on the holy fools, condemning most of their antics. The decision started a wave of persecutions; needless to say, holy fools were banned from churches.

Today, the Russian Orthodox Church is one of the most respected institutions in Russia. It would be fair to say that amid the general distrust of most institutions, there are only two with consistently high trust ratings: the person of the president (51 percent) and the church (50 percent).[268]

In February 2012, at the peak of Vladimir Putin's presidential campaign, he was shown on state television meeting with Patriarch Kirill, who publicly labelled the last twelve years of Putin's rule as a "gift from God." Although clerics from all major denominations were also present (Russia is, after all, formally a secular state with a constitution that separates the government from religion), the public meeting, where the future president and the Patriarch greeted each other with the customary kiss on the cheek, was interpreted as a bid by Putin to use the church to bolster his legitimacy.

Amid the protests and plummeting trust ratings, amid a failing anti-corruption drive, and most of all, amid mounting criticism that Putin lacked an ideology or "anything holy" at all, it was only natural that he would lean on the church, drawing a mandate from its blessing in a way that had something in common with Ivan insisting on a blessing from the Patriarch of Constantinople.

But in this secular state, where church and religion were formally separate, the Russian Orthodox Church was still eerily intertwined with the state. That month, Kremlin courtiers began to talk openly of church-state harmony.

The Moscow Patriarchate, which hadn't existed in any real sense since Peter the Great replaced it with a Holy Synod, was formally reinstated by Joseph Stalin in 1943. There was even an apocryphal account of his meetings with clergy at that time, who showed up in plainclothes, without their church garb. This, apparently, provoked a question from Stalin: "What, you fear me but don't fear Him?"[269]

After that, the KGB would maintain a close watch on leading clergy, grooming the most promising to move ahead in the church hierarchy. This was the path of Patriarch Alexis II, who, as Alexei Ridiger, was recruited into the KGB sometime after 1950, propelling his career. In fact, the close cooperation between the KGB and leading clergy like Alexei Ridiger demonstrated the very essence of the kind of church-state harmony extolled in past centuries. Patriarch Alexis II would go on, by some accounts, to play a pivotal role in taking a stand against the hardliner coup in 1991, helping bring down what, at least on paper, was an atheist dynasty.[270]

But the ties between church and state would continue; Alexis' successor, Patriarch Kirill (Vladimir Gundyayev) was also known to have KGB ties. But if the late Alexis was widely respected for his integrity, Patriarch Kirill—whether due to sheer timing or, indeed, because of the cynicism that many Russian observers ascribe to him—was less fortunate. By winter of 2012, all sorts of allegations against him were being leaked to the press. Aside from a successful tobacco importing business he and other church leaders were allegedly involved in (which was not illegal), Gundyayev was implicated in an embarrassing apartment scandal, where he was accused of pressuring the courts to allow him to annex the upstairs apartment of a former health minister. The pretext was that the neighbor's reconstruction had ruined Gundyayev's rare book collection—damages that a court estimated as being worth over a million dollars.[271]

The scandal quickly coincided with mounting reports of hit and run incidents by priests driving fancy cars—either the public was genuinely getting fed up with clerical hypocrisy, or someone was trying to discredit the church. Patriarch Kirill, who never really commented on the apartment scandal allegations—and particularly his hardliner spokesman, Vsevolod Chaplin—insisted someone was deliberately attacking the church.

It was in this environment of Orthodoxy apparently under siege that Pussy Riot, in their stated bid to drive a wedge between church and state, danced in Christ the Savior Cathedral.

As the church, and the particularly outspoken Chaplin, lashed out at the punk group, singling them out for committing what they described as a deadly sin, it was the government's decision to prosecute them that exposed the church-state harmony Pussy Riot had merely poked fun at.

If there indeed was a meeting in which Patriarch Kirill directly asked Putin for retribution, as some allege, then it wasn't just Putin leaning on the church. It was also evidence of a subordinate church seeking protection from the state. The pact seemed to have worked spectacularly. In a society where a majority condemned what Pussy Riot did, by using their stunt to accuse the opposition of unleashing "Satanic rage" against the church, in the words of Vsevolod Chaplin, the government may have succeeded in driving a wedge into the opposition. In the eyes of many Russians who were indifferent to the protesters but dissatisfied with Putin, the Pussy Riot scandal functioned as a sort of deal breaker: this government may be corrupt and illegitimate, but are those hooligans any better? Finally, Chaplin would go on and publicly state that that "the religious neutrality of the state is a fiction."[272]

But there is, perhaps, also another, somewhat esoteric explanation, in the light of the history of the centuries we have rather haphazardly explored in this chapter: The Tsar can't just ignore the ire of a holy fool—as the one force that can compete in its absoluteness, the Tsar is as dependent on the holy fool as the holy fool is on the Tsar. And so, if the holy fool bids the Tsar to go away, the Tsar must respond by either complying or unleashing all his wrath; ignoring him is not an option, for by ignoring the holy fool the Tsar would be belittling his own status before his people. But in punishing him, he acts at his own peril—for the holy fool is sacred. The challenge, thus, becomes a self-fulfilling curse.

Chapter 17

The Living Law

I know that stare. And I know of no other more terrifying than that hopeless, metallic stare."
—**Alexander Hertzen**, describing a meeting with Nicholas I, 1856

I drove up to them, sat up, and one of the fishermen turned, looked at me, and began to cross himself. I asked, "Why are you crossing yourself?" When he realized that it was really me he said, "We drank a little bit yesterday and I thought I was seeing things."
—**Vladimir Putin**, recalling an incident when fishermen allegedly took him for Christ walking on the water, 2012

Everything is so complicated, so tangled, brother. But there is no time to sort it out. Our madhouse is voting for Putin. Our madhouse will be glad.
—**Alexander Yelin**, songwriter, author of the lyrics to "A Man like Putin," performed by the girl group Singing Together, 2011

…When it comes to this, I shall prefer emigrating to some country where they make no pretence of loving liberty—to Russia, for instance, where despotism can be taken pure,

and without the base alloy of hypocrisy.
—**Abraham Lincoln**,1855

1.

IT WAS A matter of time before he looked at me; when he did, his eyes did not linger on my face, but slid down and stopped on my boots. I realized nervously that despite the sludge of early spring, I had not cleaned my boots in days.

Here stood the Basileus, the cold gray-blue eyes of the living law were cast upon me, and my boots were dirty.

Putin reportedly suffers from far-sightedness—a defect of vision which may cause him to focus piercingly on things at a distance of several meters without necessarily seeing them.[273] It's quite possible that he could not tell what color my boots were, let alone whether they were clean. But you don't just brush off that gaze; journalists who have encountered it lead their stories with it; if you meet him, what is spoken is often secondary. What people really want to know is, "What did you feel when he looked at you?"

Part of the lasting genius of George Orwell's *1984* was not just its uncanny insight into Stalinist society, but the ability to identify the central experience of absolute power: Big Brother is watching you. He will gaze at you, unmoving, as you talk, you will try not to mirror his gaze, try not to anticipate the impact your words are having on him, if they are having any at all. But by being watched, and by acknowledging who you are being watched by, you enter into a game as old as time, a personal transfer of power, an understanding, and an implicit designation of who stands above the law. It doesn't matter whether you see him or not. What matters—what always matters—is who he is looking at, and what he sees.

On December 20, 2012, I remembered my dirty boots, how he could look at you, how journalists and foreign heads of state had spun all sorts of legends about the "killer eyes" and the "icy glare," as I scanned the press hall for a place to sit where he would be able to see me. Front row seats were taken, but I didn't really want to sit in the front row anyway. I picked a seat in the second row to the side, still within his field of vision, then nibbled queasily on an unripe nectarine from the refreshment stand. This wasn't like that spring of 2011 in the government building of the prime minister, where we stood silently as he posed for a photo op with Prime Minister Benjamin Netanyahu. If I didn't need to do anything then but watch, if the whole point of that photo op was to see and be seen, then today was Putin's first press conference since formally returning to the presidency, and I was determined to ask a question. Why show up at a press conference otherwise?

"We are entering the heart of darkness," a veteran journalist in the van had joked as we drove up to the press hall. Jokes like this had followed the press pool; they were an integral part of those times when reporters were forced to sit for hours with nothing to do. They kept waiting like Byzantine courtiers for the Emperor to show up because waiting underlined his divine nature—but if it was a ritual 1500 years ago, then it was mere inefficiency today. "He drinks our blood," another journalist told me of the times he'd been kept waiting, locked in small rooms, for what resulted in little more than a glimpse. In the twenty-first century, did we have anything left but irony? Forced by circumstance to deify or demonize this?

Five hours later, the same journalist who joked about the heart of darkness, a seasoned veteran, would leave the press conference with what he described as "the heaviest feeling of depression."

My question had to do with orphans, and, like all real questions, it wasn't a question at all, but a confrontation over what had quickly spiralled into the most depressing story of Putin's thirteen years in power, the Browder story, as told in Chapter 9.

The resulting anti-Magnitsky Law, banning Americans from adopting Russian orphans, had sparked an outrage.

In a country where, whether due to climate, infrastructure, or simply the sheer exhaustion of its people, orphanages were struggling to clothe and feed 105,000 orphans and abandoned children, where 1,220 children had died while in the care of Russian adoptive families between 1991 and 2005, the government was banning American adoptions on the pretext that 19 Russian children died in the care of American families. Many had done the math: for approximately 1000 children who would not be adopted as a result of the anti-Magnitsky Act that year, the likelihood of death would increase twenty-two-fold. Before he signed the bill, I wanted to confront Putin with those statistics, and I wanted to ask if he thought the deaths of those children were worth the retaliation effort.

I was not surprised that the first question centered on the adoption ban and the Magnitsky case. Critical questions were a hallmark of Putin's conversational style; that he had the patience to field each and every one of them was certainly meant to suggest pluralism and democracy. In each of the questions, he veered off into the Magnitsky Act. Americans had snubbed Russia, this was an appropriate retaliation. As for the adoption ban, "I repeat: I must look at the details of the law, but in general I understand the mood of State Duma deputies."[274]

Over the course of about eight increasingly confrontational questions, Putin meandered back and forth, dipping below the law, only to rise above it. He encouraged people to submit a petition to the Duma, he spoke of "details of the law," tantalizingly suggesting that within the framework of the law he could even, perhaps, veto the bill, as if it had not originally come from him anyway. And then the patrimonial living law would shine through the legal-rational state, and he would say something like, "Sit down, Masha," or "How can it be normal when you are humiliated [by Americans]? Do you like it? Are you a masochist?"[275]

Given the number of people in the country who were eager to interpret his displeasure as an order to act, that cold gaze, when directed at you, was not just a PR gimmick. The journalist who was told to sit had the grace to reply, "Thank you, Vova," but there was also the danger of utterly unpredictable consequences. Another journalist's newspaper would be shut down after Putin quietly scolded the press corps for laughing at the name of her Chechen newspaper, *Kadyrov Pravda* (Kadyrov's Truth)—Ramzan Kadyrov is the ruthless leader of Chechnya; they interpreted the paper as part of his personality cult, through, as Putin corrected, the name referred to the late Akhmad Kadyrov. He reprimanded the press hall, not the woman, and yet local officials in Chechnya registered his annoyance and shut down her paper. He had been displeased; anything could happen.

The public officials who quake in the presence of "the boss," the stock market shares that plummet at the slightest hint of his "hopeless" eyes looking in the direction of any industry that displeases him, and the opposition journalists who doctor their websites after meetings with Putin will all go through the motions of life in a modern, if flawed democracy, but sense with their gut how things actually work. The non-verbal signals may appear to be coming from Putin—who expertly plays into them—but they are actually the response of those who surround him.

I knew all this as I held up a sign with my paper's name; one of hundreds, perhaps not as eagerly as the others. When he cast his eyes in my direction, I couldn't help but hide my face behind the sign. It was one thing to know the statistics, but to say them to his face, as he stared back, bored, his gaze unmoving, inexpressive, all-knowing?

Four hours of this, and the press conference was suddenly over. He had not called on me, I had not asked my question. As he stepped down toward us, we encircled him. Someone wanted that last chance to use him to make page one, someone just wanted his attention, his favor, or his grace, some wanted to show their defiance. Some asked for a photo together, some squealed, some were determined to confront him, to score points, to restore a semblance of dignity.

The cold-eyed human being who stood a meter away from me, who absorbed the attention of millions until his human nature had dissolved in it, was propelled above the laws he intoned. I took a deep breath, called out to the Tsar, spoke his name and patronymic, and faltered, tripping over the consonants: "Vldimvmich…!"

2.

On a crisp, sunlit day in late February 2012, just a week before Vladimir Putin's re-election, Oksana Abdulayeva, a kindergarten teacher from the suburban town of Serpukhov, sat in the crowd of Moscow's largest outdoor stadium at Luzhniki. She had been given free tickets by the municipal bosses of her kindergarten, and she had gladly shared the tickets with me, saying that she was told the more people showed up the better. "The labor union invites you to a holiday concert," her print-out said. Tens of thousands of people slowly gravitated towards the stadium, drawn by dancing, rope-skipping, free music, and pop stars performing their latest hits. Women with wreaths of paper flowers around their heads stood along a carpeted path leading to the stage.

Abdulayeva, given a free ride to enjoy a holiday in Moscow, watch a show, and see the city, was more than happy to go.

Did she know that Vladimir Putin planned to attend the rally? No, she did not. But she smiled and said wistfully: "That would really be nice if he did."

Except that Oksana Abdulayeva did not like, trust, or plan to vote for Putin. She told me she deeply disliked him, in fact. And yet she had no qualms about attending a rally for his benefit, a demonstration of his inevitable popularity, to be broadcast across the country.

"We had these tickets," she told me later. "We're from Serpukhov. We wanted a nice day out in Moscow."

In response to the hundred-thousand-strong protest rallies that spilled into Moscow's streets in the winter of 2011–2012, Putin's new Kremlin ideologue, Vyacheslav Volodin, retaliated by amassing hundred-thousand strong rallies of support. Factory workers, low-level civil servants, school and kindergarten teachers, and anyone else who was on the government payroll were bussed in, cajoled, and often paid to show up for these pro-Putin demonstrations. They numbered tens of thousands, they eagerly competed with the protesters, but when caught on camera many had trouble explaining why they were there.

At Luzhniki Stadium on February 23, 2012, a national holiday commemorating the armed forces, a total of 130,000[276] people showed up. Dozens of buses had parked along the blocked-off highway ramp, with one driver telling me he was recruited and paid by the Presidential Administration.

But if the demonstration at Luzhniki was trying to be a political convention, in reality it looked more like an enormous medieval fair. The people came to eat the free food and listen to the concerts, and if the contingent at the protest rallies was blatantly cosmopolitan— the hipsters with their scarves and shabby coats, Indian skirts, and trousers, the right people, as they liked to call each other—then the crowds that filled Luzhniki Stadium consisted of the gray, rugged faces of women and men living hand-to-mouth lives, scurrying between a job that earned little and produced even less and the cramped home with the broken pipes to fix. Exhausted by the daily effort of life, they looked resigned to the idea that they had nothing to gain and everything to lose. They were not there for politics, because politics seemed to irritate many of them if it existed for them at all. They were there for a nice day out, for a chance to see a few celebrities on stage.

And, much like at a real medieval fair, the top celebrity was the sovereign.

He emerged in a black jacket, a Botoxed rock star. He touched the hands of the women with the paper flowers in their hair, and ascended the stage to deliver a speech about death.

Standing as close to the stage as security would allow, I saw a small, bald man with a strange face wearing a fur-lined parka. I noticed his familiar, bored countenance, how difficult it was for that aging bureaucrat, adept at wearing whatever role his people craved, to play the dictator, the role that seemed to disgust him most of all. Cosmetic surgery dulled the once icy fire of his eyes when he tried to flash them, but he tried, and his people seemed to appreciate the effort.

"I wish I could shake your hands and hug every one of you," he said in his quiet, office voice.

"But why not, we want you to!" cried the ladies pressing up to the stage.[277]

He stumbled through an initially awkward speech, pacing the stage so that everyone could see his face. He made one or two embarrassing gaffes.

Trudging through a couple of sentences in his native bureaucratese, he suddenly raised his voice, and the effect, coming from a soft-spoken man, was stirring: "Do we love Russia?" he called out, and he demanded an answer.

He then spoke of childbirth, ordering that his people should multiply. "There are millions of us, but there must be more."

In a matter of minutes, he worked himself into a carefully-guarded rage, the kind necessary to channel pagan energy from a crowd of 100,000 people.

"We remember these words from our childhood, we remember these warriors who swore an oath of allegiance to their Fatherland, who yearned to die for it," he cried out, his voice metallic as he pronounced "death."

And then he recited a poem about the Great War of 1812:
For Moscow we shall die,
Like all the rest in battle slain!
We'll fight and die, we cried again!
And there, upon that bloody plain,
We kept our pledge to die.[278]

Somewhere between a threat and a promise, his speech culminated with a menacing scowl: "The battle for Russia continues. Victory will be ours!"[279]

Vladimir Putin said "death" exactly four times—and he was referring not to the abstract death of an enemy, but to the past and future death of his people. He was calling on us to die in his name, for Russia personified; a pale, gray man who struggled to show emotion now channeled it, manipulating a primordial yearning to share the fate of one's sacrificed ancestors.

I stood there petrified, repeating his words in English for some reason—because I sensed the insidious logic of what was happening, of that pale shadow of why people had yearned to die for Stalin. For an exhausted, overworked housewife struggling to keep up with the ignoble minutiae of everyday life, the undarned socks, dripping taps, runny noses, shorted circuits, and other, bigger casualties of spending one's energies staying warm in a cold country, of the Herculean feat of bringing children into such a world—the prospect of a glorious death could, in fact, be sweetly enticing. Today, she would never admit this to herself, let alone articulate it—but there it was, the pagan instinct that Putin was exploiting, for God only knew what purposes.

Oksana Abdulayeva, the kindergarten teacher cajoled to turn up to the rally, had been happy to see Putin.

"As a person, as a celebrity, it was nice that he showed up," she said. But it seemed as though she hadn't really articulated her thoughts on this until I asked her—and it surfaced that in reality, she resented him.

She had been trying unsuccessfully to get pregnant, but her teacher's salary wasn't nearly enough for *in vitro* fertilization.

"He keeps saying, 'Have more children,'" she said. "But how? And why? So that they can be sent to Chechnya and be killed?"

She said she would not vote for him, or for any of the other candidates. But despite her judgment and her resentment, she had, like thousands of others, turned out for a rally to support him, simply for being asked. In a week's time, 45.6 million Russians would cast their vote for Putin. Of those people, some genuinely believed in him, some liked him and thought he was smart. But there were also millions who marked the ballot much in the same way that Oksana Abdulayeva, despite her resentment and disgust, attended a rally to support him—for simplicity's sake, for lack of an alternative, for money, or for being asked.

3.

It was just past 6 AM on the morning of the presidential elections on March 4, 2012, and I was stumbling through ankle-deep snow, blinking against the flurries in the excruciating pre-dawn darkness, trying to find Alexander Pypin's car.

Pypin, a soft-spoken commercial real estate analyst in his late thirties, had found himself, to his own surprise, organizing a team of volunteer election observers in the village of Nizhneye Myachkovo, 20 kilometers (12 miles) southeast of Moscow, where he had purchased a home a few years ago. He would drive me to the polling station, where, under the watchful eyes of the election commission chairman, we would pretend to have met for the first time.

"I'm sorry I'm late," I said as I got into the back seat.

"Don't apologize to me, apologize to the Russian people," he joked.

He explained that he had gone as an observer during the December parliamentary election because he felt some light needed to be shed on the black hole that was municipal politics in the Moscow region. State officials were quietly being sold choice land plots; nosy people were getting beaten up. The violations he saw at his polling station meant that his accidental foray into politics, at least for him, was the start of an uphill, ultimately fruitless battle that he was forced to engage in. "Our people don't understand what an election is. They don't know how to make a choice," he said.

The presidential election of 2012 saw tens of thousands of middle class volunteers like Pypin flood polling stations across the country; some compared it to the Narodniki movement, the nineteenth century revolutionary-minded urban students who started "going to the people" in search of their roots, seeking to adopt what they saw as the peasants' collectivism as the basis of socialism in Russia.

My own decision to become an election observer came out of lofty intentions that quickly descended into the banal. I initially felt that the only hope for change was for those urban protesters I had stood among in Moscow to "go to the people," and to convince them that ballot stuffing was wrong. And, like many volunteers, I believed that I should also try to convince these harried, provincial women administrators who followed orders that following illegal orders was wrong.

But at that particular polling station, where everything seemed to have been decided before I even showed up, there was little use in my presence other than simply watching, because in the end, we were proven utterly powerless.

Anton Dugin, a tall, suave red-haired man in his late twenties, stood among the election observers at the provincial polling station where he was chairman, chatting them up about politics. A local administration official, he wore a well-cut suit to spend nearly twenty-four hours at a village sports hall set up with ballot booths and tables. On March 4, 2012, he seemed to be juggling two tasks: to ensure that the voting process went smoothly in accordance with the paper law, and to ensure that Prime Minister Vladimir Putin got the necessary number of votes in accordance with the living law, passed down from the Presidential Administration in the Kremlin to Dugin's boss in the governor's administration of the Moscow region.

How to achieve the former was easy: that was written down in a series of federal laws. But how to achieve the latter, well, that was entirely up to Dugin, and him alone.

"It's as if you don't know your history," he was telling two middle-aged women. "Russia has always had autocracy. It has always had a Tsar. And that has always been good for some people and bad for others."

After a few minutes, as Dugin casually moved to chat up the younger observers and distract them, one of the older women would stand up and stuff ten ballots into the box. As the younger observers stood in a commotion around the ballot box, filming its contents and noisily calling the police, Dugin, who just a few moments ago had suppressed a hearty giggle over a joke involving Putin's alleged mistress Alina Kabayeva, remained unperturbed and refused to acknowledge that any ballot stuffing had taken place. The folded pack of ten ballots was clearly visible in the transparent container, but when confronted with the protests, Dugin offered a perfectly reasonable answer: "Well, yes, it's a ballot box, and there are a lot of ballots in it. What's the problem?"

The problem was that Dugin, like most election committee chairmen around the country, hardly needed ballot stuffing and other visible examples of voter fraud to guarantee Putin a secure victory in the presidential race. Opinion polls in February placed the number of people who planned to cast their ballot for Putin at 63 percent of those who said they would go and vote—well above the 50 percent Putin would have needed to formally avoid a runoff. There had been hope—and evidence of high-level debate—that recent protests and Putin's dip in popularity would result in a two-round election that would force him to fight for his votes and do what was unthinkable for a Tsar: take part in campaign debates.

But that never happened. An unwritten order emerged from the new Kremlin ideologue, Vyacheslav Volodin—Putin's trusted United Russia handler who was brought in to replace Vladislav Surkov—that regional governors and administration officials were to ensure a victory for Putin in the first round. The aura of power could not be allowed to diminish, the Kremlin was not ready for politics, and neither were the Russian people, that message seemed to say. The elections were not a debate between politicians convincing voters of the good of their policies; they were a formality crowning a battle for power. The battle, as pro-Kremlin sociologist Olga Kryshtanovskaya told me at the time, was as it had always been in Russia—not to win but to destroy, to wrest power or to maintain it. It was no wonder that, in this context, Putin would continue presenting his campaign as a matter of life and death. "They are looking for a sacred victim," he would say of the opposition. "They'll whack him, if you'll pardon the word, and then blame the government."

That battle lay at the heart of the numbers. What the opinion polls seemed to mask was the key mystery of Putin's twelve-year rule:

the illusion of his popularity. Taken at face value, the polls presented a politician far more popular than other contenders. What they did not reflect was why people chose Putin, and the psychology behind their choice. The numbers, the façade of the election process, the polls, and the media dressed an ancient sentiment in modern clothes: even devoid of the slightest voting irregularities, even under the most pristine polling conditions, without violating a single law, the people were not choosing a favored politician. They were following orders. By picking out of five presidential candidates, they were not choosing a policy. They were deciding whether to obey or to rebel.

In the sports hall of Nizhneye Myachkovo, I was greeted by two sleepy policemen and the cordial Anton Dugin. To my request to see bound books with the list of 800 voters registered to that station, he politely waved it off as "later." And while I initially brushed this minor violation off to the bustle of setting up the polling station in time for its 8 AM opening, I would later learn that it was no coincidence.

The morning hours amounted to an endless rotation of aging pensioners. At least three women in their eighties accosted me with a shaking hand, "Where is Putin's name, little daughter? Sign it for me, I cannot see." I had to refuse: though election officials regularly told these women to approach us for help, by law I could be kicked out for simply touching her ballot.

But these old women were not the only ones who gave Putin his victory.

At half past ten, about seven weather-beaten men in working clothes piled into the room. Each one of them was holding an absentee voting certificate, which allowed them to vote away from their place of residence. As suspicious observers accosted them about their registration (they had none), one fellow volunteer whispered to me: "Where I live, United Russia got over 50 percent in the fairest of votes." The volunteer was Anatoly Zakharov, a twenty-eight-year-old engineering consultant who worked for a construction company in nearby Zhukovsky. His mother had worked as an election official at his local polling station, and from colleagues, he knew about the latest approach to obeying the living law without visibly violating the paper law.

"Everything is transparent now," he told me as we stood next to the transparent ballot box, in full view of the camera that Putin had ordered installed at every polling station. "No ballot stuffing is necessary, because there's another method that's far more efficient."

As Zakharov described it, contractors from a town's key industry—such as the Pikalevo factory—are driven to a meeting with local administrative authorities. The local officials explain, very politely, that that they need to go and vote—hinting that if they do not, they will not get coveted government contracts. They are not necessarily told who to vote for. "They understand the signal," Zakharov said. "On what basis can our contracts be annulled?" Zakharov overheard at another meeting with local officials. "On the basis that you are not a patriot."

The seven workers lined up to receive their ballots in another room out of the view of the observers. After emerging, one of them, suffering from what appeared to be a hangover, stood staring at his ballot in bewilderment. He didn't seem to have an inkling of what he was supposed to do with it, until an observer directed him to a voting booth and told him to check the box next to his chosen candidate.

After the seven men voted, they walked out, single file, and piled furtively into a silver Mitsubishi pick-up truck standing outside in the sunlit snow. As Zakharov began filming the truck, its driver, after eyeing us suspiciously for a few moments, walked over, and said: "Who are you, and why are you filming?"

Zakharov explained that he was an election observer and was filming the premises in accordance with the law. The driver, who would not give his name, looked as if he wanted to explain something to us, as if he had something weighing on his conscience. "I'm a working Russian man, don't you understand?" he told us. "I just want the right choice to be made."

No evident violations were committed by driving seven workers to vote using absentee ballots, and we didn't have the means to trace this Mitsubishi truck to see if it appeared later at other polling stations. But as I learned later from the Golos election watchdog, voting by absentee ballot appeared to be the method of choice to increase Putin's results at the 2012 elections. On informal orders from regional or local government officials, factory bosses would buy up absentee ballots given out at each polling station, and workers would be bussed in to ensure that they voted. Companies would register themselves as enterprises that had to work on weekends to ensure that they were eligible to receive absentee ballots in bulk. In total, 1.6 million people voted by absentee ballot in March 2012—an increase of about 400,000 people compared to the turnout for the Duma elections, according to the most commonly cited figures.[280] As the night wore on, the observers—Pypin, Zakharov, and a younger man named Alexei—were engaged in a polite, silent battle of wills with Dugin, struggling to comply with every letter of the paper law and force Dugin to do the same. It had become clear that the minor violations—like Dugin's reluctance to show us the lists of voters—had not been a mere oversight. Once the votes were counted, he insisted on penciling the results into the protocol on the wall, instead of writing in pen as required by law. One number remained missing in that protocol, and it was the number of ballots handed out. Very likely, had we seen the books and the list of absentee voters, we would learn that the numbers would not add up. To keep this concealed from us, Dugin just kept us waiting, hoping that after twenty hours at the polling station we would get too tired and leave.

Determined to stay to the end, Pypin and Zakharov would make a note of each violation in a calm voice, turning on their cameras. They had repeatedly demanded to see the lists of registered voters to ensure that the number of ballots handed out did not exceed the number of people who came to vote. But Dugin wouldn't budge. "We'll do it later," he said. "The women are drinking tea."

I sat down for tea with Yelena Kiselyova, one of the commission members, and asked her if the observers were getting to her. They were. An employee in the district administration, she had worked at polling stations for twenty years, she said, and people had voted "correctly," without election observers getting in the way. I would never learn what exactly she meant by "correctly."

Dugin, meanwhile, was overheard telling the other officials to try to wait until the observers left, otherwise they would never manage to "hide" discrepancies in the lists. By three in the morning, Dugin merely told observers that the lists had already been counted without them—and sat down with two other women over a calculator to come up with the right number to pencil into the protocol.

Where the observers were concerned, their paper law, the four complaints they had written out with shaking hands, proved no match for Dugin's determination to follow orders, and the authority to sidestep that paper law that he had clearly been given. In a blatant violation, he marked "zero" in the protocol for the number of complaints he had received. When Pypin asked him how that was possible given that he had received and signed four complaints, Dugin gave an Orwellian answer.

"The election commission has decided that there were zero complaints," he said with a smile.

At two in the morning, I stood demoralized as I watched the pile of ballots with a check next to Putin's name grow. Pypin would continue to battle the results with complaints to the courts, the prosecutors, and the police, but I had already given up, seeing it was pointless to nitpick: weeding out the administrative and federal violations wouldn't diminish in the slightest that towering stack of ballots.

When confronted about violating a whole slew of regulations that Yelena Kiselyova should have known about, as an administrative official who had worked in election committees for twenty years, she brushed off my accusations.

"We will work as we've always worked," she said, and cheerfully continued counting the ballots. What other way was there?

4.

Much like his boss, Dmitry Peskov, Putin's long-time and charming spokesman, did two things with baffling skill. He managed to shroud the president in mystery even while insisting on his transparency. He elaborated on the institutional limits on Putin's powers with a knowing look that seemed to nullify the very institutions he spoke of. And he never forbade journalists from asking particular questions of the president. He just indicated, with his beaming eyes and his smile, what the "right" questions to ask were. "Cameron is nothing, tariffs are everything!" he declared with a disarming grin to a group of journalists in the White House in the summer of 2011, as he "persuaded" them to leave the issue of the British prime minister's meeting with Putin and focus instead on Putin's promise to delay a hike in energy tariffs.

I met Peskov for an extended interview in the summer of 2009;

it was a period when, as prime minister, Vladimir Putin evoked more mystery than he ever did as president. Constitutionally, the president of Russia may have been endowed with virtually despotic powers in accordance with Yeltsin's constitution; but Putin's influence as prime minister showed that he could continue wielding those powers from any office. It was the big question that dominated the political news for the next three years: was there any possible interpretation that Putin was not actually in power, and a mere prime minister subordinate to the president?

I had only waited for about forty minutes in the plush reception of his White House office when Peskov emerged from the double doors, shook hands with an official, and turned to me, nodded and smiled. "So, what are you going to write?" he said, as he led me in and invited me to be seated. He was jovial, friendly in an endearing way, and there was absolutely nothing unusual, let alone sinister in that question. It was a question that any PR specialist would ask in an interview. Except that it invited a Russian reversal: In Russia, Putin interviews YOU.

He sat back, but at times he leaned forward and looked from under his brows and smiled; at these moments he was saying some of the more pointed axioms—that Putin was misunderstood and demonized, and that those who demonized him hated Russia with the very "fiber of their soul."

That Peskov was smiling left no doubt that at that moment he believed every word of what he was saying. What was more worrying was that his smile dared you not to believe him.

"What sometimes astounds me," he said, "is that back in 2000, when foreign media called or sent requests for an interview, their argument was that it would be a chance to reach the audience of country X, be it European or North American or South American, to [broadcast] information about Putin, about his personality, about his passions, about his positions on key issues, about who he is.... What is astounding is that we still get requests formulated in the same way."

He paused.

"Those who wanted to understand who Mr. Putin is—they have understood already. Those who did not want to understand him—they never will."

Peskov's agitation had a specific reason. Just a few moments before he spoke those words, he answered a phone call on his mobile. A journalist was calling about the latest murder in Chechnya of a human rights activist, and the inevitable accusations that followed blaming Putin. Peskov's face did not change as he answered the question in English. But when he turned to me it was clear that he was indignant.

"Here's a tragic case of a tragic murder of [Natalia] Estemirova. Just now I got a call from a Western journalist who is in an [emotional] state because she just got out of a press conference where… she heard the words, 'Putin. Is. To blame. For the murder of Estemirova.' As I told the journalist, the pain of the loss of one's colleague is understandable, but nothing can justify such stupidity."

What was "stupid" about blaming Putin for the death of Estemirova was not about his godly or, on the contrary, his demonic powers. It was the ignorance of all the good he had done in Chechnya. "To say that about Putin is to completely rule out all those efforts that he has made in the last nine years in bringing peace, stability and the rule of law."

Peskov could not reveal too much of the truth—that Putin's maneuvering space was severely restricted regarding Chechen strongman Ramzan Kadyrov, a man accused of torturing and killing people, but who loyally kept the threat of separatism at bay. For by revealing this, Peskov would be puncturing the myth of omnipotence that had come to surround Putin.

And so the logic was simple: state power did not deny its godliness when it was credited with good things, but grew indignant when bad things were attributed to that same omnipotence.

"Everything that Russia does is received negatively," Peskov lamented. "And, likewise, the demonization of anyone and everyone who has anything to do with Russia."

I think it's worth discarding, for a moment, all these attempts to demonize, deify, or otherwise justify Vladimir Putin and look at him closely as we would at an animal in his habitat (no judgment!), considering his actions from the perspective of his environment and his history.

The second president of the Russian Federation was born during the post-war deprivations of the late Stalinist period, in 1952. His parents were middle-aged factory workers sharing a communal apartment, who had lost their first two children during the siege of Leningrad. The daily squalor of the life led by George Orwell's Winston Smith is only a slightly exaggerated approximation of the basic domestic conditions that Putin may have spent his early years in.

Putin recalls of his childhood: "Once I saw a huge rat and started pursuing it, until I cornered it. It had nowhere to run. Then it turned around and sprang on me. It was unexpected and very frightening."[281]

It is easy to imagine some of the values such a childhood could give rise to: comfort, stability, a bit of luxury in the form of Brioni suits—but of those, most of all, comfort. And also—pity, the kind of pity that keeps one from shooting a dying horse, or from firing a corrupt, inefficient, but loyal minister. And maybe, too, an insecurity, a slight chip on your shoulder. When someone snubs your men, your loyal men, you understand, and perhaps forgive, their extrajudicial revenge. Even if they murder a journalist on your birthday to demonstrate their loyalty.

Whether due to their absence of squalor or the presence of the very sense of ideological mission that life lacked, Putin took a liking to Soviet spy movies, like the classic *17 Instances of Spring.*

While still in school, he went to the local KGB and said he wanted to work for them. He was told to get a law degree and come back.[282]

He did, in 1975.

In the 1980s, after spending years tapping, tailing, and intimidating dissidents, he started speaking like those very dissidents during his posting in Dresden. "Volodya had already absorbed all of this dissident wisdom back in Leningrad," according to a friend of Putin cited by Yuri Felshtinsky and Vladimir Pribylovsky. "He spoke of many dissidents with esteem. He was especially respectful of Solzhenitsyn."[283]

This is important, for he had no allegiance to the idea of Communism, merely to the people that he served.

In 1991, he went to work for Leningrad's first democratic reformer, Mayor Anatoly Sobchak, as the head of City Hall's International Relations Committee. Putin warned his boss dutifully that he was a KGB agent. He resigned from the KGB on the day of the hardliner coup, August 20, 1991, when he no longer had a choice in what side to pick.

And thus began possibly the most interesting and significant period of his life, as he used the only job experience and know-how he had—his career in the KGB—to bring foreign investment to St. Petersburg's new free market.

In 1991, he asked his friend Pyotr Aven, then chairman of the Foreign Economic Relations Committee, to get a federal licence for a city program allowing City Hall's International Relations Committee to export commodities in exchange for food. According to a notorious inquiry by Leningrad deputy Marina Salye, he won unauthorized tenders for friends in the timber industry. The friends got rich, the food was never seen, and St. Petersburg's grocery shelves remained empty.[284]

In 1991, as head of the International Relations Committee, Putin headed an enterprise that took control of 51 percent of the city's gambling business, and, according to some allegations, pocketing some of the profits and distributing the rest among his friends.[285]

Putin himself described this process as "attempts to bring order to St. Petersburg's gambling business."

"To do this we created a municipal enterprise that didn't own any casinos, but controlled 51 percent of shares in the city's gambling establishment." According to Putin himself, the enterprise consisted of the "main controlling organizations," which were the FSB and the tax police. As shareholders, they (the exact word Vladimir Putin used is "the government") were to profit from the dividends. Except that they never did, for the gambling establishments were "laughing at us and showing us losses."[286]

In a country stripped of its governing ideology, when the centuries-old tax farming mechanism had kicked in, Vladimir Putin found himself in the middle of the action.

His subsequent rise to power through the Presidential Administration, the Security Council, and the FSB was part luck and part bureaucratic cunning. But what emerges again and again in biographical and political accounts is the lack of supreme ambition: the top job fell on Putin as if out of the blue. Insiders described the struggle involved in "getting Putin into the job," while his wife Lyudmila spent New Year's Eve 1999 weeping after Yeltsin publicly resigned.[287]

He had not created this system; he had adapted to it. And he had adapted so well that the powerful circle of hundreds of men inside and close to the Kremlin crystallized around him and pushed him to the top, to stand above the laws when they failed to function, which was most of the time, and to rule over them and protect them.

A leader is only as corrupt as the system that produces him. Given that inevitability, it was hard to expect that whoever replaced this small, gray man would not stand above the law.

The idea of an autocratic government as little more than a protection racket is not new—some historians, and free market theorists in particular, have explained the emergence of government as a pillaging gang that settled down and had the leading "roving bandit" wear a crown, in the words of political theorist Mancur Olson.[288]

Russia's Primary Chronicle, that twelfth century document of disputed origins, hails the voluntary invitation of Scandinavian princes by Slavic tribes to rule over them in 862, laying the ground for the myth of a mystical spiritual union between the people and their conquerors that would continue to be taken seriously as late as nineteenth century Russia. A likelier version, of course, is that those same Scandinavian princes started pillaging the thriving Volga River trade route connecting Byzantium with Scandinavia, but soon realized that a permanent protection racket could extract more rent, and so settled down and formed fiefdoms.[289]

Similar fiefdoms had sprouted in Europe, perhaps over a smaller, more crowded territory. But in one major way, the process of legitimization diverged, and it seemed to have diverged very early on.

There are usually two ways that brute force can become legitimate, transforming a "roving bandit" into a king: through the law, or through itself. Russian power has usually sought to legitimize through itself; but post-Soviet Russia has seen a curious mix of both approaches, each of which functions as though the other did not exist, and yet each coming to the other's rescue. Where the legal-rational state fails, the patrimonial kicks in.

By the seventeenth century, foreign visitors to Muscovy were struck not just by the absolute nature of its sovereign, but by the absence of lawyers. "Their laws provide that everyone plead his own case or have some kinsman or servant of his assigned to this, for they have no lawyers at all," a certain Jacques Margeret wrote in 1606.[290]

Part of the reason for this may have lain not so much in the weakness or corruption of the courts, but the absence of contracts to litigate.

The historian Richard Pipes, who famously argued for a link between property rights and freedom, describes two uniquely Russian geographical circumstances that unwittingly suggest exactly the opposite—that in Russia, despotism came from a surplus of freedom.

In the first circumstance, Pipes wrote that factors of climate created a situation in central and northern Russia where it was not profitable to invest more in one's land plot than was necessary for basic sustenance. In other words, no matter how much you tend your field, you will still get less grain for your effort than in France or Italy. These low profit margins devalued land and dampened the incentive to protect ownership rights.

The second concerned a uniquely Russian brand of feudalism. If in Europe the service of a vassal to a lord was dictated by a mutual contract that sprang up over generations of such service, then in Russia the contract was one-sided. The vassal came to serve the lord exclusively on the lord's terms. How could such a situation sustain itself? According to a very simplified scenario, if the vassal found the service too burdensome, he moved to another land—he was free to do so. But precisely because he was free to do so, no mutual contract bound his lord to any obligation—and if it was this contract that would lead to institutions like independent courts and the rule of law in Europe, the very idea of a contract, a mutual agreement, was not internalized in Russia.[291]

The Soviet critic Iurii Lotman took this a step further—identifying "agreement" (magical) and "self-giving" (religious) as two models of social culture and interaction, one based on contract, the other on submission. He traced how the latter predominated in medieval Russia, where the very idea of a contract governing relations was looked down upon. Under this religious model, one submitted fully to power without the constraints of a contract. "The concept of government service that arose in these conditions presumed an absence of agreements between the two sides: from one side there was the full and unconditional giving of the self, and from the other there was grace." A medieval literary character would not be ashamed to call himself a "dog" in demonstrating his loyalty to his prince.[292] Utter freedom and utter despotism, thus, arose from economic conditions early on, and there could not be one without the other. There would be few of the "networks of mutual dependence" described by Pipes that, while constraining the individual freedom of Western vassals, also protected them from the tyranny of their lord. The Russian boyar was either free to go where he pleased, for the land was vast, or he was an utter slave, a "dog" to his sovereign, "on the table, and on the balcony."

In the absence of functioning laws and "networks of mutual dependence," the legitimacy of the crown came from within. This form of legitimization had its own, particular appeal. The fourth century courtier Themistius, somewhat cynically, described this appeal in regard to Emperor Theodosius I: "For he is the animate law, not merely a law laid down in permanent and unchangeable terms… God sent kings on earth to serve men as a refuge from an immovable law to the safety of the animate and living law."[293] It is easy to see how businessmen like William Browder could be drawn to that living law, without immediately seeing how quickly one could also wind up "on the table and on the balcony."

But a self-sustaining living law also needed an idea, some form of New Jerusalem to justify its implicitly quasi-divine nature. Russia's manifest destiny would be used by Ivan the Terrible, Peter the Great, and Joseph Stalin to justify whatever blood they needed to spill on the way to achieving their holy mission—be that a New Jerusalem in the case of Ivan, a window into Europe in the case of Peter, and industrialization in the case of Stalin.

Vladimir Putin, born just seven years after the last heroic exploit of Russia's manifest destiny—the victory in World War II—came from a generation that had no more strength for heroic feats. After rising to the apex of the state, he paid only marginal dues to the legal rational state that struggled to legitimize his rule, and could not be held accountable to it. But if his predecessors answered only to God and a divinely-inspired mission, he didn't have the faith or the strength to be a messiah-prince. So he just pretended to be Chuck Norris.

As he aged, however, he was beginning to fail at that. His appearance in a hang-glider in August 2012, leading a flock of storks in migration, drew little but irritation from many Russians (seeing him on TV and not in a moment of supplication). Vague reports of a back injury morphed via Facebook into rumors of a sarcoma (that few took seriously). Attempts to continue looking young at sixty through evident plastic surgery (which was never admitted) only drew ridicule.

The mass protests of 2011–2012 can be seen as a reaction of the middle classes to that lack of mission, the notion that they were being ruled by a corrupt opportunist, or even a false Tsar. It was not surprising that to remedy this, Putin's government resorted to the latent caesaropapism of Russia's past, drawing on the legitimizing force of the only other institution with a modicum of trust: the church. In the words of sociologist Vladimir Shlapentokh, Putin was trying to privatize God.

But if those attempts—coupled with a repressive crackdown (which helps bring out the government's quasi-sacred nature)— succeeded partially in disorienting a marginal opposition that itself lacked any ideology or political program, they had not succeeded in guaranteeing legitimacy. Putin was drawing on a traditional force, on church-state harmony, even as he tried to uphold a legal-rational state. By meandering back and forth between the two, he risked exposing himself as a false Tsar, and further awakening the need for a real one.

5.

Vladimir Putin had probably heard me say his name, just as he had heard a few others. He continued answering a question about corruption—it consumed him. "Look at me, I'm talking to you," he told a journalist standing next to me. He had not turned in my direction, each was supposed to wait her turn (I had realized with some dismay that, aside from nervous security guards, mostly women had encircled the president). Since I had mustered the courage to say his name to him once, I could easily say it again, I should have said it again, I was a journalist, the fear of irritating him, the unpredictable consequences of his answers, should not have stayed me. But what would I say once he turned to me? Ask him to consider the statistical likelihood of more dead orphans before signing the bill? He knew this already, just as he already knew that he would sign the bill. I could only elicit his annoyance or his favor, depending on what he saw in me. I also suspected that, by looking at me, he could discern even better than I whether I was in real opposition to him or not. And somehow, I didn't want him to know it, because I didn't want to know it myself. But there was something else that stopped me from continuing, that allowed me to just let it go and walk away: it was the sudden sense that what we were engaging in was not exactly a press conference, and we were not exactly journalists anymore. It was a more ancient exchange that I realized I didn't want to be a part of. I didn't want to ask him for anything.

Epilogue
Russia without Putin

I believe that power originates from the impenetrable depths of the human psyche. From the same place as love.
—**Vladislav Surkov**

Freedom is a religious problem. The insolubility of the soul. The inevitability of the separation of everything from everything.
—**Vladislav Surkov**

RADIK SAT ON top of an APC, smiling radiantly into the May sun, as he and a couple of masked men with Kalashnikovs and a Russian flag rode up to the barricaded regional administration building of Ukraine's breakaway Donetsk region.

"Where are you from?" I asked him.

"Donetsk," he said. Radik couldn't have been more than twenty. He wore unmarked fatigues, with the red, black and blue sticker of the self-proclaimed Donetsk People's Republic on him and the APC. One of his calves was wrapped in scotch tape, holding a knife in place.

"Where's this thing from?" I asked, patting the top of the APC. Everyone was looking for a smoking gun that Russia was arming the insurgency. Did the equipment come from raided depots in Ukraine, or was it passed on over the border by rogue supporters of the insurgency within the Russian military? Did it matter all that much?

"Got it from near Donetsk."

"Why?"

"*Tak nado.* That's the way it has to be."

He seemed there to show that they could; that militants like him were adamant about holding a referendum on independence from Ukraine the following day. Radik beamed as he explained that after the referendum, Russia would annex the Donetsk region, just as it had done two months earlier with Crimea. He was certain of it.

Other local residents were not.

"I don't know who those guys in the Donetsk People's Republic are," said one long-time Donetsk resident. He asked not to disclose his name because, as he put it, he'd still have to live in the same city with them after I left.

I understood his concerns: having entered the separatist stronghold once, with its Russian flags, its trash, its half-drunk men with masks and fatigues and Kalashnikovs, its reputed cellars for suspected "fascists," its catch-and-release of suspicious-looking journalists, you were never quite sure when you'd make it out.

"I don't understand what their referendum is about, and I don't understand what they want," said the resident. But nor did he trust the government in Kiev, which, having itself been propelled into power on the wings of an insurgency, hardly knew how to deal with another insurgency blowing up in the east.

That it had come to this, a civil war in Ukraine with activist militants on both sides trying to avenge previous deaths until they swelled into the thousands, was both an accident and an inevitability. Maybe Radik was right and this was just the way it had to be. The messy breakup of the Soviet Union had never really been complete, leaving behind all sorts of volatile Russian-speaking and other ethnic enclaves within republics that found themselves sovereign nations virtually overnight. The checkerboard of languages and nationalities across the post-Soviet space was a legacy, in many ways, of Joseph Stalin's attempts to impose a melting pot, relocating nationalities by force, forging societies in a top-down effort, and never preparing for the eventuality that empires break up with disastrous consequences for the people that inhabit them. Throughout the 1990s, violent ethnic conflicts would flare up as a result across the former empire; in Georgia, Tajikistan, Azerbaijan, even within Russia, in Chechnya and Ingushetia, Russians whose grandparents had been relocated decades ago to enhance diversity would often become victims of the violence. Given the linguistic, social, and economic divides within Ukraine, perhaps the clashes were merely waiting to happen.

For the Russian nationalists both in Russia and Ukraine, the civil war that was unfurling was their own Russian Spring, their leader proclaiming Russia's manifest destiny. Emboldened by a pro-Western revolution in Kiev that, with a visit from CIA chief John Brennan and US money, had all the outward show of political support from Washington, they rallied around a cause they could get behind with every molecule of their souls. Suddenly, the disparate flurry of fragmented nationalist groups united under a single banner of protecting the Russian people in what was once the cradle of Russian civilization. Their members activated their ties with war veterans, military intelligence, and the FSB, and, inspired by Putin's show of military might, picked up Kalashnikovs and flooded south into Ukraine's Donetsk and Lugansk regions. "Tsar, their lives are more important than your wallet," supporters of Ukrainian intervention said of Russians in Ukraine at a Moscow rally in June 2014. "Putin, save Donbass."

The disenfranchised former and acting security officers we saw in Part II mobilized for the cause, with hundreds deploying themselves to East Ukraine. Here was the sacred mission at last, the national ideology so many had yearned to see in the Kremlin.

"Putin, give us orders," an FSB major who identified himself as Alexander said to me. "We need just one day and Ukraine will be ours. We have 300 men in Donbass. We just need a command."

The liberal opposition was pushed to the margins and further atomized as Putin's approval ratings shot up to 85 percent. Even some of the leaders of the street opposition, who two years earlier vowed to overthrow Putin, themselves in jail or under house arrest like Sergei Udaltsov, not only supported the Kremlin's intervention in Ukraine, but felt it hadn't gone far enough.

Some Russians in east Ukraine, and particularly in Crimea, gazed upon the Kremlin's new-found decisiveness with awe and envy.

"Everybody here worships him. We never had a president who would do anything for the people," a sixty-year-old woman in a dilapidated apartment block in Simferopol would tell me.

For Vyacheslav Fomenko, an entrepreneur in Donetsk, the envy was more complex. Watching his country splitting apart, seeing a government in the capital that was openly hostile to Russian speakers like him, he remained skeptical. "Russia finally got their tsar. Putin. Maybe, if we'll wait long enough, we'll get one too. I want one. Because why should I have to hate my country?"

★ ★ ★

The thing that had triggered the civil war was really an afterthought. In late November 2013, Ukraine's President Viktor Yanukovich had suddenly backed out of signing an association agreement with the EU, widely seen as a first step towards eventual EU accession. It was clear, from the start, why this had happened: if he signed, Ukraine couldn't join the Eurasian Union, a free trade zone spearheaded by Russia as a new Soviet Union, except without the communism. While an economic liability and more financially volatile than Kazakhstan and even Belarus, Ukraine was nevertheless crucial to the Eurasian Union on a symbolic level, as a cradle of Russian culture and civilization. It was in Kievan Rus that Orthodox Christianity was adopted. If Vladimir Putin embarked on the Eurasian Union as part of a historic mission to become the "gatherer of Russian lands," Ukraine had to remain within his sphere of interests.

There was also another, more practical reason for that, far more important and perhaps even existential for Putin than grand visions of empire: he needed to ensure that NATO stayed out of Ukraine.

And so there had been pressure from Putin, inevitably in the form of threat to up the price for Russian gas, which Ukraine depended on and which it was already having a catastrophically dire time affording. To sweeten the pill, Putin had also offered $15 billion in loans.

Russia's deal, at least in the short term, may have been more appealing to Ukraine's economy: a discounted gas price of $270 per thousand cubic meters (35,000 cubic feet) and no export duties compared to the average price in Europe of about $380; less strings attached than on the bailout offered by the IMF, with its obligatory austerity measures aimed at getting Ukraine's economy in shape; and trade with Russia and other Eurasian Union countries. Russia was a smaller market to do business with than Europe's, to be sure, but Ukraine, and East Ukraine in particular, already had the Soviet-era industrial and infrastructural ties in place towards doing business with Russia. Locals in the East, Yanukovich's chief constituency, felt they would be disenfranchised by a deal with Europe—the economy was bad already, and reorienting it westward when it was so embedded with Russia's would be painful.

But for western Ukraine, where cities like Lviv saw themselves as part of Europe and a large part of the population spoke mainly Ukrainian, the promise of Europe seemed the only hope for viable change. Lacking hydrocarbons, Ukraine's economy had sputtered along for more than two decades, hardly improving since the 1990s. Ukraine's government was as spectacularly corrupt as Russia's, and it was almost as repressive. But unlike the Kremlin, Yanukovich's government didn't have a monopoly on politics; there was a viable opposition in parliament, and every four years there were elections where it was hard to predict who the winner would be. Most importantly, it hadn't developed that sacred inevitability that was so characteristic of the Kremlin.

The corruption, repression, and economic backwardness had swirled together, in the minds of the Kiev protesters, into a stifling blanket of Russianness that needed to be shaken off. That was why the first demonstrators to turn up on Maidan rallied for closer integration with Europe, which they hoped would serve as a jolt to revive the economy and clean up its politics.

But then, when the government's riot police, the Berkut, moved in and violently tried to clear the square, all hell broke loose. In a matter of weeks, Euromaidan became about toppling Yanukovich's corrupt regime. It had spiraled from a European protest about issues into the kind of existential revolt more typical of Russia. Politics disintegrated, leaving only the show of force: riot police were filmed forcing protesters to stand naked in sub-zero temperatures. And what was initially a demonstration of peaceful students, was now joined by masked, armed radicals from Ukraine's two far right movements: Svoboda and Pravy Sektor. After months of standoff between the protesters and the Berkut, the violent clashes began. Cobblestones were unearthed, barricades built from tires and barbed wire, Molotov cocktails, and then the guns, once they became available, though no one quite understood how they were procured, and by whom. By the time Yanukovich was forced to flee the country on February 22, well over 100 people had been killed—by Berkut, by radical protesters, and by mysterious snipers who shot people on both sides.

Just like that, Yanukovich's government was gone. A pro-Western interim government came in headed by the opposition. To curry favor with the demonstrators still camped out on Maidan, or simply as part of the revolution's continuing rebellion against all things Russian, the new authority's first move was to propose making Ukrainian the single state language. If passed, the move would in effect have stripped Russian, which was more commonly spoken in eastern regions like Donetsk, Lugansk, and Crimea than Ukrainian, of official status. Russian would no longer be taught in schools, and the many in the East who didn't speak Ukrainian would be forced to learn it. The new interim president, Oleksandr Turchynov, quickly rescinded the proposal, but the damage had already been done: the suggestion itself, coupled with anti-Russian remarks made by pro-Western politicians, had frightened and angered the East to the extent that Russians there, particularly in Crimea, where Russia had a naval presence, began to mobilize. It also gave Russia, which had likely already developed a plan to take Crimea, the perfect excuse to move in.

Pro-Russian protests flared up in Crimea's Simferopol on February 23. Local politicians with Russian ties, acting in the manner of the Maidan demonstrators, seized government buildings and proclaimed themselves as the new authorities. Sergei Aksyonov, a former businessman with Russian connections and a shady past, was elected prime minister of Crimea in a snap vote held in a building surrounded by armed militants. Politically, Aksyonov had Russia's full backing: Russian state TV called what happened in Kiev an "illegal armed coup" and warned of genocide, while Putin pledged to protect the Russian-speaking people of Crimea and East Ukraine from the "fascists" in power.

Where Crimea was concerned, Russia was well-placed to do what it wished. The peninsula, which was gifted to Ukraine in 1954 by Soviet leader Nikita Khrushchev, had been somewhat of a point of contention among Russian nationalist hardliners in the military since the breakup of the Soviet Union. Giving a region away within the USSR was one thing, but they reasoned that Crimea was Russian and it had no place being part of the foreign country Ukraine had since become. More importantly, since 1783 Crimea had been the home of Russia's Black Sea Fleet, and Russia had a lease agreement with Kiev that allowed up to 25,000 military personnel to service its naval base in Sevastopol.

Propelled in Moscow, meeting local sentiment half-way, the events were set in motion. Professionally armed soldiers bearing no insignia turned up in the streets of Simferopol and Sevastopol in the last week of February. Self-mobilized militias bearing Russian flags started calling for secession from Ukraine and joining Russia. On March 1, Putin asked the Federation Council to authorize sending the Russian army to Ukraine. An invasion seemed imminent.

Where Crimea was concerned, rather than overt invasion more effective in the tangled, precarious social landscape of an empire that had never quite finished breaking up was propaganda, grass roots support, and subterfuge. The new pro-Russian prime minister Sergei Aksyonov asked Russia to join it, in the name of protecting the people. Self-mobilized militia, veteran officers who served in the Soviet Union with Russian comrades, so that it wasn't clear whether they were Russian or Crimean, patrolled the streets, stormed weapons depots with hardly any resistance, and coordinated, at least on some level, with the Russian command of the Black Sea Fleet. Vladimir Putin would continue to deny that Russia had any intention of annexing Crimea right up until the day after the March 16 referendum, when it did.

The simple answer to why Putin annexed Crimea but not the other eastern Ukraine regions was because he could. In Crimea's case, the plan to take back the peninsula, as a potential option waiting for the right moment to be set into motion, had been developed long before, military experts would say. The decision to carry it out was sudden, and formed probably sometime in late February or early March.

Why then, and why the rush? The truth of the matter is that Crimea was annexed with hardly a shot fired. The threat of invasion, propaganda, and a strategy that largely allowed the self-mobilized pro-Russian militias to do their work, was enough. There was no resistance from Kiev. Local Tatars and Ukrainians opposed to the move held several protest rallies, but being outnumbered their only option was simply not to turn up for the referendum.

On the surface, the decision to annex Crimea was sold on the popular premise that "Crimea's ours," the hashtagged meme that swept Russia's Twitter in spring 2014, and on the supposed need to protect the Russian-speaking population. This was the rallying call, the sudden resurgence of Russia's manifest destiny. But the more practical reasons that a normally risk-averse Putin went ahead with a decision that would isolate him internationally, provoke Western sanctions, and thus jeopardize the business interests of his closest cohort was more foreign than domestic: NATO and the Black Sea Fleet.

Russia's naval base in Sevastopol, and thus its naval presence in the Black Sea, was contingent on an increasingly unpopular agreement with Ukraine. In 2010, Russia's lease of the territory was prolonged until 2042 in exchange for gas subsidies under the Kharkiv Pact. The Ukrainian opposition, which simply did not show up when the treaty was ratified in parliament, had since widely called the pact illegitimate and unconstitutional. It was clear that a new pro-Western government would soon scrap the lease, forcing Russia to leave the base by 2017.

This was coupled with the ever-present threat of Ukraine eventually joining NATO, which pro-Western factions in Ukraine had been keen on. Once Ukraine was on the way towards NATO membership, Russia would have effectively given up the Black Sea to NATO without any form of counterbalance. Annexing Crimea, thus, wasn't about imperial expansion. It was about the need to defend what already was, in substance but not in name, an existing empire. Like Putin's behavior on the domestic arena, it was a manifestation of the natural state of things, concealed by a network of international laws that, in Russia's case, openly clashed with that archaic natural state.

Would Putin move further with the Ukrainian mainland? With the seizure of government buildings by Russian-aligned militias and the referendum on independence, it looked in April that Lugansk and Donetsk would go the way of Crimea. Why else was the Kremlin, in all essence, fueling a covert war on the ground?

If the hope was for a Crimea-style referendum, that never

materialized. The new Kiev government cracked down on the separatist rebels, and by the end of the summer nearly 3000 people were dead and hundreds of thousands displaced. Without ever actually invading, Russia found itself fighting a shadow war it was not prepared to admit. And when, in August, the first Russian regular soldiers came back from Ukraine in coffins, their government would not acknowledge where they fought, and they would be buried in secret funerals. Russian nationalists began to grumble that Putin was selling out to the West. In September, amid a precarious ceasefire, an AP reporter found a mass grave dedicated to the rebels: "They died for Putin's lies," said the engraved epitaph.

In 2014, what Putin expertly did in Ukraine was sit back and let things happen to his advantage—unleashing a nationalist force that he could not contain and channeling it to unite the country around him, around a religious mission. Why did he need to rely on that ancient force that was beyond his control to rein in once unleashed?

Aside from geopolitical maneuvering to secure influence over Ukraine, there were powerful internal factors driving Russia's intervention. As the 2012 protests had shown, Putin's own future wasn't fully certain. The aftermath of Kiev's Maidan suggested what could happen to Russia in the event that a liberal revolution succeeded in toppling an authoritarian regime: a violent split between the modern-minded west versus the patrimonial east, as dormant separatist hubs would explode.

There was another domestic factor pushing Putin to act, and it was psychological. For six years, the government had funneled a good share of its resources—both monetary and ideological—towards the Sochi Winter Olympics in February 2014. Rife with corruption and scandal, a lot of effort went into maintaining the kind of stability necessary to pull off such an ambitious project. There was talk, even, that political decisions, from a parliamentary reshuffle to decisions involving the volatile North Caucasus region nearby—in particular, Ramzan Kadyrov's Chechnya—were put on hold until after the Olympics in order to avoid destabilization. Many predicted a new wave of corruption scandals and sackings.[294] Such tension leading up to one single sporting event—no matter how big—creates inevitable uncertainty after the fact. Would the Olympics prove to have been a force holding things together? Would the absence of an ambitious, consolidating project, amid a stagnating economy, exacerbate political and economic instability and the centrifugal forces that have perennially plagued such a large country as Russia? The end of the Olympic Games coincided with the toppling of Yanukovich's regime in Kiev. There couldn't have been a better time for a new consolidating project to emerge—after all, the demand for one had been growing. In Russia, to a greater extent than for smaller countries, there is hardly any other unifying force strong enough to maintain the country's integrity and keep it under the sovereign's dominion.

And so, when Tatyana Gruzdeva, one of the demonstrators at a Moscow "Save Donbass" rally, declared that she was behind the sovereign body and soul, she was merely expressing the primal culmination of sentiment when a force stronger than yourself demonstrates intent to protect you and your own kind from what you perceive as a foreign threat. That Putin had suddenly reacted by amassing troops on the Ukrainian border and annexing Crimea was simply what a leader that they felt they deserved had to do. *Tak nado*. It must be.

But was it meant to? When a jetliner carrying 298 innocent people—Dutch, Malaysian, British—was shot down by what appeared to be a surface-to-air missile fired, according to preliminary evidence, by pro-Russian insurgents in the self-proclaimed People's Republic of Donetsk, the world turned against Putin in earnest. He stood before a choice. Would he stop backing the pro-Russian insurgency in Ukraine and betray the people who had rallied around him following his annexation of Crimea, his threats of sending troops, and his promises of support to the rebels? Would he betray the security service officers and the ordinary people yearning for a mission? Or would Putin stand by the nationalist forces he had unleashed, bringing crippling sanctions and isolation to his country—utterly alienating the middle class he tried so hard in the past to foster? He could not avoid both.

Betrayal, in security circles, is the worst sin one can possibly imagine. It is said that Putin, a security veteran himself, respects both friends and enemies alike—it is the traitors he has no sympathy for. At the core of Russia's actions in Ukraine was nothing less than the *Russian idea*: part cult, part military doctrine, part religion. And in the summer of 2014, the Russian sovereign stood in front of an existential threat: that of being forced to betray the Russian idea.

★ ★ ★

Power, in the Russian tradition, legitimizes itself. But it must be propped up by its *idea*, its divine mission, for that legitimization to work. This is not necessarily because the people want it this way, but because there is usually little alternative.

Why is this the case? Why can't a society just elect a leader who will rule in accordance with the law, in accordance with democratic procedure? Because first there must be laws a society has agreed upon.

I have evaded this question throughout the book, primarily because such a question presumes we are dealing with a problem that needs to be fixed, whereas I believe we are instead dealing with a problem that first needs to be understood.

The dominant assumption about Russia—held for over a hundred years by both Russian philosophers and outside observers—is that Russians tend to forge an intrinsically collectivist society, where the interests of the group predominate over those of the individual. The idea, which pitted Russian society against a presumably individualistic West, is so dominant that communists used it to justify their ideology, arguing that communism was a natural destiny for collectivist Russia, while capitalist reformers during the 1990s tried to "cure" Russians of collectivism by imposing an individualistic doctrine. It is telling that both attempts proved, to various degrees, disastrous. Perhaps the collectivism that the communists tried to exploit, and the market capitalists tried to cure, was actually lacking?

If we look back at the kind of relationships described between people in this book, we will notice a startling pattern: many of the stories that have been told are about the inability of various people to agree on a common interest and achieve it.

Sergei Kvitko's appeal to Putin to gasify his home was made after all attempts to solve the problem together with his neighbors and local government officials had failed. The residents of Pikalevo blocked a highway when negotiations between workers and managers, managers and owners, owners and the local administration, had broken down.

Law enforcement officers described in Part II used their positions of power to solve personal, individual goals of enrichment, and conflicts inevitably arose among officers in their pursuit of enrichment because the only governing mechanism was one's closeness to power.

The young activists who joined pro-Kremlin groups did so because, given a staggering lack of community in their own towns, the government was their only venue for activism. The protesting creative class failed to find a common language with many of those who eagerly joined the Kremlin's campaign for traditional values.

Those who visit Russia and travel beyond the confines of Moscow are often struck by the vast expanses. But among those expanses, they also see newly-built houses surrounded by high, impenetrable walls, as if their whole objective is to isolate themselves from their neighbors and from outsiders.

The roads, meanwhile, and the poorer homes, will often be dilapidated, broken, and desolate. Inside the walls of the rich, the lawns will be groomed and gardens will be planted, but outside, just a few meters away, one will often find a sprawling heap of rubbish.

When one looks for a Russian national identity, one will find more factors dividing society than unifying it. When an August 2013 survey asked 1600 Russians what group they identified themselves with the most, 32 percent said they were "their own person and didn't identify with any group." The next category—11 percent—identified themselves not as Russians, but as the middle class. Just 4 percent identified themselves as ethnic Russians.[295]

Interpersonal trust among Russians, while not at the bottom of the list, is still considerably lower than in other countries. According to the Levada Center, only 27 percent of Russian respondents said that they believed other people should be trusted. That figure was 69 percent in Sweden, 42 percent in the United States, and an average of 45 percent among 29 countries.[296]

More striking still were statistics on how likely Russians were to get involved in voluntary work to help strangers in their community. According to two studies in 2011 and 2012, between 1 and 3 percent of Russians said they had volunteered through NGOs in the past year. When informal voluntary work was factored in, a

2011 Gallup poll found that less than 15 percent of the Russian population volunteered. That was far below third world neighbors like Turkmenistan (58 percent) and Uzbekistan (46 percent).[297]

Far from collectivist, these figures—and the view from any rural window—paint a society that is atomized and even individualistic. Lack of communication—which leads to lack of community—emerges as a central problem.

Soviet attempts at collectivization tried to remedy this problem. Note that the very word "collectivization" presumes the *lack* of a collective, implying one that needs to be imposed by force. Collectivization attempts during the end of Stalin's rule—in the late 1940s and early 1950s, when a majority of the population lived in the countryside—faced a crucial hurdle: the lack of roads connecting communities. In autumn and spring, dirt roads were impassable; even today, this is the case for some federal highways, which become impossible to navigate during the autumn rains and the spring thaw. Lack of roads has been both a cause and an effect of lack of community. (As one study suggests, some farms took advantage of the lack of roads to remain out of the government's reach and expand their holdings.)[298]

There are also the centrifugal forces resulting from 21 internal, non-Russian ethnic republics, some of whose residents do not speak Russian. The various ethnic, economic, and social interests, sprawled out over one sixth of the world's landmass, led Russia scholar Natalia Zubarevich to conclude that we are dealing not with one Russia, but with four.[299]

Putin's state has particularly struggled to find a unifying factor: forging a national identity, and preparing for the 2014 Winter Olympics as a goal that everyone, from construction companies to schoolboys playing hockey, could strive for. But that left a big question of what would unify the country after the Olympic Games—not that the preparation efforts, riddled with corruption and embezzlement, have had much success. The Russian Spring, the annexation of Crimea and the covert, grass-roots campaign in East Ukraine filled that lacuna, melding with the resurgence of Orthodox Christianity in its perennial quest to keep the country together. Only the prospect of what nationalist ideologues referred to as a "holy war" for Novorossiya, New Russia, was capable of such unprecedented unifying fervor.

If we are dealing with an atomized society, divided by space, ethnicity, climate, and economics, if we are dealing with broken communication between individuals and small groups, then what does that say about the relationship with supreme power?

Very often, Russian authoritarianism has been explained as an extension of Russia's intrinsic collectivism. The political philosopher Hannah Arendt, meanwhile, identified "the primary concern of all tyrannical governments" as an attempt to bring about isolation, writing that tyrannies strive to sever political contacts between men.[300] But perhaps authoritarianism, and the patrimonial state in particular, is merely what arises in the absence of political bonds between people?

That kind of state, with tendencies towards absolutism, reflects not just the vulnerability of the people in the face of state power, but also the people's own implicit expectations of what state power should be like. If there is so little to unite a society apart from language and culture—which, incidentally, is not shared by a number of ethnic republics—people will look to state power to fulfil that role. The harder it is to establish horizontal networks and bonds, the more one is tempted to conflate God and Caesar, looking to his powers to step in where society has failed.

Separateness and atomization—and the compensatory, often dysfunctional collectivization that these factors produce—should not be viewed as a disease that needs to be fixed, but as a circumstance that needs to be understood and accepted. Russia may never have the close-knit communities that helped foster the kind of democratic and legal institutions that flourished, over hundreds of years, in Europe. Or, it could be that, in a digitalized world, new, unforeseen avenues of community-building will arise— because they are already arising. Russian society may continue looking to the state to play a central, unifying role—as, in times of crisis, will other societies. The use of one's public office for self-enrichment might never be eradicated in Russia, because it has not been eradicated anywhere, but it may be accepted and regulated in order to avoid catastrophic human rights violations like the death and trial of Sergei Magnitsky or the corruption scandals we have related in this book. It could well be that Russia might eventually come to terms with itself as a feudal, fragmented state—stopping the cycle of revolution and despotism that have largely been the key forces fighting feudalism and fragmentation. Russia might never have the rule of law in the Western sense, but it could, perhaps, find a better equilibrium between the legal-rational and the patrimonial states.

Or it may simply fall apart and go the way of empires that grappled with similar problems before it: Byzantium, the Ottomans, and Austro-Hungary, giving way to an entirely new kind of Russian state.

For now, however, the Russian is in many ways rather alone, gazing upward, willingly giving up his powers to a higher being that he looks to for answers, because finding answers alone is too difficult.

Acknowledgements

I AM INDEBTED to a great number of people who helped make this book possible. The following are just a few.

My husband, Mikhail Vizel, not only encouraged me to write this book, but inspired the idea when he told me, one day in 2007, that I should try to see past the politics at what was really happening in Russia.

Anthony Louis spent an enormous amount of time advising me on the text, an editor and a critic at once.

Karl Sabbagh and Michel Moushabeck brought this book to the audience for which it was originally intended: the British and the American.

Vladimir Sharov and Vladimir Shlapentokh, in different ways and from different continents, inspired and encouraged this work.

Stanislav Konunov traveled with me to Pikalyovo and helped gather interviews for this book.

Andy Potts, Tim Wall, and Natalia Antonova gave me support and advice, reading earlier versions of the draft.

My agents, Julia Goumen and Natasha Banke, put their faith in this project when it was just beginning. The phrase "make it happen" was made for them.

Finally, I would not have had the strength to write this book without the support of my family.

★ ★ ★

The people who agreed to speak to me and share their thoughts and experiences make up much of the content of this book. Some requested to remain anonymous. I am grateful for all their help, because a lot of these stories are their stories, as varied, contradictory, and multifaceted as all people and books are.

Notes

1. During a Q&A session with youth groups at the Seliger forum in August, 2011, Vladimir Putin fielded such a question. A girl who identified herself as Natalia told Putin, demurely, that she wanted to marry a military officer and asked what her "outlook" would be if she did so. "You'll have two or three children, that's for certain," Putin told her.

From an official transcript and video on the prime minister's website. http://premier. gov.ru/events/news/16080/

2. An oprichnik was a member of Tsar Ivan the Terrible's secret police during the 1560s. In modern Russia, the term is often used negatively to describe security officers.

3. Ignatius, Adi. "A Tsar is Born." *Time.* December 19, 2007. American journalists were so enthralled by Putin's stare that they devoted the leading paragraph to it.

4. If US President George Bush saw Putin's soul, then Russian President Boris Yeltsin, upon anointing his successor, described his eyes as "interesting."

5. Sakwa, Richard. *The Crisis of Russian Democracy: The Dual State, Factionalism, and the Medvedev Succession.* Cambridge University Press: New York, 2011.

6. Shlapentokh, Vladimir. *Rossiya kak feodalnoye obshchestvo.* Stolitsa-Print: Moscow, 2008.

7. Pastukhov, Vladimir. *Restavratsiya vmesto reformatsii. Dvadtsat let, kotoryie potryasli*

Rossiyu. OGI: Moscow, 2012, p. 229.

8. From a documentary about Putin aired on NTV on October 7, 2012. *Tsentralnoye Televideniye.* http://www.youtube.com/watch?v=c-0Y6FAxZ1E

9. Hertzen, Alexander. *Byloye i dumy.* From: Complete collection, Pravda: Moscow, 1975. Volume 4, pp. 159-160.

10. According to a Levada Center poll conducted in September 2012, 20 percent of women said they would like to marry Putin. http://www.levada. ru/05-10-2012/20-rossiyanok-khoteli-vy-iti-zamuzh-za-vladimira-putina

11. From an interview with Marina Razbezhkina, whose students produced a documentary film *Winter Go Away,* about the protests. "Rossiya na Marse, kuda ne doletet." *Russky Reporter.* October 2, 2012. http://rusrep.ru/article/2012/10/02/russia

12. The United Nations High Commissioner for Refugees officially expressed concern over the disappearance of Leonid Razvozzhayev in front of a UNHCR office in Kiev in October 2012. http://unhcr.org.ua/en/2011-08-26-06-58-56/news-archive/827-press-release-the-un-refugee-agency-is-deeply-concerned-about-the-disappearance-of-asylum-seek-er-from-russian-federation

13. Barry, Ellen. "Russian Opposition Figure Says Abductors Threatened His Children." The *New York Times.* October 24, 2012.

http://www.nytimes.com/2012/10/25/world/europe/leonid-razvozzhayev-says-abductors-threatened-his-children.html

14 Svetova, Zoya. "Umalivshiye osnovu." *The New Times*. June 11, 2012. http://newtimes.ru/articles/detail/53272/

15 The name has been changed at the request of the person.

16 Sologub, V. A. *Perezhitye dni*. Russky Mir, 1874, p. 117. http://az.lib.ru/w/weresaew_w_w/text_0130.shtml

17 Pushkin, A. S. *Puteshestvie iz Moskvy v Peterburg. Sobraniye sochinenii v 10 tomakh*. Russkaya Virtualnaya Biblioteka. http://www.rvb.ru/pushkin/01text/07criticism/02misc/1050.htm

18 "Premier vserossiiskogo teatra." *Gazeta.ru*. http://www.gazeta.ru/culture/2011/04/29/a_3599681.shtml

19 See Sakwa, Richard. *Putin: Russia's Choice*. Second Edition. Kindle Edition, 2009.

20 Based on an interview, conducted on conditions of anonymity, with a hotel administrator in the town of Pikalevo, May 2011.

21 Based on an interview with a driver at the Pikalevo minerals plant in May 2011. With reference to Putin's staged performance, both the hotel administrator and the driver spoke in similar terms.

22 Cassiday, Julie A; Johnson, Emily D. "Putin, Putiniana, and the Question of a Post-Soviet Cult of Personality." *The Slavonic and East European Review*. Volume 88, No. 4. October 1, 2010, pp. 681-707.

23 Gudkov, Lev. *"Priroda putinisma."* Russian Alternatives conference, December 8, 2009.

24 The t-shirts were distributed by the Foundation for Effective Politics in the spring of 1999. The author used to have one; now, threadbare, it has retired to the spare clothes drawer of the family dacha.

25 Petrov, Nikolay. "Elections." *Between Dictatorship and Democracy: Russian post-communist political reform*. Michael McFaul, Nikolay Petrov, Andrei Ryabov. Washington, 2004: Carnegie Endowment for International Peace, p. 48.

26 As quoted in: Baker, Peter; Glasser, Susan. *Kremlin Rising: Vladimir Putin's Russia and the End of Revolution*. A Lisa Drew Book/Scribner. New York, 2005. (Kindle Edition).

27 Based on an interview with one of several applicants in Moscow's central Reception Office, conducted by the author in February 2011. All further information about Sergei Kvitko's case is based on his own words, unless otherwise noted.

28 "Priyemnyie Putina ishyut istochniki finansirovania." *Kommersant*, No. 13 (4068). January 27, 2009.

29 According to a document of the gasification program posted on an official Tula region website. http://tula.news-city.info/docs/sistemsd/dok_ierizb.htm

30 From an official transcript of a speech by Putin dated September 25, 2008. http://archive.premier.gov.ru/visits/ru/6068/events/1975/

31 Ivanov, Maxim. "Overwhelmed with Pleas." *Kommersant*. July 30, 2009.

32 http://blog-medvedev.livejournal.com/22187.html?thread=167595

33 http://yarik-kolosov.livejournal.com/642.html

34 Glavvrach RDKB. "Godovaly Yaroslav Kolosov seichas na lechenii v Germanii." *RIA Novosti*. May 18, 2011. http://www.rian.ru/society/20110518/376193906.html

35 Lally, Kathy. "Medvedev meets the press." The *Washington Post*. May 18, 2011. http://www.washingtonpost.com/world/europe/medvedev-meets-the-press/2011/05/18/AFQ6QX6G_print.html

36 From an official transcript on www.premier.gov.ru

37 From a telephone interview with a caseworker at the reception office in October, 2011. The caseworker spoke on conditions of anonymity.

38 Pushkin, Alexander. *Boris Godunov*. Kessinger Publishing, 2004.

39 Kolesnikov, Andrei. "Ne ukaraulili sem poselkov." *Kommersant*, No. 138. July 31, 2010.

40 Ibid.

41 Sharov, Vladimir. *Iskusheniye revolutsiyei (Russkaya verkhovnaya vlast)*. Moscow: Arsis Books, 2009, p 23.

42 See Arutunyan, Anna. "Is Russia Really that Authoritarian?" *Foreign Policy in Focus*, January 11, 2007. http://

www.fpif.org/articles/is_russia_really_
that_authoritarian.

43 "Despite Putin's calls to bolster social
order and implement federal laws over
the entire country, the Kremlin allowed
local leaders to see themselves as feudal
lords as long as they remained loyal
to the Kremlin and were prepared to
support Putin in his fight against his
enemies." Shlapentokh, Vladimir. *Rossiya
kak feodalnoye obshchestvo*. Stolitsa-Print:
Moscow, 2008. See pp. 187-188.

44 Levinson, Alexei. "Nashe my: Vertikal, vid
snizu." *Vedomosti*, 207 (2725). November 2,
2010.

45 Kolesnikov, Andrei. "Ne ukaraulili sem
poselkov." *Kommersant*, No. 138. July 31,
2010.

46 According to Boris Sviridov, a legal expert
at the Constitutional Housing Right
Committee, a Moscow-based NGO, in an
interview with the author.

47 From an interview with Sofyin in June
2011. These and subsequent interviews
were conducted in Pikalevo by the author
together with Stanislav Konunov.

48 "Vse budet Pikalevo." *Gazeta.ru*. June
5, 2009. http://www.gazeta.ru/poli-
tics/2009/06/05_kz_3207526.shtm. See
also: Belton, Catherine. "Debt pressure
rises for Deripaska." *Financial Times*.
February 23, 2009. http://www.ft.com/
cms/s/0/627e2eac-01d6-11de-8199-
000077b07658.html#axzz1TxYigXAL.

49 RBC St. Petersburg. March 27,
2009. http://spb.rbc.ru/free-
news/20090327151015.shtm

50 Arutunyan, A. "Small town
erupts." *The Moscow News*. May 25,
2009. http://mnweekly.rian.ru/
news/20090521/55377597.html

51 Courtesy of Mikhail Panfilov's personal
video archive.

52 The Public Opinion Foundation. From
a poll of 2000 respondents across 100
residential areas in 44 Russian regions.

53 Ivanov, Alexei. *Khrebet Rossii: Azbu-
ka-Klassika*. Moscow: 2010, pp 107-111.

54 Clarke, Simon. *The Development of Capital-
ism in Russia*. (Routledge Contemporary
Russia and Eastern Europe Series). Kindle
Edition. T & F Books UK. 2009.

55 Ibid.

56 Kononov, Nikolai. "Kollaps na troikh."
Forbes [Russian edition]. April 2009.

57 From an interview in June 2011. The day
after the interview, we would learn that
Sofyin had been fired by Basel management.

58 The name of the person has been changed
to protect him.

59 Adapted and translated into English by
Anna Arutunyan from: Vladimov, Georgy.
Verny Ruslan: Istoriya karaulnoy sobaki.
Vagrius, Moscow: 2004.

60 Andrei Soldatov and Irina Borogan. *The
New Nobility: The Restoration of Russia's
Security State and the Enduring Legacy of the
KGB*. Kindle Edition. 2010.

61 Kryshtanovskaya, Olga. *Anatomiya rossiyskoi
elity*. Zakharov, Moscow: 2005.

62 As cited in: Peter Baker and Susan Glasser.
*Kremlin Rising: Vladimir Putin's Russia and
the End of Revolution*. A Lisa Drew Book/
Scribner. New York, 2005. (Kindle Edition).

63 *Moskovsky Komsomolets*, April 7, 1995, As
cited in: Peter Baker and Susan Glasser.
*Kremlin Rising: Vladimir Putin's Russia and
the End of Revolution*. A Lisa Drew Book/
Scribner. New York, 2005. (Kindle Edition).

64 Kryshtanovskaya, Olga. *Anatomiya rossiyskoi
elity*. Zakharov, Moscow: 2005.

65 Andrei Soldatov and Irina Borogan. *The
New Nobility: The Restoration of Russia's
Security State and the Enduring Legacy of the
KGB*. Kindle Edition. 2010.

66 Peter Baker and Susan Glasser. *Kremlin
Rising: Vladimir Putin's Russia and the End
of Revolution*. A Lisa Drew Book/Scribner.
New York, 2005. (Kindle Edition).

67 Ibid.

68 As cited in: Andrei Soldatov and Irina
Borogan. *The New Nobility: The Restoration
of Russia's Security State and the Enduring
Legacy of the KGB*. Kindle Edition. 2010.

69 Zhivov, V. M.; Uspensky, B. A. *Tsar I Bog*.
As cited in: Sharov, Vladimir. *Iskusheniye
Revolutsiyei(Russkaya verkhovnaya vlast)*.
Arsis Books, Moscow: 2009.

70 Uspensky, B. A. *Tsar I samozvanets*. As cited
in: Sharov, Vladimir. *Iskusheniye Revolutsi-
yei(Russkaya verkhovnaya vlast)*. Arsis Books,
Moscow: 2009.

71 Massa, Isaac. As cited in: Sharov,

Vladimir. *Iskusheniye Revolutsiyei (Russkaya verkhovnaya vlast)*. Arsis Books, Moscow: 2009.

72 From an interview given to the author in October 2011. Kabanov recalled this incident in response to a question about Andrei Soldatov's 2010 book, *The New Nobility*, which describes the increasing powers and violations of the FSB which coincided with the rise of Vladimir Putin. While it accurately portrays the brutality and unaccountability of the security service, and the rights abuses committed in the name of fighting terrorism, the book offers only a brief section on the economic crimes committed by the FSB. The brief examples and quotes offered by Soldatov, which were cited earlier in this chapter, helped formulate questions for my own investigation into the motives behind this kind of behavior, motives which I felt were not examined in *The New Nobility*.

73 Peter Baker and Susan Glasser. *Kremlin Rising: Vladimir Putin's Russia and the End of Revolution*. A Lisa Drew Book/Scribner. New York, 2005. (Kindle Edition).

74 Ibid.

75 Kryshtanovskaya, Olga. *Anatomiya rossiyskoi elity*. Zakharov, Moscow: 2005.

76 *Great Soviet Encyclopedia*, 3rd Edition.

77 Humphrey, Caroline; Sneath, David. "Shanghaied by the Bureaucracy: Bribery and Post-Soviet Officialdom in Russia and Mongolia." *Between Morality and the Law: Corruption, Anthropology and Comparative Society*. Edited by Italo Pardo. Ashgate Publishing: 2004, pp 85-99.

78 See Huskey, Eugene. "Cadres Policy in the Russian Transition." *Leading Russia: Putin in Perspective*. Oxford University Press, New York: 2005, pp 161-178.

79 Soldatov, Andrei. "Why Putin Will Inherit an Unhappy FSB in 2012." The *Moscow Times*. October 13, 2011.

80 A video of this press conference was archived by *RIA Novosti*, under the title "Pochemy v rossiiskikh SIZO prodolzhayut gibnut lyudi?" http://ria.ru/press_video/20111019/464471081.html

81 "Kity na beregu." *Vedomosti*, No. 172. September 14, 2006.

82 "I. O. genprokurora prigodilsya dlya mebeli." *Kommersant*, No. 106, June 15, 2006. http://Kommersant.ru/ doc/682324?isSearch=True&stamp= 634588780138873531

83 See Raff, Anna. "Customs Men Raid Tri Kita Furniture." The *Moscow Times*. August 26, 2000. http://www.themoscowtimes. com/business/article/customs-men-raid-tri-kita-furniture/259328.html

84 Shleinov, Roman. "Osoby control dlya mebeli." *Novaya Gazeta*. November 1, 2004. http://2004.novayagazeta.ru/ nomer/2004/81n/n81n-s29.shtml

85 "I. O. genprokurora prigodilsya dlya mebeli." *Kommersant*, No. 106. June 15, 2006. http://Kommersant.ru/ doc/682324?isSearch=True&stamp= 634589044545059536. See also: "Kto takoi Yuri Zaostrovtsev." *Kommersant*, No. 45. March 15, 2004. http://Kommersant.ru/ doc/457494?stamp=634589043578934871

86 As quoted by Igor Pylayev in "Grandmebeltorg." *Delovaya khronika*. October 29, 2002.

87 Shleinov, Roman. "Osoby control dlya mebeli." *Novaya Gazeta*. November 1, 2004. http://2004.novayagazeta.ru/ nomer/2004/81n/n81n-s29.shtml

88 "Kto takoi Yuri Zaostrovtsev." *Kommersant*, No. 45. March 15, 2004. http://Kommersant.ru/doc/457494?-stamp=634589043578934871

89 That business is conducted personally rather through paperwork is another symptom of the total lack of either legislative protection or institutional mechanisms. Entrepreneurs trust meetings, not mailed requests to a far larger extent than in the West. See Amos, Howard. "Know-Who More Important than Know-How." The *Moscow Times*. January 11, 2011.

90 The name has been changed at the request of the businessman to protect him from possible problems with security.

91 See *Kommersant*-Online. January 27, 2011. http://www.kommersant.ru/ doc/1574455/print

92 Butorina, Yekaterina. "Chuzhoi sredi svoikh." *Vremya novostei*, No. 142. August 11, 2004.

93 A video of this press conference was archived by *RIA Novosti*, under the title "Pochemy v rossiiskikh SIZO prodolzhayut gibnut lyudi?" http://ria.ru/press_video/20111019/464471081.html

94 "Kak razvivalos delo 'Trekh kitov.'" *Kommersant*, No. 57. April 2, 2010. http://www.kommersant.ru/doc/1347136

95 For more on Shchekochikhin, the allegations of poisoning, and his role in investigating the Tri Kita case, see: Abdullaev, Nabi. "Mystery Shrouds Death of Journalist Shchekochikhin." The *St. Petersburg Times*. July 4, 2008. http://www.sptimes.ru/index.php?action_id=2&story_id=26446

96 "Putin: Rassledovat delo 'Trekh kitov' budet sledovatel iz Lenoblasti." *RIA Novosti*. June 16, 2006. http://ria.ru/economy/20060616/49576574.html

97 Vrazhina, Anna. "Sila Slova." *Lenta.ru*. October 9, 2007. http://www.lenta.ru/articles/2007/10/09/cherkesov/

98 "Glavny obvinyayemy po delu 'Trekh kitov' prigovoren k 8 godam.' *RIA Novosti*. April 1, 2010. http://ria.ru/general_jurisdiction/20100401/217637390.html

99 "Kity na beregu." *Vedomosti*, No. 172. September 14, 2006.

100 Fishman, Mikhail. "Shchit i kit." *Russian Newsweek*. November 13, 2006.

101 Cherkesov, Viktor. "Nelzya dopustit, chtoby voiny prevratilis v torgovtsev." *Kommersant*, No. 184. October 9, 2007. http://www.kommersant.ru/doc/812840?-stamp=63459065676981202б

102 Andryukhin, Alexander. "Militsioner-ubiitsa Yevsyukov: A ya niskolko ne raskaivayus. Vsled za mnoi parovozikom poidut moi nachalniki." *Izvestia*. May 8, 2009. http://www.izvestia.ru/news/348339

103 From an official protocol statement published on the site of lawyer Igor Trunov, who represented Yevsyukov's victims in court. http://www.trunov.com/content.php?act=showcont&id=6445

104 Kachkayeva, Elina. "Yevsyukov grabil supermarket Ostrov, poka byl uchastkovym." *Komsomolskaya Pravda*. October 10, 2009. http://www.kp.ru/daily/24379.5/560425/

105 Based on interviews with Chichvarkin's lawyers, Yuri Gervis and Vladimir Zherebenkov, conducted in February–March 2010. See also: Ivanov, Igor. "Ogon, voda i telefonnyie trubki." *Russian Newsweek*. November 2, 2009

106 Ivanov, Igor. "Ogon, voda i telefonnyie trubki." *Russian Newsweek*. November 2, 2009.

107 Ibid.

108 "Ex-tamozhennik Sheremetyevo poluchil 9 let kolonii za kontrabandu telefonov dlya 'Yevroseti.'" *Newsru.com*. April 1, 2009. http://www.newsru.com/arch/russia/01apr2009/tamoj9.html

109 Ibid.

110 Ibid.

111 Ibid.

112 Ibid.

113 Latynina, Yulia. "Kto dovel Yevsyukova." *Novaya Gazeta*. February 15, 2010. http://www.novayagazeta.ru/data/2010/016/01.html

114 Belovsky, Ignat. "Yevsyukov v dele s Chichvarkinym." *Gazeta.ru*. July 28, 2009. http://www.gazeta.ru/social/2009/07/28/3228691.shtml

115 Interview with Boris Levin. *Gazeta.ru*. November 18, 2010. http://www.gazeta.ru/social/2010/11/18/3440461.shtml

116 Shvarev, Alexander. "Militsia yuga Moskvy obezglavlena." *Rosbalt*. April 20, 2009. http://www.rosbalt.ru/moscow/2009/04/20/634943.html. And Shvarev, Alexander. "Delo Chichvarkina: Militseiski Sled." *Rosbalt*. February 3, 2009. http://www.rosbalt.ru/moscow/2009/02/03/615210.html

117 "Yevsyukov prokhodit svidetelem po delu Chichvarkina." *Rosbalt*. July 22, 2009.

118 Shvarev, Alexander. "Militsia yuga Moskvy obezglavlena." *Rosbalt*. April 20, 2009. http://www.rosbalt.ru/moscow/2009/04/20/634943.html

119 Interview with Boris Levin. *Gazeta.ru*. November 18, 2010. http://www.gazeta.ru/social/2010/11/18/3440461.shtml

120 Ivanov, Igor. "Ogon, voda i telefonnyie trubki." *Russian Newsweek*. November 2, 2009.

121 Shvarev, Alexander. "V dele Chichvarkina poyavilsya Yevsyukov." *Rosbalt News Agency*. July 22, 2009.

122 Belovsky, Ignat. "Yevsyukov v dele s Chichvarkinym." *Gazeta.ru*. July 28, 2009. http://www.gazeta.ru/social/2009/07/28/3228691.shtml

123 Shevtsova, Lilia. *Putin's Russia*. Carnegie Endowment for International Peace: Washington, 2004, p. 429.

124 Ibid., p. 404.

125 Humphrey, Caroline; Sneath, David. "Shanghied by the Bureaucracy: Bribery and Post-Soviet Officialdom in Russia and Mongolia." *Between Morality and the Law: Corruption, Anthropology and Comparative Society*. Edited by Italo Pardo. Ashgate Publishing: 2004, pp. 90–91.

126 Ibid.

127 Humphrey, Caroline; Sneath, David. "Shanghied by the Bureauacracy: Bribery and Post-Soviet Officialdom in Russia and Mongolia." *Between Morality and the Law: Corruption, Anthropology and Comparative Society*. Edited by Italo Pardo. Ashgate Publishing: 2004, pp. 90–91.

128 http://www.youtube.com/watch?v=R4vB2a15dOU

129 "Mayor Dymovsky—MK: Mne nadoyelo byt tryapkoi." *Moskovsky Komsomolets*. November 9, 2009. http://www.mk.ru/social/article/2009/11/08/381478-mayor-dyimovskiy-mk-mne-nadoelo-by-it-tryapkoy.html

130 From an interview given to the author in January 2010. See also: Arutunyan, A. "Russia's whistle-blowers in peril." *The Moscow News*. February 1, 2010. http://themoscownews.com/news/20100201/55407384.html

131 Mayetnaya, Yelizaveta; Sedakov, Pavel. "Bedny mayorik." *Newsweek*, No. 47. November 2009.

132 Arutunyan, A. "Dymovsky freed from jail." *The Moscow News*. March 9, 2010. http://themoscownews.com/news/20100309/55419006.html

133 Arutunyan, A. "Dymovsky freed from jail." *The Moscow News*. March 9, 2010. http://themoscownews.com/news/20100309/55419006.html

134 "Yedinoross Andrei Makarov predlozhil likvidirovat MVD." *Kommersant*, No. 4276 (221). November 26, 2009.

135 Zorkin, Valery. "Povtorenie proidennogo. K shestnadtsatiletiyu rossiiskoi konstitutsii." *Rossiyskaya Gazeta*, No. 5062 (238). December 11, 2009.

136 As cited in: "Vstrecha s Putinym dlya menya oskorbleniye." *Gazeta.ru*. November 20, 2011. http://www.gazeta.ru/news/lastnews/2009/11/20/n_1426817.shtml

137 "Seeing Red." *Institutional Investor*. September 1, 2002. http://www.institutionalinvestor.com/Popups/PrintArticle.aspx?ArticleID=1027279

138 Transcript of speech by William Browder: "Hermitage Capital, the Russian State and the Case of Sergei Magnitsky." Chatham House. December 15, 2009 http://www.chathamhouse.org/sites/default/files/public/Research/Russia%20and%20Eurasia/151209browder.pdf

139 "An enemy of the people. The sad fate of a loyal Putinista." *The Economist*. March 23, 2006. http://www.economist.com/node/5661601

140 Hoffman, David. *The Oligarchs*. Perseus Books, Cambridge, MA, 2003.

141 "Perviy: glava Hermitage Capital Browder uklonyalsya ot nalogov v Kalmykii, yakoby nanimaya invalidov." *Gazeta.ru*. March 10, 2013. http://www.gazeta.ru/business/news/2013/03/10/n_2791385.shtml

142 Clover, Charles. "Russia alleges $70m fraud against Browder." *Financial Times*. March 5, 2013. http://www.ft.com/intl/cms/s/0/06df1c16-85b0-11e2-9ee3-00144feabdc0.html#axzz2jcUicOSx

143 "Putin unaware why businessman Browder barred from Russia." *RIA Novosti*. July 17, 2006. http://en.rian.ru/russia/20060717/51436114.html

144 In a taped interview, Browder used the words "He clearly wasn't my friend," but subsequently omitted the phrase in a transcript sent to him to check, for an article that was to appear in *The Moscow News*. I use this phrase here with the following clarification: Browder was clearly joking, and did not mean to indicate that Putin had ever been his "friend" in the literal sense, for he had never spoken to him personally—these words were a figure of speech, however telling.

145 "Vtoroye delo Braudera v Rossii: khishcheniye aktsiy Gazproma." *RIA Novosti*. March 5, 2013. http://ria.ru/incidents/20130305/925918569.html

146 Browder's interview to *Snob* magazine, taken by Masha Gessen. *Snob*. May 5, 2011. http://www.snob.ru/magazine/en-

try/36099?preview=print

[147] Butrin, Dmitry. "William Browder priznal sebya nevyezdnym." *Kommersant*, No. 47. March 20, 2006. http://www.kommersant.ru/doc/658889

[148] A collection of these documents can be accessed at http://russian-untouchables.com, a site operated by Sergei Magnitsky's supporters.

[149] Ibid.

[150] Belova, Yelena. "Ex-nalogovika iz 'spiska Magnitskogo' Olgu Stepanovu zapodozrili v khishchenii bolee 50 milliardov rublei." *Gazeta.ru*. November 15, 2012. http://www.gazeta.ru/social/2012/11/15/4854881.shtml

[151] Matlack, Carol. "Renaissance Capital: A Moscow Survivor." *BusinessWeek*. December 29, 2010. http://www.businessweek.com/magazine/content/11_02/b4210058424523.htm

[152] Arutunyan, Anna. "Prosecutors fingered in casino racket." *The Moscow News*. February 17, 2011. http://www.themoscownews.com/news/20110217/188428343.html

[153] As cited in: Galeotti, Mark. "Who's the Boss: Us or the Law? The Corrupt Art of Governing Russia." *Bribery and Blat in Russia*. eds: Lovell, Stephen; Ledeneva, Alena; Rogachevskii, Andrei. School of Slavonic and East European Studies. University of London.

[154] "Grease my palm. Bribery and corruption have become endemic." *The Economist*. November 27, 2008.

[155] According to a 2010 report by the Institute of Applied Law at the European University of St. Petersburg, as cited by *Vedomosti*. "Kholostoi khod." February 17, 2010.

[156] Galeotti, Mark. "Who's the Boss: Us or the Law? The Corrupt Art of Governing Russia." *Bribery and Blat in Russia*. eds: Lovell, Stephen; Ledeneva, Alena; Rogachevskii, Andrei. School of Slavonic and East European Studies. University of London.

[157] Ibid.

[158] Translated by J. Henry Harrison. London: F. Bowyer Kitto, Bishopsgate Without. E.C.: 1869.

[159] Onexim Group. Company profile. *Kommersant*. December 1, 2011. http://www.kommersant.ru/doc/1827999

[160] The readings took place on August 4, 2009, at the Gary Tatinyants Gallery, and were attended by the author. All dialogue from the readings is based on the author's notes, taken at the reading.

[161] See *Vedomosti*, July 13, 2011. "Postavil pered vyborami." See also: Arutunyan, A. "Medvedev asks business to pick." *The Moscow News*. July 14, 2011. http://www.themoscownews.com/politics/20110714/188843435.html

[162] Jensen, Donald N. "How Russia is Ruled." *Business and State*. ed. Peter Rutland. Westview Press, 2001.

[163] Felshtynsky, Yuri; Pribylovsky, Vladimir; *The Corporation: Russia and the KGB in the Age of President Putin*. Encounter Books, New York: 2008, pp. 61-68.

[164] These allegations were made following an extensive investigation headed by then deputy of the Leningrad City Council Marina Salye. In 2010, Salye began giving interviews again, and the details of her report re-emerged, coinciding with a growing campaign of corruption allegations against Putin. Ivanidze, Vladimir. "Spasaya podpolkovnika Putina: vtoraya popytka." *RFE/RL*. March 3, 2010. http://www.svobodanews.ru/content/article/1983851.html. See also Felshtynsky, Yuri; Pribylovsky, Vladimir; *The Corporation. Russia and the KGB in the Age of President Putin*. Encounter Books, New York: 2008, pp. 60-80.

[165] Baker, Peter; Glasser, Susan. *Kremlin Rising: Vladimir Putin's Russia and the End of Revolution*. A Lisa Drew Book/Scribner. New York, 2005. (Kindle Edition).

[166] "Slovar russkogo publichnogo yazyka kontsa XX veka." *Kommersant Vlast*, No. 24. June 23, 2003.

[167] Krantz, Patricia. "Fall of an Oligarch." *Businessweek*. March 1, 1999. http://www.businessweek.com/1999/99_09/b3618098.htm

[168] Karatsuba, I.; Kurukin, I., Sokolov, N.; *Vybiraya svoyu istoriyu*. Kolibri: Moscow, 2005, pp. 618-619. See also: Hoffman, David E. *The Oligarchs: Wealth and Power in the New Russia*. Public Affairs: New York, 2003, pp. 297-315.

[169] Ibid.

170 Hoffman, David E. *The Oligarchs: Wealth and Power in the New Russia*. Public Affairs: New York, 2003, pp. 319.

171 Ibid. pp. 322.

172 See Cohen, Stephen. *Failed Crusade*. Norton: New York, London, 2001, p. 33.

173 Liesman, Steve; Higgins, Andrew. "Seven-Year Hitch." *The Wall Street Journal*. September 23, 1998, p. A1.

174 Freedlan, Chrystia. *Sale of the Century: Russia's Wild Ride from Communism to Capitalism*. New York: Crown Publishers, 2000. p. 157.

175 Popova, Nadia. "Chamber to Oversee VEB Loan to RusAl." The *Moscow Times*. November 1, 2008. http://www.themoscowtimes.com/business/article/chamber-to-oversee-veb-loan-to-rusal/372105.html

176 For more on the members of the board and their powers, see http://veb.ru/en/about/officials/nabl/.

177 The letters were obtained and published by *Slon.ru* in December 2009. http://slon.ru/russia/vsya_pravda_o_prosbah_deri-paski_k_putinu-194826.xhtml

178 Lapechenkova, Irina. "Fosagro rasschitivayet sozdat sovmestnoye predpriyatie." *RBC Daily*. October 5, 2011. http://www.rbcdaily.ru/2011/10/05/industry/562949981659020

179 From a press conference attended by the author on September 14, 2011.

180 Pomerantsev, Peter. "Putin's Rasputin." *London Review of Books*. October 20, 2011. http://www.lrb.co.uk/v33/n20/peter-pomerantsev/putins-rasputin

181 "Top Kremlin aide says Putin is God's gift to Russia." *Reuters*. July 9, 2011. http://in.reuters.com/article/2011/07/08/idINIndia-58163920110708. See also: "Former Kremlin ideologue Surkov calls Putin 'white night.'" *The Moscow News*. July 29, 2013. http://themoscownews.com/politics/20130729/191804851/Former-Kremlin-ideologue-Surkov-calls-Putin-white-knight.html

182 As cited by *Kommersant*. Nagornaya, Irina. "Nado umet sebya prodavat!" *Kommersant*, No. 30. February 2, 2002. http://www.kommersant.ru/doc/311788/print

183 From an interview given by Vladislav Surkov to *Vedomosti*, No. 26. February 15, 2010.

184 Arutunyan, A. "Skolkovo's trickle-down effect." *The Moscow News*. July 16, 2012. http://www.themoscownews.com/business/20120716/189966349.html

185 According to an official transcript. See official site of Russia's chairmanship of the G8. http://g8russia.ru/news/20060704/1166957.html

186 See Tirmaste, Maria-Luisa. "Biznesmeny zanyalis Pravym delom." *Kommersant*, No. 208. November 17, 2008. http://Kommersant.ru/doc/1068728. Gozman, who had once led Union of Right Forces, admitted that the merger was organized by the Kremlin, but also said it was "shameful and disgraceful."

187 Igumenov, Valery. "Vozvrashcheniye Potanina." *Forbes* (Russian edition). March 16, 2010. http://www.forbes.ru/ekonomika/lyudi/46337-vozvrashchenie-potanina

188 Harding, Luke. "Russian billionaire arrested in Alpine prostitution inquiry." *The Guardian*. January 12, 2007. http://www.guardian.co.uk/world/2007/jan/12/russia.france

189 "Prokhorov to sell 16.6% stake in Norilsk Nickel for $10 bln." *RIA Novosti*. August 5, 2008. http://en.rian.ru/business/20080805/115754795.html

190 Raghavan, Anita. "Last Man Standing." *Forbes*. March 30, 2009. http://www.forbes.com/forbes/2009/0330/109-last-man-standing.html

191 "Prokhorov's $200 Million Purchase of Nets Gains Approval from NBA Owners." *Bloomberg*. May 12, 2010. http://www.bloomberg.com/news/2010-05-11/prokhorov-s-200-million-purchase-of-nets-gains-approval-from-nba-owners.html

192 "M. Prokhorova khotyat lishyt vlozhennykh v Pravoe delo millionov." *RBC*. September 19, 2011. http://top.rbc.ru/politics/19/09/2011/616077.shtml

193 From an official transcript on the prime minister's site. http://premier.gov.ru/events/news/9480/index.html

194 Klyuchkin, Anton. "Slovo Putina boitsya." *Lenta.ru*, citing Interfax news agency. March 4, 2010. http://lenta.ru/articles/2010/03/04/say/

195 Ibid.

[196] See Vinogradova, Yelena; Nepomnyashchy, Alexei; Tovkailo, Maxim. "Putin's Ride Boosts Ripe-Lemon Kalina Sales." *Vedomosti*. September 30, 2010. Reprinted in English in The *Moscow Times*. http://www.themoscowtimes.com/business/article/putins-ride-boosts-ripe-lemon-kalina-sales/417680.html

Prokhorov himself would later acknowledge this effect. "We only have one brand—Putin. But that is clearly not enough," he said in a speech at Moscow's International University on October 11, 2011. Zhuravlev, Alexander. "V Rossii odin brend—Putin." *Kommersant-Online*. October 11, 2011. http://www.kommersant.ru/doc/1792739

[197] From an interview given by Dmitry Medvedev to *Moskovskie Novosti*. June 24, 2011. http://www.mn.ru/newspaper_firstpage/20110624/302769706.html

[198] If a meeting is not officially publicized, witnesses will rarely go on the record to confirm it. Stanislav Belkovsky and a source in Right Cause speaking on conditions of anonymity told the author that they knew this meeting had taken place.

[199] See Belkovsky, Stanislav. "Pravoye Delo. Chto eto bylo?" Openspace.ru. September 17, 2011. http://www.openspace.ru/society/russia/details/30255/?expand=yes#-expand

[200] In an interview to the *Rosbalt News Agency*. August 18, 2011. http://www.rosbalt.ru/main/2011/08/18/880855.html

[201] According to statistics gathered by the foundation itself. http://nobf.ru/about/about/

[202] Motorina, Anna; Farizova, Syuzana. "Prokoratura trebuyet vydat deputata Roizmana." *Kommersant*-Yekaterinburg, No. 83. May 17, 2007. http://www.kommersant.ru/doc/766259

[203] Arutunyan, Anna; Khrustalyeva, Olga. "Prokhorov quits party." *The Moscow News*. September 15, 2011. http://www.themoscownews.com/politics/20110915/189047189.html

[204] Vinokurova, Yekaterina. "Chto proizoshlo v Pravom Dele." *Gazeta.ru*. September 15, 2011. http://www.gazeta.ru/politics/elections2011/blogs/3769065.shtml

[205] Smirnov, Sergei. Dmitriyenko, Dmitry. "Prohorov ne pojdet na dumskie vybory v dekabre." *Vedomosti*. September 15,

[206] From an interview given to *Dozhd TV* on September 15, 2011.

[207] Beshlei, Olga. "Oligarkh na vydanye." *The New Times*, No. 43. December 19, 2011. http://newtimes.ru/articles/detail/47892/

[208] In an interview given to *Forbes* magazine, January 26, 2012. http://www.forbes.ru/sobytiya/lyudi/78770-mihail- prohorov-vazhnyi-psihologicheskii-moment-ne-mogu-byt-chim-zamom

[209] Arutunyan, A. "Cash, Signatures and Moderation." *The Moscow News*. January 16, 2012. http://www.themoscownews.com/politics/20120116/189373436.html

[210] Baker, Peter; Glasser, Susan. *Kremlin Rising: Vladimir Putin's Russia and the End of Revolution*. A Lisa Drew Book/Scribner. New York, 2005. (Kindle Edition), loc. 5859.

[211] Browne, John. *Beyond Business*. Weidenfeld & Nicholson, 2010. From an excerpt published in *The Times*, February 5, 2010.

[212] Translated from an official transcript from the presidential site, www.kremlin.ru

[213] Skrynnikov, R. G. *Ivan the Terrible*. Moscow: AST, 2001.

[214] From an interview with the author on September 24, 2011. See also: Arutunyan, Anna. "All the Prime Minister's Men." *The Moscow News*. September 26, 2011. http://www.themoscownews.com/politics/20110926/189071296.html

[215] Ibid.

[216] See Arutunyan, Anna. "US leans towards Medvedev." *The Moscow News*. March 14, 2011. http://themoscownews.com/politics/20110314/188493495.html

[217] From an official transcript posted on the Prime Minister's site, www.government.ru

[218] Putin's spokesman, Dmitry Peskov, initially denied that Putin knew anything about the calendar. But when asked by Naomi Campbell, Putin said: "I like the girls a lot, they're beautiful. The girls in the erotic calendar were courageous and they were not scared. As student journalists, they couldn't fail to understand what might have been said to them after doing this. Nonetheless, they were not deterred and did the calendar anyway. So, frankly, that's what I liked the most." Campbell, Naomi. "When Naomi met Vladimir." *GQ*. Janu-

ary 31, 2011. http://www.gq-magazine. co.uk/comment/articles/2011-01/31/ gq-comment-naomi-campbell-interview-vladimir-putin-fitness- tigers/fitness-regime

219 "'Twelve Moods of Putin' hits Russia." *BBC Europe*. December 6, 2001. http://news.bbc.co.uk/2/hi/europe/1694236.stm

220 As cited by *Bolshoi Gorod*. June 8, 2007. http://www.bg.ru/article/6756/

221 Brezhitskaya, Yelena. "PuTin vidim, chitayem Puin. Chto pokupaem?" *Stavropolskaya Pravda*. November 7, 2008.

222 Sivun, Oleg. *Brend: Pop-art Roman*. Novy Mir, 2008. No. 10.

223 From an interview given to Svetlana Romanova. *Slon.ru*. October 7, 2010. http://slon.ru/russia/da_gde_vy_vse_vidite_v_nashem_kalendare_politiku-475994.xhtml

224 Pravda, February 1, 1935. 28 August 1936, T.H. Rigby, Stalin. (Englewood Cliffs, N.J., Prentice-Hall, 1966), pp 111-12. As cited in:, McCauley, Martin. *Stalin*. Third Edition. Pearson Education Limited, UK, 2003.

225 See Ennker, Benno. "Struggling for Stalin's Soul." *Personality Cults in Stalinism*. Eds. Klaus Keller, Jan Palmer. Gottingen, 2004.

226 See Tucker, Robert C. "The Rise of Stalin's Personality Cult." *The American Historical Review*, Vol. 84, No. 2. April 1979.

227 According to studies published in March, 2013 by the Carnegie Center. http://www.carnegie.ru/2013/03/01/%D1%87%D1%82%D0%BE- %D0%B4%D1%83%D0%B-C%D0%B0%D1%8E%D1%82-%D0%BE-%D1%81%D1%82%D0%B0%D0%B-B%D0%B8%D0%B-D%D0%B5-%D0%B2- %D1%80%D0%BE%D1%81%D1%81%D0%B8%D0%B8-%D0%B8- %D0%B7%D0%B0%D0%BA%D0%B0%D0%B2%D0%BA%D0%B0%D0%B7%D1%8C% D0%B5/fo27#

228 Ibid.

229 Garbuznyak, Anna. "Zapad dolzhen uvidet pravilnuyu kartynku." *Moskovskie Novosti*. November 25, 2011. http://mn.ru/politics/20111125/307770840.html

230 Karatsuba, I.; Kurukin, I.; Sokolov, N.; *Vybiraya svoyu istoriyu*. Kolibri: Moscow, 2005.

231 According to the philologist Mikhail Vaiskopf, the allegory of a "marriage" between the Russian ruler and the land or the people was appropriated from ancient, pre-Christian cults and superimposed on a theocratic worldview imported from Byzantium. Citing poetry from over a span of some 300 years, Vaiskopf noted the clearly erotic connotations of how Romanov rulers were described. Vaiskopf, Mikhail. "Brak s vlastelinom: eroticheskie aspekty derzhavnoi ritoriki." *Novoye Literaturnoye Obozreniye*. No. 100. 2009. http://magazines.russ.ru/nlo/2009/100/va8.html

232 Mayetnaya, Yelizaveta. "Sudba barabanschitsy." *Izvestia*. December 20, 2011. http://www.izvestia.ru/news/510240

233 Shleinov, Roman. "Dengi Nashikh." *Vedomosti*, No. 225. November 29, 2010. http://www.*Vedomosti*.ru/newspaper/article/250636/dengi_nashih

234 "Paren iz nashego ozera." *Kommersant-Vlast*, No. 29. July 30, 2007. http://www.kommersant.ru/doc/790656

235 Shleinov, Roman. "Dengi Nashikh." *Vedomosti*, No. 225. November 29, 2010. http://www.*Vedomosti*.ru/newspaper/article/250636/dengi_nashih

236 The Institute of Sociology of the Russian Academy of Science published these findings in: *Rossiiskoye obshchestvo kak ono yest*. Moscow: Novy Khronograf, 2011.

237 Bershidsky, Leonid. "What Alexei Navalny Learned from Obama." *Bloomberg*. August 26, 2013. http://www.bloomberg.com/news/2013-08-26/what-alexei-navalny-learned-from-obama.html

238 Kashin, Oleg. "Kogda Navalny stanet prezidentom Rossii." *Slon*. September 10, 2013. http://www.bloomberg.com/news/2013-08-26/what-alexei-navalny-learned-from-obama.html

239 Ignatova, Olga; Protsenko, Lyubov. "Kazhdomy svoi kandidat." *Rossiiskaya Gazeta*. July 4, 2013. http://www.rg.ru/2013/07/04/kandidati.html

240 Navalny said he was "forced" to answer journalist Aider Muzhdabayev's open letter, and posed his response on his Facebook page on July 22: https://www.facebook.com/navalny/posts/627702410582179. His brusque response was attributed by some supporters to his recent brush with jail.

[241] Zlobin, Nikolai. "Vsem uteretsya." *Ekho Moskvy*. July 25, 2013. http://echo.msk.ru/blog/nzlobin/1122290-echo/?utm_source=twitterfeed&utm_medium=twitter

[242] Tselikov, Andrey. "To Some Opposition Bloggers Alexei Navalny is 'Fuhrer.'" *Global Voices*. September 14, 2013. http://globalvoicesonline.org/2013/09/14/to-some-opposition-bloggers-alexey-navalny-is-fuhrer/

[243] The remark was made to oppositionist Duma deputy Ilya Ponomaryov shortly after the protests during a chance meeting in the hallways of state Parliament. Ponomaryov reported the exchange on his Livejournal blog and on Twitter. http://ilya-ponomarev.livejournal.com/482999.html. Peskov later confirmed that he had said something of the sort in a private conversation, but downplayed its importance in an interview to Oleg Kashin. "U vsekh lagerei konets odin."

[244] The incident was captured on camera and shown by news channels. http://www.youtube.com/watch?v=yeL1xv21oro

[245] Blyth, Kristen. "Religious Radicalism in Russia: Hell, Heaven and the State." *The Moscow News*. February 4, 2013. http://themoscownews.com/russia/20130204/191202860.html

[246] Ibid.

[247] Shargunov, Sergei. "Tost, kotory ustarel." *Svobodnaya Pressa*. July 15, 2012. http://svpressa.ru/society/article/57016/

[248] As cited in: Svoboda, M. "Obraz tsarya vo 'Vremennike' Ivana Timofeyeva." *Trudy otdela drevnerusskoi literatury*. Vol. 52. RAN, Institute of Russian Literature (Pushkinsky Dom), St. Petersburg: 2001, p. 389.

[249] Ibid.

[250] Ibid.

[251] Uspensky, B. A.; Zhivov, V. M. "Tsar i Bog: Semioticheskiye aspekty sarkalizatsii monarkha v Rossii." Uskepsny B. A., *Izbrannye Trudy*. Moscow, 1994, p. 193.

[252] Valdenberg, Vladimir. *Drevnerusskiye ucheniya o predelakh tsarskoi vlasti*. Territoriya budushchego: Moscow, 2006. First published in 1916, pp. 12-13.

[253] Evans, J. A. S. *The Age of Justinian: The Circumstances of Imperial Power*. Routledge: London, 1996. p. 62.

[254] Wiles, Maurice. *Documents in Early Christian Thought*. p. 224.

[255] Russel, Norman. *The Doctrine of Deification in the Greek Patristic Tradition*. Oxford University Press: New York, 2004. p. 23.

[256] Dobbins, J. "The Imperial Cult Building in the forum at Pompeii." *Subject and Ruler: the cult of the ruling power in Classical Antiquity*. Ed.: Small, Allistair. JRA Suppl. Ser. 17. Ann Arbor 1996, 99–114.

[257] Bibikov, M. V. "Velikiye vasilevsy Vizantiiskoi imperii: k izucheniyu ideologii I emblematiki sakralizatsii vlasti." *Slovo*. http://www.portal-slovo.ru/theology/37836.php?ELEMENT_ID=37836&SHOW-ALL_1=0

[258] Bibikov, M. V. "Blesk i nishcheta vaslevsov." *Obrazy vlasti*. eds. Mikhail Boitsov, Otto Gerhard Oexle. Nauka: Moscow, 2008, p. 14.

[259] Meyendorff, John. *The Byzantine Legacy in the Orthodox Church*. St. Vladimir's Seminary Press, 2001, p. 45.

[260] Rowland, Daniel B. "The Third Rome or the New Israel?" *Russian Review*, Vol. 55, No. 4. October 1996. pp. 591-614.

[261] Ibid., p. 255.

[262] Image published in Ibid, p. 267.

[263] Ibid., p. 269.

[264] De Madariaga, Isabel. *Ivan the Terrible*. Yale University Press, 2006. p. 53.

[265] Ivanov, Sergei. *Blazhenniye pokhaby. Kulturnaya istoriya yurodstva*. Yazyki slavyanskikh kultur: Moscow, 2005. pp. 265-287.

[266] Ibid.

[267] Ibid.

[268] According to a poll by the Levada Center released in November 2012. http://www.levada.ru/02-11-2012/doverie-institut-am-vlasti

[269] Belkovsky, Stanislav. "Papa ukazal put patriarkhu." *Moskovsky Komsomolets*. February 15, 2013. Belkovsky would be called in for questioning after several parliamentarians complained that the article was extremist. In the article, Belkovsky calls for fundamental church reforms, citing, for instance, its subordination to Stalin. At the end, Belkovsky suggests that Patriarch Kirill join a women's monastery.

[270] Garrard, John; Garrard, Carol. *Russian Orthodoxy Resurgent: Faith and Power in the New Russia*. Princeton University Press,

2008. pp. 25-37.

271 Latynina, Yulia. "Patriarch Kirill's Apartment Buried in Sand." The *Moscow Times*. March 29, 2012. http://www.themoscowtimes.com/opinion/article/patriarch-kirills-apartment-buried-in-sand/455684.html

272 Shuster, Simon. "The Priest Who Beat Pussy Riot: The Orthodox Point Man with the Kremlin." *Time* magazine. August 20, 2012. http://world.time.com/2012/08/20/the-priest-who-beat-pussy-riot-the-orthodox-point-man-with-the- kremlin/#ixzz24BRjcWT9

273 Gamov, Alexander. "Preemnik Yeltsina stradayet dalnozorkostyu." *Komsomolskaya Pravda*. August 10, 1999. Like most aspects of Putin's personal life, this cannot be verified. However, when Putin first visited *Komsomolskaya Pravda* as the director of the FSB in 1998, the journalist Alexander Gamov noticed that he was wearing a pair of glasses on a string, and, while not seeing things right in front of his face, was able to see things across the room.

274 From an official transcript posted on the presidential site, Kremlin.ru

275 Ibid.

276 According to official police figures, as cited by *RIA Novosti*. http://ria.ru/politics/20120223/572376143.html Moscow police have been known to exaggerate figures for pro-Putin rallies, while downplaying figures for protests.

277 This remark was overheard by my colleague, Natalia Antonova, who was standing a few meters away from me next to the stage.

278 The translation used here is that of Eugene M. Hayden; in the original Russian, the second line reads literally, "as our brothers die."

279 From an official transcript, as cited by *RIA Novosti*. http://ria.ru/vybor2012_putin/20120223/572995366.html

280 Barabanov, Ilya; Beshlei, Olga. "Antidot ot Nablyudatelya." *The New Times*, No. 9. March 12, 2012. http://newtimes.ru/articles/print/50844/

281 From a series of interviews Putin gave in 2000 to Andrei Kolesnikov, Natalia Timakova, and Natalia Gevorkyan. *Ot pervogo litsa: Razgovory s Vladimirom Putinym*. http://archive.kremlin.ru/articles/bookchapter1.shtml

282 Ibid.

283 Felshtinsky, Yuri; Pribylovsky, Vladimir; *The Corporation: Russia and the KGB in the Age of President Putin*. Encounter Books, New York: 2008. p. 41.

284 In 2010, Marina Salye began giving interviews again, and the details of her report re-emerged, coinciding with a growing campaign of corruption allegations against Putin. Ivanidze, Vladimir. "Spasaya podpolkovnika Putina: vtoraya popytka." *RFE/RL*. March 3, 2010. http://www.svobodanews.ru/content/article/1983851.html

285 Felshtinsky, Yuri; Pribylovsky, Vladimir; *The Corporation: Russia and the KGB in the Age of President Putin*. Encounter Books, New York: 2008. pp. 85-90.

286 From a series of interviews Putin gave in 2000 to Andrei Kolesnikov, Natalia Timakova, and Natalia Gevorkyan. *Ot pervogo litsa: Razgovory s Vladimirom Putinym*. http://archive.kremlin.ru/articles/bookchapter6.shtml

287 Baker, Peter; Glasser, Susan. *Kremlin Rising: Vladimir Putin's Russia and the End of Revolution*. A Lisa Drew Book/Scribner. New York, 2005. (Kindle Edition). Loc. 1256-68

288 See Olson, Mancur. "Dictatorship, Democracy and Development." *American Political Science Review*, Vol. 87, No. 3. September 1993.

289 Hedlund, Stefan. *Russian Path Dependence: A People with a Troubled History*. Routledge, 2005.

290 As cited in: Kollman, Nancy. *Crime and Punishment in Early Modern Russia*. Cambridge University Press, 2012. p. 48.

291 See Pipes, Richard. *Russia Under the Old Regime*. Penguin Books, 2004. pp. 50-52.

292 See: Lotman, Iurii Mikhailovich. "Agreement and self-giving as archetypal models of culture." *The Semiotics of Russian Culture*. Ed. Ann Shukman. Department of Slavic Languages and Literatures, University of Michigan, 1984.

293 Burns, J. H. (ed). *The Cambridge History of Medieval Political Thought c. 350–c. 1450*. Cambridge University Press, 1988. p.64.

294 Nechepurenko, Ivan. "Big Changes

Afoot—But Only After Sochi." *The Moscow Times.* April 11, 2013. http://www.themoscowtimes.com/sochi2014/Big-Changes-Afoot-But-Only-After-Sochi.html

295 Arutunyan, Anna. "Russia shrugged: Searching for a national identity." *The Moscow News.* September 18, 2013. http://www.themoscownews.com/russia/20130918/191929261/Russia-shrugged.html

296 Gudkov, Lev. "Doveriye v Rossii: smysl, funktsii, struktura." *Novoye Literaturnoye Obozrenie,* No. 117. 2012. http://magazines.russ.ru/nlo/2012/117/g25.html

297 Arutunyan, Anna. "Russian volunteerism: An uphill battle." *The Moscow News.* September 26, 2013. http://www.themoscownews.com/russia/20130926/191945280/Russian-volunteerism-An-uphill-battle.html

298 Haber, Maya. "The Disaster of Collective Farms Under Khrushchev." A review of *Reform in the Time of Stalin: Nikita Khrushchev and the Fate of the Russian Peasantry,* by Auri Berg. *Dissertation Reviews.* September 27, 2013. http://dissertationreviews.org/archives/5294

299 Zubarevich, Natalia. "Chego zhdat chetyrem Rossiyam." *Vedomosti.* September 24, 2013. http://www.Vedomosti.ru/opinion/news/16681621/chetyre-rossii-chto-dalshe?full#cut

300 Arendt, Hannah. *The Origins of Totalitarianism.* Harcourt, Brace & Company, New York: 1979, p. 474.

Index

Since the topic of this book is Vladimir Putin and his role in modern Russia, entries for "Putin, Vladimir" are restricted to a small range of topics of particular interest.

1984, book 213, 270

Abdulayeva, Oksana, kindergarten teacher 273-74, 276-77

Abramovich, Roman, oligarch 151, 198

Agapetus, sixth century deacon 251, 259

Ageyev, Viktor, police chief 123, 132, 134-35

Aksyonov, Sergei, prime minister of Crimea 298-99

Aleshina, Maria, student 214, 230

Alexei, tsar 253, 262

Alexis II, Patriarch 266

Alyokhina, Maria, Pussy Riot member 14, 250

Andropov, Yuri, KGB director 100

Anisimov, Alexei, United Russia party official 44-45, 47, 50-52

anti-Magnitsky Law 158, 271

Antropova, Svetlana, union leader 67, 71-73, 79

Apatit, company 180

Ardashnikov, Yakov, businessman 128

Arendt, Hannah 306

Arkhipov, Yevgeny, lawyer 116

Astakhov, Pavel, children's ombudsman 51

Aven, Pyotr 171, 174, 198, 287

Badalyants, Koren, plant director 82-83

Bakatin, Vadim 92

Baker, Peter, journalist 99

Bakulov, Petr, businessman 240

Baronova, Maria, activist 245, 247

Barto, punk group 215

Baryshnikov, Oleg, deputy police chief 123

BaselCement Pikalevo 71-73, 79, 179

Basil, Saint 265

Bastrykin, Alexander, Investigative Committee chief 241

Bekbulatovich, Simeon, Tartar prince 204

Belaya Lenta, protest movement 145, 148

Belkovsky, Stanislav, political commentator 181, 208

Belykh, Nikita, governor 241

Berdiaev, Nicolas, philosopher 213

Berezovsky, Boris, oligarch 93, 171, 173-75, 183

Berkut, Ukrainian police 297-98

Bibikov, Mikhail, historian 260

Biryukov, Yuri, deputy prosecutor general 116

Biryukova, Inna 144-145

Black Sea Fleet 299-300

Bolotnaya Square, demonstration 245-46

Bowring, Bill, human rights lawyer 157

Brennan, John, CIA chief 295

Brezhnev, Leonid 87, 127

British Petroleum 175, 198

Bronshtein, Alexander, oligarch 179

Browder, William, CEO 155-165, 167, 176, 290

Browne, John, BP chief 199

Bulbov, Alexander, Federal Drug Control Agency 118

Bush, George W., US President 130

Bushuyeva, Tatyana, lawyer 125, 132, 134

Chaplin, Vsevolod, Archpriest 21, 249, 267

Chekalin, Grigory, deputy prosecutor 142

Cherkesov, Viktor, drugs investigator 96, 117-19

Chernositov, Vladimir, police chief 142-43, 145

Chevron Texaco 198

Chichvarkin, Yevgeny, telecoms tycoon 122, 125-29, 131-34, 136

Chubais, Anatoly, reformer 186

Clarke, Simon, sociologist 81-82

Colbert, Jean-Baptiste, French statesman 95

Communist Party 46, 186, 199, 205

Connie, Vladimir Putin's dog 214

Constantine, Emperor 259-60

Crimea, Ukraine 2, 9-10, 294-95, 298-301

Custine, Marquis de, French writer 63

Demetrius I, Macedonian king 259

Deripaska, Oleg, factory owner 68-72, 77-79, 177-179

Donbass, Ukraine 295, 302

Donetsk, Ukraine 10, 293-296, 298, 300, 302

Dorenko, Sergei, journalist 249

Dugin, Anton, polling station chairman 278-80, 282-83

Dvorkovich, Arkady, economic adviser 169

Dymovsky, Major Alexei, policeman 139-151

Empire of the Czar: A Journey Through Eternal Russia, book 61

Estemirova, Natalia, murdered human rights activist 285

Eurasia Union, 296

Eusebius of Caesarea, fourth century bishop 259

ExxonMobil 198

Fadin, Andrei, journalist 174

Faizulin, Marat, customs official 109-110

"Father Boris," Orthodox priest 10-12, 25

Felshtinsky, Yuri 286

Feodorovich, Mikhail, tsar 257

Feygin, Mark, defence lawyer 22-23

Filipp, Metropolitan 262

Financial Times, newspaper 55, 161

Frazer, Sir James, anthropologist 62, 224

Fridman, Mikhail, oligarch 169, 171-72, 174, 178

FSB, Russian Federal Security Service 37, 87-94, 98-99, 102-104, 106-110, 287

Galeotti, Mark 101-103, 167

Gallup, polling organisation 305

Ganiyeva, Alisa, writer and journalist 36-38

Gazprom, oil company 73, 156, 160-62

Gervis, Yuri, FSB officer 93, 104, 127-29, 132-133, 135

Ginsberg, Allen, poet 184

Glasser, Susan, journalist 99

Godunov family 204

Godunov, Boris, tsar 55, 169, 174, 258

Golikova, Tatyana, health minister 51

Gorelov, Andrei, factory worker 56, 59-61, 64

Gozman, Leonid, politician 186-87, 192

Grant, shopping mall 110

Grebenshikov, Boris, rock musician 43

Gref, German, economics minister 129-30, 137

Gryzlov, Boris, United Russia leader 34

Gudkov, Gennady, deputy 96, 99, 247

Gudkov, Lev, head of Levada Center 40

Guelman, Marat, political scientist 249, 252

Gulichev, Colonel Igor, Cossack 251-52, 254-55

Gundyayev, Vladimir, later Patriarch Kirill 266-67

Gusinsky, Vladimir, oligarch 174, 176

Hermitage Capital, investment company 116, 155-60

Hertzen, Alexander, writer 269

Hoffman, David, journalist 160

holy fools 20, 24, 263-65, 268

Humphrey, Caroline, anthropologist 100, 136-37

Huntington, Samuel, political scientist 166

Ivan IV, tsar 97

Ivan the Terrible, tsar 22, 96-97, 101, 174, 180, 204, 258, 262, 264, 290

Ivanov, Alexei, writer 81

Ivanov, Sergei, defence minister 118-19

Ivanov, Sergei, historian 264-65

Ivanov, Victor, drug control chief 147

Jensen, Donald N., historian 173

Jungle Book, book 209

Justinian, Byzantine emperor 22, 249, 259, 260

Kabanov, Kirill, Captain, former FSB officer 87-90, 92-93, 95, 98-99, 101, 103-104, 118

Kabayeva, Alina 279

Kadyrov Pravda, Chechen newspaper 272

Kadyrov, Akhmad 272

Kadyrov, Ramzan, Chechnyan leader 272, 285, 301

Karastelyov, Vadim 145, 148

Karpov, Major Pavel 165

Kashin, Oleg, journalist 184, 240-41

Kasyanov, Mikhail, former prime minister 186, 192, 199, 200

Khabirov, Radi 193

Kharcheva, Alisa, student 215-17, 221, 223-24

Kharkov Pact 300

Khloponin, Alexander 187

Khodorkovsky, Mikhail, oil oligarch 22, 32, 34, 37, 78, 100, 126, 157, 161-63, 172, 174-76, 181, 183, 194, 196-200, 241

Khrushchev, Nikita 91, 222-23, 298

Kiev, Ukraine 294-95, 297-99, 301-302

Kipling, Rudyard 209

Kirill, Patriarch 21, 25, 248, 250, 253, 265-67

Kiselyova, Yelena 282-83

Kokh, Alfred, businessman 175

Kolesnikov, Andrei, journalist 29, 170-72

Kolosov, Yarslav, sick Moscow child 51

Kommersant, newspaper 58, 169, 171

kormleniye, tax farming 89, 101-102, 124, 130

Korzhakov, Alexander, bodyguard 175-76

Kovalev, Oleg, Ryazan governor 50

Kovaleva, Natasha (alias), youth worker 228, 232

Krasovsky, Anton, journalist 197

Kruse, Elbert 121

krysha, protection 102-103, 107, 110, 164

Kryshtanovskaya, Olga, sociologist 279

Kucheruk, Sergei, interior minister 143

Kudeshkina, Olga, judge 116

Kudrin, Alexei, finance minister 34, 187, 189, 196-97

Kurbsky, Prince 264

Kuritsina, Sveta 230, 235

Kurta, Alexander, businessman 133

Kuzmin, Valery, customs officer 129

Kuznetsov, Artyom, interior ministry 159-61, 164-66

Kvitko, Sergei 43-44, 47-50, 53-54, 303

Levada Center, polling organisation 40, 63, 304

Levin, Boris, Yevroset security chief 126, 132-33

Levinson, Alexei, Levada Center 63

Liberal Democratic Party 46

Liga Mars, import company 109

Lincoln, Abraham 270

Lipman, Maria, political analyst 224

LogoVAZ, company 174

Loseva, Olga, student 235

Loskutov, Vladimir, investigator 108, 117

Lotman, Iurii, cultural historian 289

Loyal Ruslan, novel 90

Magnitsky, Sergei, lawyer155, 157-58, 160-61, 164-66

Maidan square 297-98, 301

Makarii, Metropolitan 262

Makarov, Andrei, deputy 146

Malis, Oleg, businessman 126

Manturov, Denis, trade minister 180

Margeret, Jacques 288

Martynov, Boris, police chief 144

Maslikov, Anatoly, director general, BaselCement Pikalevo 72, 75-76, 79

Matorina, Vika, student 219

Matuzova, Yelena, Pikalevo employee 67-68, 73, 75-77, 80, 82

Medvedev, Dimitry5, 12, 15-16, 21, 33, 50-51, 55, 60, 72, 75-77, 88, 104, 119, 123, 141, 143-46, 159, 165, 167, 169, 171, 181, 184-91, 194-96, 203-207, 209, 228, 233

Medvedev, Valery, police chief 143, 145

Metakhim, company 71

Miroshnichenko, Boris, head of Department K 137

Miroshnichenko, Igor, icon bearer 254

Nadezhdin, Boris 191

Narinsky, Ivan, entrepreneur, 112

Nashi, Russian youth organisation 214, 218-19, 221-22, 225, 227-35, 253-54

National Bolshevik party 38

NATO 296, 300

Navalny, Alexei, lawyer and politician 17-18, 100, 207, 238-44, 247-48

Nechiporenko, Oleg, KGB general 99-95

Nemstov, Boris, politician 191-92

Nero, Roman emperor 259

Netanyahu, Benjamin, Israeli prime minister 271

New Times, publication 196, 249

Nezavisimaya Gazeta, newspaper 37

Nicholas I, tsar 14, 35, 61, 130, 226, 247

Nikitin, Alexander, United Russia delegate 205

Nikon, Patriarch 262

Nordstream, gasification project 57

Norilsk Nickel 175, 186, 188-89

Norman, Russel, scholar 259

Novaya Gazeta, newspaper 117

Nurgaliyev, Rashid, Interior minister 122, 130, 137, 147, 146-47

Obraztsova, Katya, student 214, 221-226, 229

Olson, Mancur, social scientist 288

Onexim Bank 170, 175, 188

oprichniki, loyal soldier of the sovereign 97, 262, 265

oprichnina, the lands of the tsar 96-97, 204, 209

Orwell, George, author 270, 286

Oslon, Alexander, pollster 41

Owen, Kevin, journalist 13

Ozersky, Dimitry, poet and songwriter 29

Panfilova, Yelena, investigator 164

Parnas, political party 191

Pashkin, Mikhail, police chairman 142

Pastukhov, Vladimir 2-3

Paul I, tsar 105

Pekhtin, Vladimir, deputy 238

Pelevin, Viktor, writer 232

Peskov, Dimitry, Putin spokesman 2, 21, 142, 145, 195, 243, 246, 249, 283-85

Peter the Great, tsar 35, 263, 266, 290

Petrov, Andrei, electrician 73-81

Petrov, Nikolai, scholar 41

PhosAgro, chemical holdings company 179

Pikalevo, factories 67-80, 82-83, 177, 179, 259, 281

Pipes, Richard, historian 289-90

Polezhayev, Alexander, poet 14-15

Politkovskaya, Anna, murdered journalist 216, 224

Polovinkin, Vasily, estate agent 232

Ponomaryov, Ilya, protester and deputy 247

ponyatiya, unwritten law, 'that which is understood' 112-113, 160, 198

Poroshenko, Petro, Ukrainian president 301

Potanin, Vladimir, oligarch 174-75, 181, 188-89, 156

Pribylovsky, Vladimir 286

Prilepin, Zakhar, writer 38

Prokhorov, Mikhail, oligarch 170, 181-83, 187-98, 200, 207

Pronin, Vladimir 123

Pugachev Rebellion 69, 81

Pugachev, Yemelian, leader of insurrection 246

PUIN, baked beans 220

Pushkin, Alexander, poet 35, 41, 55, 69, 184

Pussy Riot, punk group 6, 9, 11-14, 20-25, 248-54, 267

Putin, Lyudmila 287

Putin, Vladimir, approval ratings 40

Putin, Vladimir, childhood 286

Putin, Vladimir, corruption allegations against 224

Putin, Vladimir, fan clubs 214

Putin, Vladimir, in person 31

Putin, Vladimir, interaction with businessmen 77

Putin, Vladimir, interaction with locals 39

Putin, Vladimir, KGB career 286-87

Putin, Vladimir, marketed as a brand 219

Putin, Vladimir, business dealings 174

Putinka, vodka 219

Pypin, Alexander, election observer 277, 282-83

Ranchenkov, Artem, Lieutenant Colonel,

police investigator 22

Ridiger, Alexis, later became Patriarch Alexis II 266

Right Cause *(Pravoye Delo)*, opposition party 182, 187-92, 196, 200-201

Rodina, political party 185

Rogozin, Dmitry 185

Roizman, Yevgeny 192-93, 200

Romanov, Andrei, policeman 123

Rosneft, state oil company 163

RosPil, website 238

Rossiyskaya Gazeta, newspaper 147

Rowland, Daniel, historian 262

Rumyantsev, Marat, reserve officer 139, 147-50

RusAl, aluminum empire 177-79

Russian Orthodox Church 11, 250, 256, 265-66

Russian Pioneer, journal 169-170

Russian Spring 9, 295, 305

Ryabov, Dmitry (alias), reporter 32-35

Sakwa, Richard 2

Salye, Marina, deputy 287

Samutsevich, Yekaterina, Pussy Riot member 14, 19, 21, 23-24, 250

Satarov, Georgy, political expert 98

Savchenko, Oksana, doctor 240

Sechin, Igor, as chairman of Rosneft 163, 178, 188

Sechin, Igor, as energy minister 34

Semyonov, Ivan Timofeyevich, clerk 257

Serdyukov, Anatoly, defence minister 165

Serdyukov, Valery, governor 71-72, 77, 80

Sergeyeva, Tatyana, volunteer 64-65

Sevastopol, Crimea 299-300

Shantsev, Valery, governor 56-61, 63-64

Sharov, Vladimir, historian 62

Shatrov, Artyom, nightclub director 220

Shchekochikhin, Yuri, journalist 117

Shekino district, gasification 48-49

Shevtsova, Lilia, scholar 135

Shishkin, Sergei, Cossack leader 251

Shlapentokh, Vladimir, sociologist 2, 291

Shoigu, Sergei, Emergencies Minister 59-60

Shuvalov, Igor, government official 187, 189

Sibneft, oil company 175, 198

Sidanko Oil 175

siloviki, security personnel 96, 100, 131, 136-37

Simferopol, Crimea 298-99

Singing Together, pop group 218-19

Sivun, Oleg, novelist 220

Smolensky, Alexander, oligarch 174

Sneath, David, anthropologist 102, 136-37

Sobchak, Anatoly, mayor of St. Petersburg 173, 286

Sobyanin, Sergei, Moscow mayor 18, 239, 242-43

Sochi, Winter Olympics 10, 301-302

Sofyin, Sergei, plant director 70, 82-83

Soldatov, Andrei, security expert 94, 104

Sollogub, Vladimir, Count 35

Solzhenitsyn, Alexaksandr, writer 286

Sorokin, Vladimir, writer 232

Stalin, Joseph 39-40, 53, 221-24, 266, 290, 294

Stepanova, Olga, head of Moscow Tax Office 165

Stroganov, Anika 180

Surkov, Vladislav, Kremlin ideologist 183-86, 191-97, 200, 221, 225-26, 231-34, 238, 249, 256, 259, 279

Syrova, Marina, judge 23

Tabak, Vladimir, student 217, 221-23

Takmenev, Vadim, TV presenter 14, 19

Taube, Johann 121

The Captain's Daughter, short story 69

Themistius, fourth century courtier 290

Theodosius I, Emperor 290

Timofeyev—see also Semyonov, Ivan Timofeyev 257-59

Tolokonnikova, Nadezhda, Pussy Riot member 14, 20, 250

Tolstoy, Alexei Konstantinovich, writer 87, 169

Tolstoy, Leo, writer 155

Tri Kita, furniture contraband scandal 108-10, 117-19, 130

Troitsky, Artem, music critic 235

Trunov, Igor, lawyer 124-25, 131

Turchynov, Oleksandr, intirim Ukrainian president 298

United Russia, political party 16, 33, 43-46, 48-49, 184, 186-87, 203, 205-206, 228, 236, 238, 279-80

Ustinov, Vladimir, prosecutor 102, 117

Valdenberg, Vladimir, historian 259

Varfolomeyeva, Dasha, Buryatia child 52

Vasilyev, Andrei, editor 169, 171

Veber, Sergei, mayor 72-76

Veretinsky, Fyodor, district prosecutor 72, 75

Verkhnyaya Verya, village affected by forest fires, 55-57, 64-65

Verzilov, Pyotr 20

Vesti, TV channel 48

Vladimir, Russian prince 261

Vladimov, Georgy, writer 90

Vlaskin, Andrei, courier 132-134

Vokin, Mikhail, lawyer 132, 134

Volkhova, Julia (alias), fire victim 56-57, 65-66

Volkov, Alexander, customs official 109-110

Volkov, Leonid, campaign manager for Navalny 242-43

Volodin, Vyacheslav, ideologist 231, 274, 279

Voloshin, Alexander, chief of staff 183, 186, 188

Vorobyev, Andrei, United Russia party official 205

Vremennik, work of Ivan Timofeyovich Semyonov 257

Vrubel, Dmitry, artist 218

Waller, Glenn, Australian ambassador 176

Wladislaw, King of Poland 174

Yanukovich, Victor 296-98, 302

Yabloko, political party 238

Yakemenko, Vasily, head of Russian State Agency for Youth 214, 225-26, 228-29, 231-33

Yegorova, Olga, judge 116

Yelin, Alexander, poet and songwriter 219, 269

Yeltsin, Boris 4, 40, 91-93, 95, 135, 168, 173-76, 185-86, 188, 284, 286

Yevroset, telecommunications company 126, 129-34, 137

Yevstafiev, Gennady, retired security officer 94

Yevsyukov, Major Denis, policeman 122-25, 131-35, 140

Yukos, oil company 157, 163-64, 175-76, 183, 198

Yumashev, Valentin, politician 188

Yumasheva, Tatyana, daughter of Boris Yeltsin 186

Zaitsev, Colonel Pavel 105-11, 115-19

Zakharov, Anatoly, volunteer 280-82

zakon, the written law 160

Zaostrovtsev, Yuri, chief of FSB economic crimes department 110-11, 118-19

Zatulin, Konstantin, United Russia lawmaker 206

Zhirinovsky, Gennady 186

Zhukov, Colonel Yevgeny, FSB officer 109-10, 118

Zlobin, Nicolai, political expert 243

Zorkin, Valery, Constitutional Court chairman 147

Zuyev, Sergei, furniture magnate 109-11, 116-17, 119

Zyuganov, Gennady 174, 186